from Nick
    Brussels,   19/4/89

Lynne Stanley

GW00322829

CLASSIC
INDIAN
VEGETARIAN
COOKING

CLASSIC INDIAN VEGETARIAN COOKING

JULIE SAHNI

DORLING KINDERSLEY · LONDON

A Jill Norman Book

First published in Great Britain in 1987
by Dorling Kindersley Limited,
9 Henrietta Street, London WC2E 8PS

**Illustrations by Richard Pfanz
Decorations by Lorraine Harrison**

British Library Cataloguing in Publication Data
Sahni, Julie
    Indian vegetarian cooking
    1. Vegetarian cookery   2. Cookery, Indian
    I. Title
    641.55'636'0954 TX837
    ISBN 0-86318-242-9

Typeset by Goodfellow & Egan (Phototypesetting) Ltd., Cambridge

Printed in Great Britain by Billings

◆

To my son Vishal Raj
— a total joy
— a lover of good food
— for rolling and puffing
perfectly round balloons
of poori bread since
the age of four.

◆

CONTENTS

◆

(continued)

INTRODUCTION

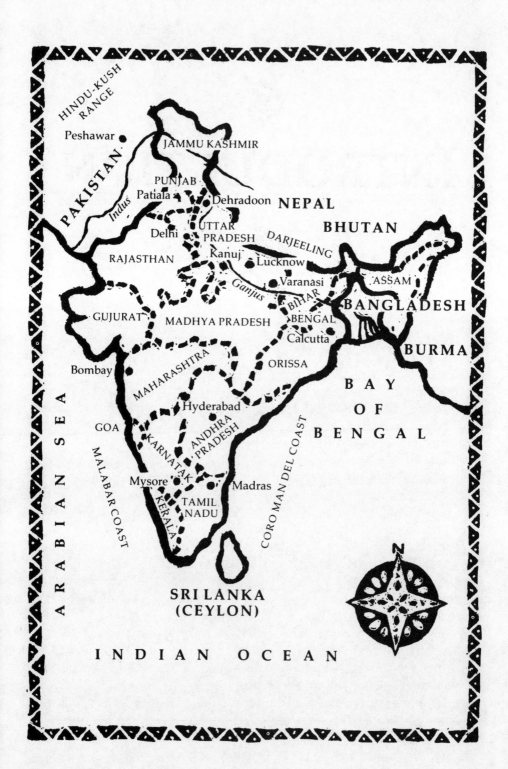

It was well into the fourth day of *Jaith* (May–June) by the lunar calendar. The face of the moon was in a quarter-turned position while the zodiac moved back and rested slightly inclined. There was no sign of Saturn, and the family priest declared it was a perfectly auspicious day for the wedding of my sister. Before researching this day the priest had investigated the astrological charts of my sister and her husband-to-be for compatibility, fertility (she now has two sons), and an eternally tranquil married life.

Although determining a well-omened day for this holy event might require considerable astrological calculation, the auspicious times for weddings are fairly well defined in the ancient holy Vedic books – from March until June. Only during this period can the supreme god of preservation, Lord Vishnu, be evoked for blessing the couple – a necessary step in a holy Vedic wedding. At other times Vishnu is believed to be away in Raja Bali or attending to the important sacrificial rites of the monks in the Himalayan mountains.

This is the religious explanation, but it also happens to be the most logical. The months following the auspicious wedding period (July to September) are marked by heavy monsoon rains, thereby making any celebration outdoors impractical. The summer months (March to June) are also scorchingly hot, generally bringing all activities to a grinding halt. Most important, the harvest season precedes the auspicious months. Since most Indians still depend upon agriculture for their livelihood, the money from the crops helps defray the expenses of the wedding and ensures abundant food for the feasting.

The wedding, I was told, was being celebrated in the south at the request of the bridegroom's family. So there we all were, with bedding, steel trunks, cooking vessels, jewellery, and all manner of paraphernalia, trekking down some seventeen hundred miles from New Delhi in the dead of summer, in a crammed, steaming-hot train. If this was not lunacy enough, our family cook, a Kanauj Brahmin, carried all her meals, including her drinking water, for this journey of several days, since she would not eat food cooked by anyone other than her clansmen, because she is an orthodox vegetarian.

My father, a complete non-believer in rituals and deity worship of any kind, would normally never consent to such an undertaking, but he was eager to taste the wonderful cooking of the temple chefs of that area, who are known the world over for their magnificent vegetarian banquet presentations. To me, as a young teenager, the journey represented adventure and excitement, with the train ride topping the

list. The train moved slowly, passing through many states: Northern Province, Central Province, Maharashtra, Andhra Pradesh, and Tamil Nadu. In every state a totally different experience awaited us. Each place represented a distinctly different culture: the physical characteristics of the people, their language, clothes, climate, scenery, and naturally their food. The dining car attached to the train served delicious New Delhi-style food: braised vegetables in aromatic sauces, spicy *dal*, yogurt *raita*, rice pilaf, *chapatis*, pickles, and chutney. But as the train made stops at each railway station along the way, I gorged on an array of delicacies: pistachio *barfi* in Agra; mustard-fragrant fritters in Bhopal with steaming sweet tea served in *kolladh*, unglazed terracotta disposable mugs; crunchy snacks with *kari* leaves and *ajwain chivra* and *bhel* awaited me in Nagpur, where sweet and sour sprouted-bean salad was the local favourite. As the train entered the deep south, the food got hotter. I still remember trying to brush off the red chili pepper flakes sticking to the rice grains in the lemon pilaf and scraping off the green chili and coconut chutney from the foamy dumplings served in banana leaves at the Vijayawada station in Andhra. And then there was that wonderful aroma of coffee that lingered in the air at all the stations in the south. It was served with scalded milk and sugar, in small stainless steel glasses. And I drank it southern-style: with a little practice, I poured the coffee into my mouth by holding the glass half an inch away. I did not let my lips touch the rim of the glass, since in the south, disposable drinking vessels are not widespread.

The wedding ceremony, one day full of rituals, feasting, and celebrations, was to take place in a lovely classic structure called a *chattra*, next to a temple of Lord Shiva. The courtyard surrounding the building was lined with the famous coconut and date palms of southern India. The fragrant jasmine and rose patches and the statues of the different deities gave the whole place a feeling of tranquillity.

In the morning the air was filled with the smell of freshly roasted, ground, and brewed coffee. I ate steaming savoury puddings, tiny puffy breads with braised potatoes in a shallot-and-ginger sauce, accompanied again by that wonderful coffee. To beat the heat I sipped a special lemonade made with tamarind water, palm jaggery (unrefined sugar), and the essence of fresh ginger. There were snacks and sweets to munch on all through the day – chick-pea noodles, griddle cakes, cardamom-laced jaggery and wheat dumplings, silky crêpes with fiery dips and spice powders, and ample varieties of

asafetida-laced fritters. I ate many of them on disposable plates made of banana leaves.

My sister was missing all this, for she had to attend to the various rituals (*pooja*) in order to be prepared for the great occasion. The auspicious time for the marriage ceremony determined by the priest was late morning; hence everyone was busy getting the wedding altar (*mandap*) with its holy fire (*agni*) ready. The sweet pipe and drum music, traditional at weddings, played melodiously in a slow rhythm while the priests gathered sandalwood, turmeric paste, rice, coconut, bananas, betel nut and betel nut leaves, sweets and fruits, holy grass, holy water from the temple, and clarified butter (*usli ghee*, the holy food of the Vedic Aryans, our ancestors). These ingredients were to be offered to the supreme Lord Vishnu to appease him and seek his favour, using the fire god as messenger. The local town gardener brought beautiful garlands of roses, marigold, marjoram, and jasmine that the bride and the groom would exchange. My mother brought silver coins and gold-brocaded silk saris to be offered up to the various gods (these finally ended up with the presiding priest) and to the elderly relatives, to seek their blessing, which in many cases was more important than the blessing of the lower-ranking gods such as the Mouse God (*Chooha Dev*) or the Monkey God (*Hanuman*).

As the preparations neared completion, the air started becoming thick with the aromas of lentils cooking with turmeric and sesame, tamarind boiling with jaggery, and spices roasting. I followed the scents to the large backyard. There they were – the famous temple vegetarian chefs: bare-chested and barefoot, wrapped from the waist down in gold-brocaded white cloth. They wore a bright yellow sacred thread (*janaeo*) around their necks and across their chests and had holy ash smeared on their foreheads and arms. Gently chanting a Vedic hymn, they stirred large batches of lentil and vegetable stews and braised vegetables, some with fried spices, some with roasted lentils and spices, others with yogurt and herbs, in large gleaming brass and copper pots as big as bathtubs!

There were helpers grinding coconut and chilies for the relish and stews and pulverizing almonds for the puddings and *halwa*. One person did nothing but crack and grate the enormous pile of coconuts that resembled a small mountain. At Vedic ritual celebrations and associated feasts, all the food has to be made on the premises that day, including combining, roasting, and grinding the spice blends for the many dishes. In Hindu ceremonies the food needs to be blessed by all

the appropriate gods, but in fact it ensures absolute freshness and the most perfect taste in the ingredients.

The magical gastronomic experience my father and everyone else waited for was finally coming. The pipe music suddenly became louder, and the tempo of the drum increased, signalling that the auspicious hour was not too far away. I rushed back to the *mandap*.

My sister Reena, dressed in a flowing red silk sari with a gold border, sat in front of the holy fire. Around her neck she wore several gold chains and necklaces, and gold bangles jangled on her wrists. On her forehead she wore a large *bindi*, the red dot of *kamala* powder that is the mark of a married Hindu Brahmin woman. Her eyes sparkled with the dark *kaajal*, a mascara made by mixing burned and powdered almond shells with the special *sarapunnaga* oil. Her tiny waist was circled by an elegant gold belt, and silver rings adorned her small toes, which had been painted crimson with a paste of turmeric and *kamala* powder. The diamonds in her ears and nose sparkled as she blushed in nervous anxiety. She was sitting beside her husband-to-be, flushed, vulnerable, and looking stunningly beautiful – suddenly no longer a carefree teenager but a young bride, now part of a Hindu Brahmin household with all the responsibilities this position entailed.

The exchange of garlands was followed by several fire sacrifices (this involved pouring *ghee* into the fire to create flames while special Vedic hymns were recited) to call upon the supreme gods of the Aryans – earth, water, wind, thunder, and sun. At the exact moment (*mohort*) of the auspicious time, the groom tied the holy cord (*mangala sootra*) around the neck of his bride. The cord was coated with sandalwood and turmeric paste and carried a gold pendant, the emblem of the exclusive high-priest caste of the Brahmins. The groom then gently placed my sister's foot on a holy stone (a symbol of the mighty mountains the original ancestral Aryans came from) and pledged to maintain the tradition of the Brahmins. Finally they both walked around the fire seven times to complete the holy union while the family and guests threw rice on the couple to wish them prosperity and fertility.

Once married, they sat for the second time in front of the holy fire and continued the sacrifices, this time for the Hindu gods, starting with Lord Shiva; Lord Vishnu and all his incarnations, including the fish, pig, tortoise, horse; Rama; Krishna; and their consorts. No god could be left out. Even the carriers of the gods – goose, bird, and bull – were included in the prayers.

While all this high-level diplomacy with the gods was going on, most of the guests wandered off to the banquet floor, where a twenty-two course vegetarian feast awaited them: several different types of vegetables, braised, stir-fried and steamed; lentil stews; steamed cakes and sauces – all served with rice, *ghee*, yogurt salad, *dal*, bread, wafers, pickles, chutneys, pudding, sweetmeats, and fresh fruits – served all at once!

The bride and groom do not participate in the banquet. Instead they are fed separately, near the marriage altar, with more rituals. At the conclusion of the entire ceremony, the couple is given some toys to play with and some lentil wafers (*papad*), which they then proceed to smash into bits on each other's head! This somewhat curious tradition is a holdover from ancient times, when the bride and groom were often as young as three or four years old and needed some relief from the solemn rituals of the wedding.

Today I can close my eyes and savour the delicious scents of that banquet and the tingling sensation I felt when I first looked at that exquisitely prepared enormous meal, and the final rapture I felt after I had devoured all the food! Reflecting on my sister's wedding so many years later, I am also reminded of the innumerable animals, birds, sea creatures, and all of nature's elements that the Hindus worship as if they were gods. Many years later I visited the temple for rats (*Chooha Devi Mandir*) in Rajasthan, and the temple for the monkeys in Hardwar. I observed the festival that celebrates the snake god Cobra (*Naag Panchami*) by offering him milk and honey in a *thali* at night, and the festival of the harvest, at which five-course meals are offered to the birds and eleven-course meals to the cattle. These rituals took place before the participants could be served anything to eat.

The Hindu philosophy of peaceful coexistence with nature, the principle of nonviolence, suddenly seemed to fall into place. I realized that this was a culture that respects every living creature equally. What our forefathers established was a form of preservation of God's creatures. Vegetarianism thus came naturally and effortlessly.

As a child I was brought up by my parents and the family cook in a Hindu Brahmin household as a strict vegetarian. I ate no meat and did not miss it, for our family vegetarian meals were always tasty, wholesome, and downright satisfying. Today I am not a practising vegetarian, but I frequently include several vegetarian dishes and meals in my diet, for I find them refreshingly light. I also like them because they provide exciting new flavours and textures.

THE
PRINCIPLES OF
INDIAN
VEGETARIAN
COOKING

VEGETARIANISM IN INDIA

◆

Worldwide, there are two reasons for the practice of vegetarianism: first the belief that abstinence from animal flesh is conducive to a healthful diet, and second the belief that the consumption of meat involves the taking of life from living creatures.

In the Western world the first reason is the predominant one, and Western vegetarians, for the most part, adopt a meat-free diet in the belief that the human body does not require meat in order to maintain good health. Some pursue this concept further, holding the belief that eating meat is not only unnecessary but is in fact harmful, resulting in excessive cholesterol in the blood, which can lead to heart disease, high blood pressure, and strokes. The widespread use of chemical growth hormones in animals raised for our consumption has also given rise to a general concern about increased risk of cancer.

In India the religious or moral aspects are perhaps the most central to the practice of vegetarianism. The taking of a life is repugnant to the majority of Hindus, who constitute the largest group (83 per cent of India's 680 million population) of practising vegetarians in India. Additionally, many Hindus believe in reincarnation and thus feel that any living creature could well harbour the soul of a human being awaiting rebirth as a human. Perhaps the most extreme example of protecting the sanctity of life is the Jain practice of carrying a broom at all times. Thus when a Jain walks, his path can be swept carefully clean, moving any insect aside that otherwise might be trodden underfoot. The Jains even refrain from eating certain vegetables and fruits during the rainy season, because they contain worms and insects, and the Jain would not want any harm to come to those creatures. The Jains also avoid farming in any form: they do not want to endanger the life of any living creatures in the soil. Jains thus have specialized in business and commerce, at which they excel.

In both West and East there are varying levels of vegetarian practices. The most basic consists of eliminating red meat from the diet. The next strictest level avoids, in addition, the consumption of fowl. The next adds fish and seafood to the list of forbidden foods, and the most stringent of all eliminates eggs from the diet because eggs are considered to be embryonic chickens. Some Hindu sects, such as the

Brahmins from the holy cities of Banaras or Kanauj, carry this concept even further – they forbid the consumption of specific vegetables such as garlic and onions. These holy Brahmins believe that the primary function of these vegetables is to enhance the flavour of meat – a most undesirable association.

Thus the world of vegetarian practice and belief is highly complex, and many different forms are practised in India.

This book is written in the belief that many Western vegetarians can add variety and a whole new world of adventurous flavours to their meals. Whether or not the Indian motives apply in the West, there is certainly a great deal to be learned from a vegetarian cuisine that has existed for over four thousand years.

You will see that some of the menus and recipes frankly reflect a desire to imitate the taste of meat as closely as possible. Others reflect a desire even to eliminate those vegetables, fruits, and seasonings that are associated with the preparation of meat, chicken, or fish or in some way resemble flesh, such as tomatoes, beetroot, and watermelon.

Whatever your own motives and personal predilection, it is my fervent hope that the vegetarian recipes in this book will expand the scope of your palate and suggest many ways of adding new dimensions of flavour to your life.

In this book references are frequently made to Hindus (particularly of the Brahmin caste) and to Jains (an offshoot of Hinduism), as these are the two groups of strict vegetarians in India. The main body of the recipes is derived from their repertoire. Many other groups, such as the Sikhs and the Buddhists (offshoots of Hinduism), the Parsis (a sect the members of which emigrated from Persia in the ninth century to escape religious persecution), the Moslems, the Jews, and the Christians, although they are not exclusively vegetarian, eat very little meat, chicken, or fish for economic reasons. They rely very heavily on vegetables and vegetarian products; thus their vegetarian dishes are extremely interesting and flavourful. The book includes those recipes as well.

A NOTE ABOUT SALT The recipes in this book use much less salt than is called for in traditional ways of cooking those dishes. Its reduction, or sometimes omission, is compensated for by other flavourings such as sour, peppery, bitter, astringent, and sweet. Black salt, used in several recipes in this book, is readily available in Indian groceries. If you are are unable to find it, simply eliminate it – do not substitute white table salt as the black salt has little or no salinity. It is primarily used for its digestive and aromatic properties.

VEGETABLES AND FRUITS

◆

Vegetables and fruits have always been an extremely important part of the diet of all Indians. Furthermore many Indians, either for economic or religious reasons, are strict vegetarians. Fortunately this does not mean that the Indian diet is in any way monotonous, as India is blessed with the largest variety of vegetables in the world. In addition, Indians cook with the varieties of unripe fruits that grow there, increasing the range of possibilities even more.

Almost all the vegetables and fruits used in Indian vegetarian cooking are commonly available in Britain, therefore I do not describe them in any great detail in this book. Discussed at some length, though, are those vegetables and fruits that are available here but only to a limited degree. These include taro root and leaves, drumsticks, cluster beans, fenugreek greens, pointed gourd, and sapota. These items can be found in Indian, Asian, and other ethnic shops. Make an effort to try some of the new vegetables and fruits, as they will expand the scope and variety of your cooking.

VEGETABLES

◆

Vegetables are best cooked as they are harvested (something commonly done in India), as they are at their freshest then. Remember that the dishes in this book will taste as good as the ingredients you put into them. Fresh, tender vegetables with sweet fragrances will make all the difference in the world.

AMARANTH LEAVES *Chaulai*

Amaranth, also known as Indian summer spinach, is commonly referred to in India as *chaulai*. It looks and tastes very much like Indian spinach except for its colour, which can range from dark green to purple red, and its intense herbal aroma. Many varieties of amaranth grow throughout the tropics.

They can roughly be grouped into three categories: *Amaranthus blitum*, *Amaranthus tricolor*, and *Amaranthus caudatus*. The first two are grown primarily for their edible leaves. The second, also known for its thick, succulent stems, is called *tandoo keerai*. The third variety mainly yields seeds, another delicacy in Indian cooking.

◆

BITTER GOURD *Karela*

The bitter gourd, with its green, very coarsely wrinkled rind, like the skin of a crocodile, has been growing in India since ancient times. There are two distinct varieties of bitter gourd plants, *Momordica charantia* and *Momordica balsamina*. The former yields cucumber-like fruits, while the latter, ovoid-shaped fruits with narrow pointed ends.

Bitter gourd, as the name suggests, has a characteristic bitterness that is an acquired taste. Much of its bitterness is removed by soaking or boiling the vegetable in a salt-turmeric mixture before cooking.

◆

BOTTLE GOURD *Lauki ya Doodhi*

The bottle groud (*Lagenaria siceraria*), a vegetable of the *cucurbitacea* family, has been cultivated in India since Vedic times. The thin green skin is peeled off before cooking to reveal a pale ivory-colour, tender flesh. Its flavour can best be described as somewhat like chayote or cucumber. Because this gourd retains its shape even after prolonged cooking, it is often stuffed. It is also used in stews and soups and for making fudge. Always buy a young immature gourd that feels firm to the touch and has a firm, not spongy, central core and as few seeds as possible.

BUCKWHEAT LEAVES *Faafar*

The buckwheat plant *Fagopyrum* has been growing in the northern and north-eastern Himalayas since ancient times. Three distinct species – *cymsum* (known as *banogal*), *esculentum* (*faafar*), and *tataricum* (buckwheat) – grow almost year-round. Indians cook the succulent leaves in the same way as spinach. Buckwheat greens are particularly welcome in winter, since the plant thrives in cool, moist climates when other greens don't.

Buckwheat leaves are delicious braised in lentil and bean sauces, stir-fried in mustard oil with turmeric, and puréed in sauces.

Spinach and amaranth make reasonably good substitutes.

◆

BUTTER BEANS *Sem*

Butter beans, also known as hyacinth beans or *lablab* beans, have been cultivated in India since ancient times. There are two distinct varieties. We are interested in the *Dolichos lablab-typicus* variety because it yields succulent, edible green pods. The *sem* beans resemble broad beans, except they are a darker green and have a slightly wrinkled, rough surface. Broad beans can be used as a substitute.

◆

CHAYOTE *Chow-Chow*

This delicate, pear-shaped fleshy fruit with a single flat seed is a favourite of southern Indians, who call it *chow-chow*, or *sheemai* (foreign) *kattrikkai* (aubergine), which boggles my mind, as it in no way resembles an aubergine.

Chayote, fruit of the plant *Sechium edule*, is native to Mexico and Central America. It was introduced in southern India by the Portuguese in the seventeenth century. Southern Indians either cook it in a stew or simply steam it and dress it with a spicy coconut dressing (p. 294).

◆

CLUSTER BEANS *Guar ki Phalian*

These beans grow in clusters, hence their name. They belong to the *leguminoseae* plant family *Cyamopsis tetragonoloba*. Native to India, cluster beans grow in many parts of that country. The bean pod has a distinct spicy coriander-like aroma. Its slight bitterness is considered by Indians to enhance its taste. Be sure the beans you select are bright green and show no signs of yellowing. They keep well in the refrigerator for up to a week if you store them wrapped loosely in a plastic bag.

◆

DRUMSTICK *Sehjana ki Phali*

Sehjana ki Phali is called drumstick not because of its similarity to a turkey leg but because the pods, the edible part of this plant *Moringa oleifara*, are shaped, when dried, like the sticks used to beat a drum. The green pods have thick, rubbery skins and fleshy pulp and seeds. The flavour is often compared with asparagus and drumstick is considered a delicacy in Gujarat, Bengal, and southern India. Fresh drumsticks are difficult to obtain, but tinned drumsticks imported from India are acceptable, since for most vegetarian dishes in this book, drumsticks are parboiled before being added to a dish at the end of cooking.

◆

FENUGREEK LEAVES *Methi ka Saag*

Fenugreek, native to Ethiopia, eastern Europe, Mediterranean regions, and, of course, India, is the most exotic smelling of all greens. The leaves come from the same plant – *Trigonella foenumgraecum* – that yields the bitter pulse used as a spice in cooking.

Fenugreek leaves possess a natural bitter flavour for which one needs to acquire a taste, although most Indians seem to be born with it. Indians usually serve them with other greens such as spinach, or beet leaves. They are also wonderful in lentil stews and stuffed breads. They are especially tasty cooked with starchy roots because their strong flavour is mellowed by the blandness of these vegetables.

Fenugreek leaves, sun-dried and used as herbs, are the leaves of a special, highly scented variety of the fenugreek plant, *Trigonella corniculata*. They are popularly known as *kasoori methi*. If fresh fenugreek is not available, small quantities of dried fenugreek leaves may be substituted.

◆

GREEN BLACK-EYED BEANS *Hara Lobbia*

The young, tender seeds of the pod of *Vigna unguiculata* (the black-eyed bean plant) are regarded as a delicacy by the vegetarians in the western and south-western regions of India. Indians handle this vegetable much the same way as green peas; they serve them in green salads, pilafs, braised dishes with spices, as well as in desserts.

Select crisp-looking beans that have no brown spots and, most important of all, that exude a fresh pine-like fragrance. These beans are closely related to yard-long beans which can be used as a substitute if fresh black-eyed beans are not available.

◆

GREEN CHICK-PEAS *Phalian*

Green chick-peas are the young tender pods (containing seeds) of the plant *Cicer arietinum* which, when mature and dry, are what we know as chick-peas (*channa*). In the province of Uttar Pradesh, where most of the chick-peas in India are grown, these green delicacies are particularly prized. The seeds from the pods are munched raw, served in a spicy salad by themselves, or cooked with herbs and seasonings like any lentil preparation. Green chick-peas have a wonderful earthy scent and a delightful crunch. They do not have the heavy, mealy quality of dried chick-peas. Green chick-peas are difficult to find, but young, uncooked or lightly steamed broad beans make fine substitutes.

GREEN PIGEON PEAS OR GRANDULAS *Vatana*

No group of Indians know more about varieties of vegetarian ingredients, particularly fresh beans, peas, and lentils, than do the Gujaratis. Although they are called peas, these are really fresh whole unhulled lentils with the greenish-brown skin on. They are known as *vatana* by the Gujaratis and Maharashtrians. Fresh green lentils are delicious cooked in spicy gravy or with dill.

◆

GREEN UNRIPE MANGO *Kachcha Aam*

The fruit of the mango tree (*Mangifera indica*), native to India, when unripe, tart, and young, is used as a vegetable in Indian cooking. The problem is that both ripe and unripe mangoes can look alike from the outside. The unripe kind is totally green and feels much firmer and harder when pressed – as hard as an unripe peach. Unripe mangoes have a creamy white flesh and a sharp tang. They turn yellower and sweeter as they ripen.

In Indian vegetarian cooking the most common use of raw mangoes is in making pickles, chutneys, and relishes. They also lend a tart flavour to sauces and stews. Peeled, sliced, sun-dried, and ground into powder, green mangoes become an important souring agent called *amchoor*. I particularly love green mangoes in a chutney such as Madras Hot Star Fruit (or Mango) Chutney, p. 299.

See more on mango under fruits on page 33.

◆

GREEN UNRIPE PAPAYA *Kachcha Papeeta*

The unripe papaya fruit (*Carica papaya*) is considered a delicacy by the Jains and Hindu Brahmins of north India. The vegetable is peeled, the few immature seeds scraped out, and the pulp chopped before cooking.

The two most popular uses of green papaya are in making pickles and chutneys. It is also stewed with beans and lentils and braised in spicy sauces.

JACKFRUIT *Katahal*

Jackfruit (*Ortocarpus intergrifolia*) is one of great importance to Indians. The fruit's texture and distinct flavour, when cooked, closely resemble meat; hence it is popularly used by strict vegetarians in mock meat specialities.

Indigenous to India, jackfruit grows throughout all regions. Indians use the unripe fruit as a vegetable. The olive green skin, thick and studded with short spikes, is peeled to expose the edible part of the vegetable: almond-colour flesh with almond-colour seeds. It is delicious stewed with spices and herbs and folded into pilafs. Indians also love to pickle jackfruit or turn it into a sweetmeat. Tinned jackfruit of all kinds is awful-tasting; keep away from it.

Jackfruit should not be confused with the somewhat similar-looking *durian*, a native fruit of southeast Asia with purplish glutinous flesh and a strong smell, which is best avoided altogether.

◆

KALE, FLAT *Karam ka Saag*

Karam ka saag, also called *haak*, is the most adored green in Kashmir, the northernmost state of India, where it grows almost wild. *Karam ka saag* is essentially a variety of kale, flat kale to be precise, known as *Brassica acephala*. Kashmiri cooks prepare the greens in many wonderful ways – fried with spices, stewed with tomatoes, in dumplings, and in breads.

Kashmiri cooks also carefully sun-dry this vegetable – they lay the kale on their thatched roofs – and store it for use in the winter when fresh greens are no longer available.

◆

KOHLRABI *Ganth Gobhi*

Shaped like a white turnip, this vegetable, a native of northern Europe, was introduced to India by the Dutch in the later part of the sixteenth century. Because of its delicate flavour, kohlrabi is highly esteemed in Indian cooking. In north India kohlrabi (*Brassica oleracea*) is called *ganth gobhi*, meaning knotted or bulbous cauliflower, probably because it tastes like cauliflower stalks.

LAMB'S QUARTERS OR PIGWEED *Bathua*

Lamb's quarters (*Chenopodium album*) is not to be confused with lamb's lettuce (*Valerianella*), also known as corn salad or mâche. Lamb's quarters, or *bathua*, has irregularly shaped triangular leaves and a subtle grassy flavour and is popular in north India. Because of its natural viscous property in puréed form, Indians frequently combine it with other greens to act as a thickener. *Bathua* is also delicious chopped and stuffed into breads.

◆

LOTUS ROOT *Bhen ya Kamal Kakadi*

Lotus root is the creeping rhizome of the lotus plant *Nelumbo nucifora*, native to India, China, and Japan. It grows naturally in ponds and lakes, although it is widely cultivated in tanks and terraced fields for its edible rhizome. The greyish-brown vegetable comes in links resembling sausages. The links are fleshy and, when cut, exude a mucilaginous juice not unlike what is found inside okra. They do not soften even after prolonged cooking. For this reason they are favoured by vegetarians as a meat substitute. Cooked, they taste very much like mushrooms.

Lotus root is most popular with the Sindhis in the state of Gujarat, where it is commonly known as *bhen*. The Sindhis do many wonderful things with lotus root, including turning it into *koftas* (p. 188). The Mangalorians in Coorg in southwestern India add it to a spicy bean stew to provide texture (see recipe on p. 198). Tinned lotus root is available in Chinese shops.

◆

MUSHROOMS *Khombi, Dhingri, aur Guhchi*

Several varieties of mushrooms grow wild in India, mostly in the foothills of the Himalayas in the northern and eastern parts of India. Of all the varieties, three are most popular. The beehive-shaped morel (*Marchella esculenta*), known as *guhchi*, is found in the Kashmir region. Prized for its shape and aroma, *guhchi* is reserved for special occasions, to be folded into elaborate pilafs and rice casseroles (*biryani*). Chanterelle (*Cantharellus cibarius*) or *dhingri*, as it is known locally in Punjab, is much relished for its chewy, meat-like texture. It is braised or stewed in spicy sauces or simply stir-fried. The third, field mushrooms (*Agaricus campestris*), known as *khombi*, and today cultivated commercially, are eaten stir-fried with spices and in fritters. Indians traditionally eat mushrooms fresh just hours after they are picked. Because of the lack of proper packing and shipping in India, mushrooms are generally consumed in the region in which they are gathered or cultivated.

◆

MUSTARD LEAVES *Sarsoon ka Saag*

Although the mustard plant is grown in many parts of India mainly for its seeds (used as spice), in the state of Punjab the greens are treated as a delicacy. The tender young leaves are savoured for their delicate flavour as well as warming qualities in winter when the greens are generally in season.

Of all the varieties of mustard it is *Brassica juncea* that yields the most succulent leaves.

In Indian vegetarian cooking both the southern variety of giant curled mustard leaves (fresh or frozen) as well as the widely available Chinese mustard greens with their soft, satiny leaves and white or yellow blossoms, are suitable. Select crisp, tender dark green bunches that, when slightly pressed, exude a sweet, mustardy aroma.

◆

OKRA *Bhindi*

Of all the tropical vegetables, Indians love okra the most. Okra (*Abelmoschus esculentus*), a native of Africa as well as Asia, is widely cultivated throughout India today. When fresh, okra has a beautiful green colour. Avoid prickly ones with dark blemishes.

In Indian cooking, okra is stir-fried, stuffed, stewed, and folded into pilafs.

◆

OTHER LEAVES

Several varieties of succulent leaves and twigs are used in Indian cooking. These include turnip leaves, carrot and radish leaves, the tips of tamarind leaves, and drumstick leaves (p. 23), taro leaves (p. 29), young shoots and twigs of bottle gourd (p. 21), and young pumpkin. These greens are traditionally cooked with beans and peas or with starchy vegetables to give them a gentle aroma.

◆

SNAKE GOURD *Chichinda*

The snake gourd (*Trichosanthes anguina*), resembling a thin green snake, is a popular vegetable of southern India. It may be stuffed or baked, or peeled and used in stews.

◆

SPINACH *Palak*

Palak is the most popular spinach grown in the winter in India. Known as Indian spinach, *palak* is completely different from the spinach we commonly see in Britain. Indian spinach consists of the tender leaves of the beet, *Beta vulgaris benghalensis*, which gives out a delicate fragrance when cooked. *Beta vulgaris cicla*, commonly known as Swiss chard, makes an excellent substitute. Or you can enhance the flavour of common spinach by cooking chopped green pepper with it (about one small green pepper with one pound [500 g] of spinach).

◆

TARO OR DASHEEN *Ghuiyan ya Arbi*

Taro or dasheen is the tuberous plant *Colocasia esculenta*, with heart-shaped leaves. Both the tuber and its tender leaves are edible. Taro roots, called *ghuiyan* or *arbi*, are shaped like potatoes except they are smaller and have a rough, hairy skin, sometimes with dark brown rings. The white flesh, which often turns off-white or pale grey when cooked, tastes somewhat like potatoes.

Taro leaves, called *arbi* or *ghuiyan ke patte* or simply *patra*, have a delicate flavour. They are called *callaloo* in the West Indies, after the famous soup made with them.

Both taro roots and leaves are considered a delicacy in Indian vegetarian cooking. The roots are stir-fried with spices, braised, or served cold as a salad. The leaves are stuffed with spicy lentils or braised in sauces.

A word of caution: Both taro root and its leaves must be cooked before being eaten, as they sometimes have an acridity that causes irritation in the mouth due to the presence of needlelike crystals of calcium oxide in both forms of the vegetable.

Choose firm, nonspongy roots of the same size, so they will cook uniformly. They should be dark brown, with a hairy skin that has brown rings. Make sure your taro leaves are bright green, look fresh, and show no signs of wilting around the edges.

A similar-looking root with a somewhat similar flavour is *yautia* (*Xathosoma sagitti folium*), which makes a good substitute for taro root.

◆

WATER CHESTNUT *Singhada ya Paniphal*

Water chestnuts are the fruit of the plant *Trapa natans*, growing naturally in ponds and lakes. They are very popular all through the north, from Assam to Gujarat. Water chestnuts are used in many ways in Indian vegetarian cooking – peeled and eaten as a snack, mixed with spices and turned into a salad, or cooked with creamy beans to lend contrast in texture. Water chestnuts are also sun-dried and ground into flour to be used in batter for fritters and for making delicious breads. They are available tinned, and occasionally fresh, from Chinese shops.

◆

YAM OR ELEPHANT'S FOOT *Zimikand ya Suran*

This giant edible root from ancient times is called elephant's foot because it does in fact look like one. One yam can weigh as much as a hundred pounds. Indian yam (*Amorphophallus campanulatus*, called *zimikand* or *suran*, is native to India. Because of its meatlike texture and spicy flavour, it is a favourite with vegetarians, particularly the Jains in Gujarat and the Brahmins in southern India.

In India *zimikand* is sold cut in pieces. Here, however, this root is not available. Cassava (*Manihot esculenta*), known also as manioc, yucca, or tapioca root, makes a good substitute.

◆

YARD-LONG BEANS *Phalian*

These beans, also known as asparagus beans, are thin, with very long pods. The Indian variety of yard-long beans, belonging to the plant *Vigna sinensis*, has been growing there since ancient times and tends to be more slender. The variety commonly available in Europe is *Vigna sesquipedalis*. It is not quite as aromatic as the Indian kind. Yard-long beans taste very much like French beans except they are stringless and have a much sweeter and more delicate taste. Make sure you choose bright green and crisp pods that show no signs of turning yellow or becoming wrinkled and dry.

FRUITS
◆

Fruits, both cultivated and those found growing naturally, have been in existence in India since ancient times. The 2,500-year-old Vedic document *Artha Shashtra* describes the cultivation of mangoes, bananas, figs, grapes and dates in great detail.

The Indian passion for fresh fruits reached its peak in the sixteenth century, with the creation of *Lakh Baag*, a garden of the Moghul emperor, Akbar, that had 100,000 varieties of mangoes. (In Hindi, *Lakh* means '100,000' and *Baag*, 'garden'.)

Most Indian fruits are sweet – very, very sweet. That's the way Indians like them for dessert. If a fruit is on the tart side, salt (many different varieties) is frequently sprinkled over it to turn it into a *chat* (the Indian appetizer salad). In Indian vegetarian cooking fruits are used in both unripe and ripe forms, in chutneys, sauces, beverages, and pilafs.

◆

CARAMBOLA OR STAR FRUIT *Kamarakh*

Carambola is the fruit of the tropical evergreen tree *Averrhoa carambola*, native to India and Malaya. The ovoid fruit with five acutely angled ridges is often called star fruit because of the star-shaped slices. There are two varieties of star fruits; one is tart to sweet with tasteless, flavourless flesh, and the other is extremely tart to sweetish-sour with highly aromatic, flavourful flesh. In Indian cooking only the second variety is used.

The watery, translucent, pale yellow, tart flesh of the unripe fruit turns golden yellow and sweetish-sour when ripe.

Growing primarily in southern India along the coastal regions, carambola is used in place of tamarind, especially in dishes with pale ivory-coloured sauces. Sliced carambola is spiced and pickled or turned into fragrant chutney. It is also good in stews, lentils, and salads. In northern India, where the fruit is called *kamaragh*, the ripe fruit is eaten raw, with black salt and spices as an appetizer called *chat*, or combined with other fruits as a dessert with Indian cream (*rabadi*). Crushed unripe carambola makes an excellent summer punch when combined with raw palm sugar.

◆

CUSTARD APPLE *Sharifa*

Botanically speaking, the custard apple could include many different varieties of fruit trees belonging to the *Annonaceae* family. In India, however, only *Annona squamosa*, bearing the superior fruit, is referred to as the custard apple. It may come as a surprise to Indians that their beloved custard apple, mentioned in religious books dating back some one thousand years, is indigenous to Africa.

The greenish-black fruit contains many seeds, which are enclosed inside a creamy beehive-shaped pulp. The almond-coloured flesh is juicy, delicately flavoured, and sweet. Indians love eating custard apple raw as a dessert; combined with nuts and butter, it is turned into irresistible sweetmeats, such as *barfi* and *halwa*.

◆

GUAVA *Amrood*

Guava, known as the apple of the tropics, is the greenish-yellow skinned fruit of the plant *Psidium guajava*. *Amrood*, as it is commonly known in India, is often thought to be Indian in origin, although it is a native of Central America. The flesh, studded with tiny edible seeds, ranges in colour from creamy white to pink to crimson red. The texture changes from grainy to smooth as the fruit reaches the peak of ripeness.

The most popular uses of guava in Indian cooking are in a cold salad appetizer (*chat*), and in a delicious drink with the pressed juices of guava, honey, fresh ginger, and lemon juice.

Since guava contains a high level of natural pectin, it is also used in making chutneys and Anglo-Indian jams and sweetmeats.

◆

MANGO *Aam*

The kidney-shaped mango, the fleshy, juicy fruit considered the king of fruits in India, has been growing there for over five thousand years. The name mango, incidentally, is the western pronunciation of the fruit's name in Tamil, the language of southern India, *manga*. The Portuguese, who introduced mangoes into Europe from India, took the name with them. Mango, the fruit of the plant *Magnifera*, is considered a summer fruit. An Indian's craze for this fruit can be understood only by noting the innumerable varieties (over 1,000) grown all over India. Mangoes can range in size from a small lemon to a large pineapple, and in colour from light green to bright orange-red. Because of the arid climate and tropical heat, Indian mangoes develop a sweetness and perfume unmatched by any others in the world.

The golden yellow flesh of ripe mango is wonderful to eat by itself, but in Indian vegetarian cooking it is used in pilafs, chutneys, spicy sauces, curries, yogurt drinks, puddings, and ice creams.

Incidentally, the amoeba-like shape seen so commonly in the printed fabrics called paisley is a stylized mango!

◆

MULBERRY *Shahtoot*

No visitor to India can honestly claim to have experienced the country without visiting Kashmir and sampling the wonderful mulberries, the fruits of the plant *Morus nigra*, that are sold by the street vendors outside the Moghul gardens and palaces during the summer months. Mulberries range in flavour from very sweet to mouth-puckeringly sour. The black mulberries are more flavourful, hence preferred. In India white mulberry trees are cultivated not for their fruit but for the purpose of housing silkworms.

PAPAYA *Papeeta*

It always comes as a surprise to Indians to discover that one of their favourite fruits, papaya (*Carica payapa*), is in fact native to Central America. *Papeeta*, as it is known in India, is a melonlike fruit with skin that ranges in colour from green in its unripe state to yellowish orange when fully ripe. The sun-gold flesh is sweet and aromatic only when it is fully ripe. Therefore, when buying papaya, make sure you've got a ripe one by lightly pressing it with your thumb. It should 'give' slightly.

Indians generally skin, seed, and slice papaya into wedges and make a cold snack called *chat* with it. They also enjoy it by itself as a fruit or mixed into yoghurt drinks or cooked into sweets and pudding.

◆

SAPOTA OR SAPODILLA *Chikoo*

Sapota, the fruit of the tree *Achras zapota*, native to Central America, has been cultivated in the state of Gujarat in India since the seventeenth century. *Chikoo*, as it is called by the Gujaratis and other Indians, is brown-skinned and ovoid, resembling a kiwi. The slightly grainy textured flesh, pale brown and cloyingly sweet, contains a few large black seeds. The fruit is generally peeled and seeded before serving.

Since Indians have a fondness for extremely sweet tastes, it is not surprising that they love to eat this fruit all by itself. *Chikoo* is most commonly eaten in Indian salads and used in making puddings and sweets.

PULSES

◆

Pulses can be grouped into three categories: lentils, beans, and peas, all of which are called *dal* in Hindi. They are subdivided into unhulled (meaning with the skin still attached to the pulse) or hulled (skin removed and the pulse split in the process). Unhulled pulses hold their shape during cooking, thus making attractive main dishes, especially when cooked with other vegetables. However, they take longer to cook and are hard to digest. Hulled pulses, on the other hand, cook in a very short time and are easier to digest. Since they have no skin to hold them together, they fall apart during cooking and produce marvellous, velvety purées. Laced with spice-perfumed butter, *tadka*, they make delicious light side dishes known as *dal*. Dals comprise the staple of vegetarian diets because they provide the necessary protein.

◆

LENTILS

DAL

Lentils are thin lens-shaped seeds ranging in colour from yellow to walnut brown. The lentil, native to Asia Minor, has been cultivated in India since ancient times. In fact, half of the world production of pulses is concentrated in India. Because they are both easy to digest and extremely versatile to cook with, lentils are the most commonly eaten pulse in India.

The two varieties of lentils used in Indian cooking are the seeds of the plant *Lens culinaris* and the seeds of the plant *Cajanus cajan*. In Europe and America only the lentils from the plant *Lens culinaris* are used. The unhulled whole seeds, ranging in colour from greenish yellow to brownish black are cooked in soups and casseroles and used in salads.

In India these same seeds are first hulled and then split in half to make them easier to cook and digest. In India the *Lens culinaris* variety of lentils are either yellow or pink once their skins are removed. The pink lentils are tiny and known as *masar* or *masoor*.

The *Cajanus cajan* plant produces large yellow lentils known as *toovar*, or *arhar*.

Yellow lentils are popular all over India, while the pink are consumed mainly in the north – all the way from Assam to the western border into Pakistan, Afghanistan, and further. Bengalis have a particular fondness for pink lentils and also turn them into batter for crêpes, fritters, and dumplings. Both yellow and pink lentils cook to a smooth golden purée. In most recipes they can be used interchangeably, although it must be remembered that the yellow purée is thicker and takes almost twice as long to cook as the pink purée.

BEANS

DAL

◆

After lentils, beans are the next most common pulses consumed in India. Of the innumerable varieties that are popular in India, five stand out as the most favoured: mung beans (*moong dal*), black gram (*urad dal*), tepary beans (*moth dal*), kidney beans (*rajma*), and butter beans (*val*). Except for kidney beans, which are always cooked whole with the skins on, all are cooked either whole or hulled and split.

In Indian vegetarian cooking, beans are braised with vegetables, steamed with herbs and spices, or cooked into purées. In some regions they are sprouted and used in salads and appetizers or fried and eaten as snacks. They are also ground into flour, and batter to produce foamy dumplings and pancakes.

BLACK GRAM BEANS *Urad Dal*

Black gram beans are the black cylindrical seeds of the plant *Vigna mungo* (also known as *Phaseolus mungo*). The name *urad dal* usually refers to the hulled and split seed, which is ivory white in colour. This is the form in which it is most widely used, most importantly in the making of the wafers called *papad* or *puppadam*. The beans are extremely rich in protein and minerals. Combined with rice and cooked, they form an easy-to-digest superior protein, as in the universally popular vegetarian breakfast food and tiffin from south

India – *dosai* (crêpes), *uttappam* (sourdough pancakes), *idlee* (steamed dumplings), and *vada* (fried dumplings). In southern India the beans are also used as a spice (as one uses fenugreek seeds or beans).

The whole beans are called *sabat urad*. The most popular preparations in the north are cooked with yogurt, tomatoes, ginger, and spices into a thick, chunky purée, and in the south are cooked with sharp spices and crisp lotus root.

◆

BUTTER BEAN *Val*

Butter bean, also known as *lablab bean*, is the seed of the plant *Dolichos lablab-typicus*, native to India. In Gujarat, where they are most popular, the beans called *val* are generally hulled and split before being cooked into delicately braised dishes with vegetables and spices.

Because of the Gujarati influence, these beans today are also very popular with the Maharashtrians and the Parsis in Bombay.

Val beans, even without their skins, take a long time to cook and are difficult to digest. But since they have a distinct flavour and texture that Indians associate with meat, they are much loved by vegetarians.

◆

KIDNEY BEAN *Rajma Dal*

Kidney bean is the the seed of the plant *Phaseolus vulgaris*, ranging in colour from light pink to dark purplish red. These beans, always consumed whole, are called *rajma* in India. *Rajma* comes in innumerable sizes but for the purpose of marketing are divided into two categories: *badi* (large) *rajma* and *choti* (small) *rajma*. No other Indian understands these beans as well as the Punjabis, who flavour them with onions, cumin, and lots of shredded ginger. The dish is named *ramja* after the beans themselves. *Rajma* is extremely nutritious, very high in protein and carbohydrates, and makes an excellent meat substitute. But because of the type of protein, they are difficult to digest and therefore must be cooked with plenty of digestive seasonings, such as ginger and cloves, and served in small portions unless you are doing a lot of manual work, which aids digestion.

MUNG BEANS *Moong Dal*

Mung beans, also known as green gram beans, are the seeds of the plant *Vigna aureus* (also called *Vigna radiata*, *Phaseolus radiatus*, or *Phaseolus aureus*) and are native to India. The tiny green cylindrical seeds, when hulled and split, yield yellow rectangular beans. The name *moong dal* in India usually refers to yellow mung beans.

Mung beans are much loved by Indians because of their delicate flavour. They also cook quickly (in half the time taken by yellow lentils) and are easy to digest. Since mung beans are rich in protein, Indians cook them with rice to make the famous porridge served at breakfast called *khichdee* (p. 218) in the north and *pongal* (p. 219) in the south. The famous boiled rice and fish preparation known as *kedgeree* is an Anglo-Indian interpretation of the classic Indian dish. *Kedgeree* substitutes egg and fish protein for mung bean protein. In Gujarat and Maharashtra, whole mung beans are sprouted and eaten as a salad or steamed (see the technique for sprouting mung beans on p. 87). Mung bean flour is used for making bread and sweetmeats. Fried mung beans are one of the most popular and nutritive snacks in India (p. 168).

◆

TEPARY BEANS *Moth Dal*

The tepary bean is the very tiny cylindrical brownish green seed of the plant *Vigna acontifolius*, known in India as *moth*. These beans, very similar botanically to mung beans, are cooked much the same way. One popular snack, enjoyed all through the north and southwest, consists of soaking the beans and then frying them. The fried beans are then combined with spices and chick-pea vermicelli. This preparation is called *dal-moth*, after the bean.

OTHER PULSES

◆

BLACK-EYED BEANS *Lobhia Dal*

Black-eyed beans, small kidney-shaped greyish-white seeds from the pod of the plant *Vigna unquiculcata* subspecies *Catiang*, are almost a staple in the southwestern area of Coorg, Maharashtra and Gujarat. They are cooked in stews and braised in dishes with spices. They are also ground into flour for crêpes and pancakes. These beans, when cooked whole, are generally soaked before cooking to soften the skin and hasten the cooking process. In north India they are cooked in similar ways to kidney beans.

◆

CHICK-PEAS AND SPLIT PEAS *Channa Dal*

The most popular and commonly used pea throughout India is the yellow split pea *channa dal* from the pod of the plant *Cicer arietinum*. The name *channa dal* refers to the hulled split peas. The split peas are a little difficult to digest, so they are often cooked combined with vegetables.

The whole peas, known as chick-peas, come in two varieties. The Indian species, yielding small black chick-peas, called in India *kala* or *desi channa*, is most widely grown all over India. A superior variety with large white peas is cultivated in the northern and northwestern regions of India. They are called *safaid* or *kabuli channa*. The most famous preparations of chick-peas are created in Punjab, either by braising them in tangy spicy cumin- and coriander-scented sauces or by boiling them and combining them with fresh herbs and seasonings, making delicious appetizers. In the south they are turned into a snack with an intriguing taste by adding jaggery (raw sugar) and coconut. Chick-peas are also ground into a flour called *besan*, which forms the basis of batters for fritters, dumplings and sweetmeats and, of course, spicy breads.

◆

SOYBEANS *Bhat ya Patnijokra*

Soybeans, the white globular seeds from the pods of the plant *Glycine max*, which grows wild in the eastern Himalayas, is indeed an important pulse crop in India. The soybean has traditionally been used as *dal*, split and cooked similarly to butter beans (*val*). Roasted or, more precisely, popped as popcorn for a snack (called *bhunja*), or ground and mixed with *usli ghee* and jaggery into *laddoo* (sweets), they are a children's delight. In addition, a fermented product of soya is much relished in Manipur and Assam. Soybean flour has become very popular in recent years as an enricher of baking products, for both nutrition and flavour. The traditional breads made with wheat, millet, and barley flour also use soya flour. Also, soybean oil is one of the chief mediums for cooking. In India, soya milk, unfortunately, has not been accepted because of its bland flavour and beany taste. However, soybean curd is becoming very popular as a replacement for milk and cheese (*paneer*), because of the concern for health.

GRAINS

◆

Grains, called *anna lakshmi* (*anna* means 'grain' and *Lakshmi* is the Indian goddess of wealth or prosperity), are part of all Hindu religious ceremonies, from the naming of children over a bed of wheat to blessing a newly-wed couple by throwing it on them.

Many different varieties of grains are cultivated and consumed by Indians. No meal is considered complete without grains being used in one form or another. For many Indians it is an inexpensive source of food-energy proteins and calories. This has resulted in many ingenious creations of grains with special textures and flavours.

◆

BARLEY *Jaun*

Barley has been cultivated in India since ancient times. The holy Hindu scriptures refer to barley, in ancient Sanskrit as *yawa*, being used in all religious rituals. Barley plants (*Hordeum vulgare*), which are mainly grown in the northern provinces of Rajasthan and Uttar Pradesh, resemble wheat somewhat, except that the grains are rounder and plumper. Barley is well known for producing high energy while at the same time having a low fat content. For this reason the grain is mainly used in the form of flour mixed with wheat and chick-pea flours to make the everyday bread (p. 306). Barley is also roasted and coarsely ground into cereal.

◆

BUCKWHEAT *Faafar*

The same plants that yield buckwheat leaves (*Fagopyrum esculentum* and *Fagopyrum tataricum*) also yield buckwheat grains (or cereal), ranging in colour from greyish brown to greyish black. Native to India and central Asia, buckwheat is a cold-climate plant of the Himalayas. Buckwheat is either roasted and made into cereal (*dalia*) or ground into flour. In India buckwheat flour is generally combined with wheat flour for baking *chapati*. Its characteristic aroma is much favoured by the Indians in the Himalayan regions.

Buckwheat flour is rich in protein and other minerals; hence it is a good source of nutrition.

◆

CORN OR MAIZE *Makka*

Corn or maize (*zia mays*) is one of the most extensively grown grains in India. A native of North and South America, corn was introduced in India in the sixteenth century by the Portuguese. In Indian cooking corn is primarily used in the form of a finely ground yellow corn flour. Corn flour contains no gluten; as a result, corn flour breads are cooked like griddle cakes, or the corn flour is combined with wheat flour or certain vegetables possessing a viscous quality as a binder and then baked as *chapati*. The corn bread in Punjab is traditionally eaten with garlic and shredded ginger-laced mustard-green purée (*saag*, p. 246) and a lump of freshly churned butter. In addition to being used for flour, corn kernels are roasted and coarsely cracked for cereal (*dalia*) or processed for corn flour, corn oil, and corn syrup.

◆

MILLET *Bajra*

Millet (*Pennisetum typhoides*), known as pearl millet or *bajra* in India, is one of the most popular cereals in India, along with rice and wheat. Although it is native to Africa, pearl millet has been cultivated in India for centuries. As sorghum, it is grown primarily in dry farming conditions in the central and northwestern regions of India. Very popular with the Gujaratis and Rajasthanis, millet is turned into fragrant pilafs with vegetables or savoury breakfast cereals. The grain is also ground into flour for baking the popular bread *bajra ki roti* or the classic Gujarati *dhebra*, griddle-cake-like breads laced with green chilies, garlic, and spices. Millet flour is generally mixed with wheat flour for breads. This is done to make rolling easier, as millet flour has no gluten, and to make it easier to digest, as millet, a coarse grain, can be very harsh on the digestive system if taken in large portions. Finally, most important of all, the combining of flours results in improved protein in the cereal mixture, making it more nutritious.

RICE

CHAWAL

Rice (*oryza*) has been known to Indians for over six thousand years. The ancient Hindu holy books made frequent reference to *anna* ('rice grain') and *anna lakshmi* ('goddess of prosperity') as the source of life. Rice is today the staple of two thirds of the population of India. In fact, rice accounts for half of all the grains cultivated in India.

There are thousands of varieties of rice grown in India, but they can generally be grouped first by treatment: raw (standard) or processed (parboiled). Then it is classified first by the length of the grain: long, medium, or short, and then by breadth: superfine, fine, or coarse. Obviously superfine, meaning narrow or thin, long grains rank highest. It also matters if the grains are unscented or scented (such as in the case of basmati).

Of all these types the following are most popularly used.

◆

STANDARD LONG-GRAIN RICE *Arwa Chawal*

This husked, milled and polished grain of rice, called *arwa chawal*, is similar to American long-grain rice. It is a staple in most eastern and southern provinces in India. Basmati, a superior long-grain rice that costs a lot more, is reserved for special occasions. This rice, in my opinion, is best suited to southern and eastern Indian vegetarian dishes, as its neutral flavour heightens the spiciness of these regional specialities.

BASMATI (SCENTED) LONG-GRAIN RICE

The northern Indians do not eat rice on a regular basis; they are primarily wheat- and millet-bread-eating people. However, when they do, the preference (if they can afford it) is for the scented long-grain rice called basmati (literally meaning 'queen of fragrance'), grown along the foothills of the Himalayas. Cooked basmati has long, thin grains, like pieces of vermicelli, that are tender-spongy to the touch. Basmati exudes a special aroma, described as milky-nutty – musky, even when it is served all by itself, without even salt or butter. Basmati complements all northern, central northwestern, and western regional dishes, particularly those of Moghul origin. Basmati needs to age before it develops the right cooking qualities (a non-chalky and fluffy texture with an intense aroma), and so the rice is stored in *godowns* (storing decreases the moisture content and intensifies its flavour). Basmati that contains few or no broken grains is preferred. Therefore, the number-one grade of basmati contains no broken grains and has been aged for at least six months or better yet, two years. Although in India one can buy dozens of varieties, here in Britain, we can only find one kind, called simply basmati.

◆

PARBOILED OR PROCESSED RICE *Sela Chawal*

Parboiled rice, common in the Western world, originated in India several centuries ago. In this process husked rice is soaked in water and steamed, then sun-dried before it is milled. In India more than half of all the rice that is cultivated is parboiled, the reason being that the rice grown in the southern and eastern regions is primarily medium- and short-grain. This rice, especially the freshly harvested kind, has a soft, chalky texture and suffers extensive damage during milling. Also it cooks to a sticky, glutinous mass with little expansion. Parboiling firms the rice grains, thereby making milling and cooking easy. In the southern and eastern regions (specifically Malabar, Orissa, Madras, Bihar, and West Bengal), parboiled medium- and short-grain rice is popular. Parboiled rice is widely available in supermarkets, sold under brand names.

GLUTINOUS RICE *Pottoo Arshi*

In India, specifically southern India, two varieties of glutinous rice are used in cooking: white and black. Glutinous rice, incidentally, is so-called not because of its gluten content, which is nonexistent, but because the rice, when cooked, sticks together like glue.

White glutinous rice is used for steamed cakes called *pottoo* that are made of ground rice and freshly grated coconut and eaten with palm jaggery and spicy curries at breakfast.

Black glutinous rice (which really is white glutinous rice with the bran layer still attached, but called so because of its dark appearance) is highly nutritious. It is pounded and cooked with coconut, Indian raw sugar, and *usli ghee* and turned into the delicious sweet *tottoloo*, particularly enjoyed by new mothers.

Glutinous rice has always been grown in Burma, which, when it was part of India, supplied the population of south India with it. After the partition, glutinous rice became more and more difficult to import. As a result, today in the south this rice is substituted with freshly harvested short-grain rice, which has many of the characteristics of glutinous rice. Short-grain rice, when coarsely ground to the texture of cereal (needed to make *pottoo*), is called *pottoo arshi*, or Indian glutinous rice.

◆

TAPIOCA *Sago*

Sago (*Sago cycas*), known popularly as *sagodana* (*dana* means 'grains'), is essentially pressed starch extruded from the pith of the stems of *Metroxylon sago*, a variety of palm from Malaya. The pith is pressed through discs and emerges in pear-like shapes. Sago pearls used to be imported from Malaya. It is now produced locally in India from cassava (*Manihot esculenta*), known in this country as sago or tapioca. Because tapioca is easy to digest, it is the primary food given to people during convalescence in India. In general cooking the three most popular presentations of *sago* are a wonderful pudding from south India called *payasam*, a pilaf made with green chilies and spices from Maharashtra called *sagoodana ki kichdee*, and croquettes made with potatoes and herbs from Bombay.

NUTS AND SEEDS

◆

Nuts and seeds are much richer in protein, vitamins, and minerals, pound for pound, than are pulses. They are also, however, very expensive, thus making them unaffordable for the common people. Because of their delicate flavour and velvety texture in ground form, nuts and seeds are used in Indian cooking in innumerable ways – to thicken creamy smooth sauces of Moghul origin; to enrich puddings; to garnish vegetables, pilafs, and rice casseroles; to make sweets, delicious *halwas*, and refreshing beverages. Indians love nuts to such an extent that they turn them into main dishes on special occasions (*kajoo korma*, butter-braised cashew nuts with spices).

Nuts and seeds contain a large portion of oil and must be stored in cool, dry places to prevent them from turning rancid. Also, nuts and seeds taste best freshly harvested, when their natural aroma is at its peak. For best flavour do not store them longer than six months.

◆

ALMOND *Badaam*

Almond, the nut of the tree *Prunus amygdalus*, native to central and western Asia, came to India with the Moghuls centuries ago. It is the most important nut in Indian cooking, particularly in the north, used in the preparation of many local specialities from delicate almond drinks and soups to sweetmeats. Its delicate aroma and smooth, creamy texture when ground into butter have stimulated generations of Indian cooks to incorporate it into braised dishes as well as to use for velvet-smooth sauces. Moghul pilafs are incomplete until almonds adorn them.

◆

CASHEW NUT *Kajoo*

The cashew nut, the fruit of the plant *Anacardium occidentale*, although it is traditionally associated with Indian food, is surprisingly not of

Indian origin. A native of Central America, this kidney-shaped fruit with its extremely pleasant-tasting nut was introduced to India by the Portuguese some four hundred years ago. Grown along the western coast in the south, the cashew nut is mainly used in southern cooking. It is generally chopped into bits, fried, and added to a boundless number of savoury and sweet preparations from breakfast cereals to sweetmeats. Because of its high protein content, it is also dry-roasted or fried and enjoyed as a snack food. Cashew-nut butter, unlike light-textured almond butter, is creamier and pastier and is therefore used in Indian dishes with sauces to give them a thicker, richer taste.

◆

MELON SEEDS *Kharbooje ke Beej*

Seeds from melons, such as cantaloupe, are sun-dried and peeled to yield off-white edible kernels. These seeds are an important food in north Indian cooking, often used as a substitute for almonds since they are more readily available and far less expensive. In India, melon seeds are seldom purchased in shops, as most households make it a practice to collect their own. Here, however, I doubt if many of us would have the time and patience, particularly when sunflower seeds make an ideal substitute.

◆

PEANUT OR GROUND NUT *Moong Phali*

Peanut, also known as ground nut (because it grows underground) in India, was brought there by the Portuguese in the sixteenth century. The peanut plant (*Arachnis hypogaea*) is cultivated primarily in the south of India and is used extensively in regional dishes there such as in tamarind sauces, rice pilafs, and sweetmeats. Because in India peanuts cost a fraction of what almonds and cashew nuts cost, and also because they are more nutritious (high in protein and low in fat), they are the primary ingredient in many Indian snack foods. Peanuts also yield groundnut oil, one of the primary cooking oils in Indian cuisine (see p. 56).

PINE KERNELS, INDIAN *Chilgoza ya Nioza*

Pine kernels are edible white seeds obtained from pinecones of different species found in many parts of the world. Indian pine kernels (*Pinus gerardiana*) are thinner and longer than Italian pine kernels, and are also more fragrant and flavourful. *Chilgoza*, enjoyed mainly in north India, are used in desserts, puddings, and sweetmeats, and sometimes in smooth sauces.

◆

PISTACHIO *Pista*

Pistachio, the exquisitely flavoured nut of the tree *Pistacia vera*, native to central Asia, has always held an esteemed place in Indian cooking. The Moghul emperor Jahangir attributed aphrodisiac qualities to it and once prohibited its use outside the royal kitchen by declaring it 'the nut of paradise'. Although Indians enjoy roasted, salted pistachios as snacks, only the raw unsalted nuts are used in cooking. They are shelled, peeled, and sliced to garnish delicate desserts, puddings, and fragrant pilafs, and to provide texture and taste to sweetmeats.

◆

SESAME *Til*

Sesame, the seed of the plant *Sesamum indicum*, has been cultivated in India since pre-Aryan times. Of all the seeds available to Indians, sesame is the richest in protein, hence it is one of the primary foods in a vegetarian diet. Sesame seeds are used extensively in southern and southwestern cooking in pilafs, sauces, stuffings, chutneys, biscuits and sweets. Sesame seeds range in colour from pearl white-grey and brown to black. Today the white sesame seeds are preferred for their appearance, although it is the black variety that grows predominantly in the south. Black sesame seeds contain less oil, hence are preferred in sweetmeat making. They have also been the source of the highly fragrant caramel-coloured Gingelly oil (p. 56), the primary cooking oil all through the south.

WALNUT *Akhroot*

The walnut tree *Juglans regia*, growing along the lower slopes of the Himalayas, particularly in the Kashmir region, is famous for its edible fruit and its wood,which is used to make the world-famous Kashmiri carved furniture.

In Indian cooking walnuts are used in braised dishes to thicken sauces and in the preparation of sweetmeats. In Kashmir miniature green walnuts with tender, soft flesh are eaten as a salad or a dessert. They are also cooked into chutneys and conserves (*murabbaa*). Pressed walnut oil is used by the Kashmiris in sauces and dressings in festive dishes.

MILK AND MILK PRODUCTS

◆

Indians are obsessively fond of milk. No food equals it in flavour and taste. An important source of protein, milk has innumerable culinary uses. Ancient Indians considered milk the primary food of man (*Aryan*) and offered clarified butter (*gritha*)* to the great gods of heaven. Milk in all forms is an integral part of the Indian way of life. It is, in fact, the *only* animal protein for many Indians.

Indians use the milk of the many different animals that produce it and can be milked. These include the cow, buffalo, goat, sheep, camel, ass, mare, and yak. Camel's milk is restricted to the desert region of Rajasthan, while sheep's, yak's, and mare's milks are found only on the mountain slopes of the Himalayas. Goat's milk has always been associated with the poorer class of the Moslem population. Ass's milk obviously reflects an extreme state of desperation for the need of milk. A Brahmin, believing that everything put into the mouth goes first to the brain, would, of course, consider suicide first. Cow's and water buffalo's milk are the first choices and are most widely consumed.

You might conclude from all this that milk would be abundant and affordable in India. Well, milk is plentiful but it is very expensive, because the care and feeding of cows and buffalos cost a great deal. An average Indian family can spend as much as a third of its food budget on milk and milk products every month!

You can therefore understand why the cow is sacred to an Indian and milk one of life's greatest blessings. The common words uttered by elderly women to bless young girls in India are *Doodho nahao pooton phalo* ('May you bathe in or be overwhelmed with milk and have many sons and grandsons').

Brahmins worship cows, and bathe them in sandalwood water and adorn them with rose garlands and *bindi* (the sacred vermilion mark on the forehead). They serve them eighteen-course banquet meals at certain festivals!

Indians use milk in many ways – as yogurt, clotted cream, buttermilk, butter, clarified butter, cheese, thickened milk sauce, milk scrapings, and milk fudge. All these products have their own distinct flavour, texture, and aroma, hence in Indian cooking they are always considered distinctly different foods.

Gritha is the ancient sanskrit word for *usli ghee*.

MILK *Doodh*

Cow's milk with its delicate fragrance is preferred for direct use, while buffalo's milk with its higher fat content is preferred for making milk products.

Indians enjoy milk most as a drink, mixed with cool spices as a summer punch, or warm and laced with saffron threads and cardamom to cut the winter chill. Milk is also necessary in making Indian-style tea (*chah*) and southern Indian coffee. Finally, milk is widely used to enrich sauces in many savoury dishes and to make puddings, desserts, and sweetmeats.

◆

YOGURT *Dahi*

Indian yogurt is different from the yogurt we get here. It is most likely to be made of buffalo's milk; thus it is creamier and more firm textured – almost the consistency of gelatine – and it has a marvellous fermented aroma. To reproduce Indian yogurt, you are left with two options. You can modify commercially available yogurt to make it more like the Indian kind by mixing in a little sour cream, double cream, or yogurt cheese, depending upon the need of the recipe. Or you can make your own.

Yogurt is easily made at home. To make yogurt you first scald milk and cook it to room temperature. When it is barely warm (about 55°C), add a little started yogurt (about 1 tablespoon yogurt for each ¾ pint/ 450 ml milk). Mix it in well, then cover and let the yogurt set in a warm place. In an oven with a pilot light on or near a radiator is a good place. The yogurt takes anywhere from eight to twelve hours to set. When the yogurt is set, transfer the dish to the refrigerator to stop further fermentation. An inexpensive proposition is to invest in an electric yogurt maker. These work very well, especially if you are handling yogurt for the first time.

◆

HUNG YOGURT *Khadi Dahi*

Hung yogurt is a delicacy from the states of Gujarat and Maharashtra, along the west coast of India. It is made by hanging the yogurt for several hours in muslin until all excess moisture has drained off, leaving behind a soft cream-cheese-like product with a slightly fermented sour flavour. It is laced with herbs for breakfast or combined with fruits and nuts and served as a dessert. Hung yogurt is not sold commercially. It is always made at home and should be eaten within forty-eight hours for the freshest taste.

Hung yogurt is best made with a rich, creamy yogurt that has a distinct aroma. I begin by making, first, a rich batch of yogurt that compares with the Indian one. The proportions are 1¼ pints/750 ml milk combined with ½ pint/300 ml double cream. When the yogurt is set, I carefully remove the clotted cream on the surface (it can be used to make fresh butter or for certain desserts). The decreamed yogurt (with a fat content of only 10 per cent) is what I then use to make hung yogurt cheese. I place this yogurt in double or triple layers of muslin, the four corners of which I tie together. The yogurt is then hung to drain overnight or for eight hours (a door handle on a kitchen cupboard directly over the sink is a good spot). At the end of hanging, the mixture is reduced to about half its original quantity. Transfer the cheese, scraping it from the muslin with a rubber spatula, to a dish; cover and refrigerate.

◆

INDIAN BUTTER *Desi Makkan*

Indian butter (*desi makkan*) is produced from yogurt, or the clotted cheese from yogurt, or the two combined. It has a high acidity (lactic acid) and a pronounced pungent flavour. Indian butter is also prepared from clotted cream collected from several batches of milk, soured with the addition of a little yogurt, and ripened for a day at room temperature, so it can develop the desired level of acidity.

Indian butter is a delicacy for peasants all through the northern and western regions. It is traditionally enjoyed for breakfast over flaky radish bread or millet bread laced with green chilies. It is this butter that is melted and folded into lentil dishes and the classic Punjabi mustard purée, *saag*.

Desi makkan is made by adding equal amounts of water to yogurt or a yogurt-cream mixture and then churning it until it separates into lumps. The butter is used immediately or stored, floating in cold water and refrigerated. Fresh butter keeps from up to two days, after which time you should turn it into clarified butter.

CLARIFIED BUTTER *Usli Ghee*

Clarified butter (*usli ghee*) is made by heating butter long enough to allow the moisture present in the milk solids, which causes spoilage, to evaporate. The slow heating and cooking process gives the clarified butter a gentle nutty aroma, a pale yellow colour when cool, and a distinctly grainy texture. The unmistakable taste of authentic *usli ghee* is due to the lactic flavour present in the butter.

To increase the shelf life of *usli ghee* and to give it an interesting dimension, Indians add the leaves of the betel nut plant or cinnamon plant, nutmeg, cloves, peppercorns, dry ginger, or a piece of turmeric. To make *usli ghee* see the recipe on p. 57.

Usli ghee is the favourite cooking fat of Indian vegetarians, especially in pilafs, lentils, freshly baked breads, sweetmeats, delicate puddings, and desserts.

◆

INDIAN BUTTERMILK *Chach, Lassi, aur Mattha*

Indian buttermilk, called *chach*, is a by-product of Indian butter. The liquid from which the butter separates produces buttermilk. *Chach* has a unique and strong lactic flavour. It is thin, intensely flavourful, and has a distinct yogurt taste. It is this type of *chach* that is traditionally used for making the sweet beverage *lassi* or its savoury equivalent, *mattha*. Indian buttermilk is also combined with rice and salad vegetables and served as a cool, refreshing soup in parts of southern India.

The best substitute for Indian buttermilk is good-quality plain yogurt (preferably homemade) diluted with water. The proportions are given in each recipe.

◆

INDIAN CHEESE *Chenna aur Paneer*

Indian cheese is one of the most delicate of cheeses imaginable. Simple in concept and preparation, it is made by curdling milk and separating the creamy white cheese. This fresh cheese is extremely fragrant and is considered a true delicacy. *Paneer* is *chenna* that has been pressed to extract all its moisture. *Paneer* is also moulded and thus can be cut into neat pieces.

Chenna and *paneer* are important sources of protein for all Indian vegetarians. The culinary uses of *chenna* and *paneer* are phenomenal. *Chenna* is the primary ingredient in almost all the famous sweets from Bengal. *Chenna* is also used in various sweetmeats and desserts. *Paneer*, on the other hand, is treated as an important protein food. Cut into small pieces and sautéed, *paneer* is served in innumerable braised sauces, pilafs, and gravy-based dishes.

To make chenna, bring 3¼ pints/2 litres of milk to the boil. Reduce the heat, keeping the milk at a gentle rolling boil, and add one of the following coagulants: 3 tablespoons freshly squeezed lemon juice, ½ pint/250 ml sour plain yogurt, or 3 tablespooons cider vinegar diluted with 3 tablespoons water. As soon as the milk curdles and the white curd forms and separates from the greenish yellow whey, turn off the heat. Pour the cheese along with the liquid through a colander or sieve lined with a thin fabric or four layers of muslin and place it in the kitchen sink. Hold the colander under the tap and let cold water run through the cheese to wash away the excess odour of the coagulant. Bring up the four corners of the muslin and tie them together. Gently twist to extract as much water from the cheese as possible, then hang the cheese to drain for an hour (as in making hung yogurt cheese). This cheese, crumbly in texture and slightly moist, is *chenna*.

To make paneer, wrap the *chenna* back in the same muslin, place it on the work surface, and weight it down with a heavy object such as a large pot filled with water. Press the cheese for half an hour. Remove the cheese and cut into small ½ in/1 cm by ½ in/1 cm by 1 in/2.5 cm pieces. Keep the cheese immersed in a bowl of water until needed. It keeps well for up to four days, covered and refrigerated.

◆

THICKENED MILK SAUCE, MILK FLAKES, AND MILK FUDGE
Rabadi, Khurchan, aur Khoya

When milk is boiled in a large shallow pan for a long period of time, it gradually undergoes miraculous changes in colour, flavour, and texture, transforming itself from a milky white liquid to a brown fudge-like mass with a distinctly sweet aroma. *Rabadi, khurchan,* and *khoya* are the different milk products that are produced at different stages of the same cooking process. Each of these creations plays an important role in the sweetmeat making industry of India. Even though their preparation requires considerable time and skill, they are all made on a regular basis in all the pastry shops of India.

To make rabadi, the milk is cooked in a large *kadhai* or any sauté pan, with as little stirring as possible until it develops the characteristic *rabadi* aroma. The milk reduces over a period of time and concentrates to the consistency of golden syrup. To aid in the evaporation process, the skin, as it forms over the milk, is periodically broken and removed to the sides of the *kadhai* or pan, where it dries into flaky layers (called *khurchan*).

The concentrated thick milk is then combined with water and flavouring and enjoyed as the classic *rabadi-doodh* (*rabadi*-flavoured milk) beverage. The milk flakes are used as a golden flaky garnish over *halwa* and special Rajasthani sweets.

Generally at the end of cooking when the milk reaches the appropriate concentration, the milk flakes are scraped and stirred into the milk to produce *rabadi*. Thus a good *rabadi* is golden coloured and is almost of a honeylike consistency, with layers and layers of flakes of milk. It is this *rabadi* that forms the basic sauce for the classic dessert *ras malai* and many Bengali and Rajasthani sweets and as a fruit topping.

Instead of stopping the cooking, if the *rabadi* is cooked further, it concentrates into a doughlike mass that, when cooled, develops a fudge-like texture. This is called *khoya*. It is pale brown in colour and has a pronounced *rabadi* flavour. *Khoya* is a speciality of Uttar Pradesh and is the base of the famous sweet *peda*.

The classic milk fudge *khoya* is of course not made from *rabadi*. The milk in this process is boiled rapidly while being stirred constantly to reduce it to a fudge-like mass in the quickest time possible. Stirring keeps the fat from separating on top. As a result, the *khoya* is pearl-white, with a nutty aroma, and has a rich buttery consistency. It is this *khoya* that forms the basis for almost all Punjabi and Gujarati sweets and the famous sweet *gulab jamun*. Kashmiris use this to make their meat-lookalike *keema* dish *matar shufta* (p. 216).

OILS AND FATS

◆

OILS

◆

As in France, one factor that gives different regional cultures in India their individual character is the use of distinctly different cooking oils. There are many different oils, and each region specializes in one (although it may use one or two more), depending upon the natural availability and its adaptability to local cuisine.

That is why a simple dish such as quick-sautéed spinach tastes distinctly different in each region. The Bengal cook sautés it in mustard oil, the Madras in sesame oil, the Malabar in coconut oil, and the Bhopal in groundnut oil, to name just a few.

The oils (called *tel* in Indian) used in Indian cooking are generally cold-pressed, hence intensely aromatic. They are also unprocessed (what we call unrefined); thus they are caramel-coloured and fairly viscous.

In towns in India even today you can see the old-fashioned oil presses, where nuts and seeds are pressed right in front of your eyes. The freshly pressed oil, slightly warm and still frothy, is poured into metal jugs (designed especially for oil) to be carried home.

There are four important cooking oils used in Indian vegetarian cooking: coconut, groundnut, mustard and sesame. In addition, there are sunflower, safflower, and soya oils, all of which in recent years have gained tremendous popularity, primarily for health reasons. Then there are almond and walnut oils, used sparingly due to their prohibitive cost and limited production.

◆

COCONUT OIL *Narial ka Tel*

Coconut oil is the pressed oil extracted from ground desiccated coconut, called *khopra*. Although coconut palms are found all along the coastline from Gujarat to Bengal, it is the southern region that specializes in manufacturing coconut oil. Naturally the people of this region are the primary consumers. Coconut oil has a deep, nutty aroma and a characteristic rich, desiccated-coconut flavour. In Malabar, where there are more coconut trees than stars in the sky, coconut oil is used in general cooking. It is an essential ingredient of their *moolee* dishes. I find its heaviness and the fact that it is so highly saturated – to the degree that lard is – bothersome, so I limit my use of it in Indian cooking to a few Malabar dishes.

◆

GROUNDNUT OIL *Meetha Tel*

Groundnut oil, known as *meetha tel* or *moongphali ka tel*, is one of the most popular cooking oils in central and northern India. Indian groundnut oil has a deep aroma and a beautiful amber colour. The groundnut oil available here is light coloured and almost tasteless. The best way to capture some of that authentic Indian aroma and flavour is by adding some toasted peanuts, whole, chopped, or ground, to the dish.

◆

MUSTARD OIL *(Sarsoon ka Tel)*

Lush mustard plants fill the fields in the eastern and northern plains of India. The seeds, in addition to being used as a spice, are pressed to yield mustard oil called *sarsoon ka tel* or *kadwa tel*. Mustard oil has an intense mustardy aroma and a slightly bitter taste, characteristics much loved by the mountain people called Pahadi and the populace of the eastern regions of India. Mustard oil is, in fact, preferred for deep frying, cooking vegetables, flavouring peas, and pickling throughout all of northern India. It has been renowned for its medicinal properties for centuries. Used as a liniment for massaging the body, it is believed to relieve rheumatic and arthritic pain. Women in Bengal, known for their long, lustrous black hair, apply mustard oil as a hair tonic.

◆

SESAME OIL *Til ka Tel*

Indian sesame oil, deep golden-coloured with a sweet robust aroma, is an essential flavouring and cooking oil of the Brahmins and Jains of southern and southwestern India. Sesame oil, called *til ka tel* or more popularly Gingelly oil, is used in dressings, condiments, stews and soups and in braised and stir-fried dishes.

FATS
◆

All fats are referred to as *ghee* in India. Desserts, sweetmeats, and puddings, as a general rule, are cooked in fat, preferably butter (*usli ghee*), for two reasons. One is the flavour – Indians like a dish better with this taste. The second is that the butterfat in sweetmeats acts as a binder without looking and feeling greasy, which happens when you make them with oil.

◆

CLARIFIED BUTTER *Usli Ghee*

Butter in India is called *makkhan*. Clarified butter, instead of being called *makkhan ghee*, is called *usli ghee* (*usli* means 'real' or 'pure', which in this context refers to the real or original fat of the ancient Indians). Clarified butter or *usli ghee* is essentially French brown butter with the brown residue strained off. *Usli ghee* has a light caramel colour and a heavenly aroma. Since there is no moisture present, it keeps well covered, at room temperature, for several months.

To make clarified butter (*usli ghee*), place 8 oz/250 g unsalted butter in a heavy-bottomed saucepan and put on a burner. Keep the heat low until the butter melts completely, stirring often during the process. Increase the heat to medium-low and let the butter simmer until it stops crackling, thus indicating that all the moisture has evaporated and the milk residue is beginning to fry. As soon as the solids turn brown (10–12 minutes), turn off the heat and take the pan off the stove. Let the residue settle to the bottom of the pan, then strain the clear butterfat (*usli ghee*) into another container. This *usli ghee*, when it is completely cool, will turn a creamy colour.

◆

INDIAN VEGETABLE SHORTENING *Vanaspati Ghee*

Vegetable shortening in India is called *vanaspati* (vegetable) *ghee*. It is a creamy lemon colour and has a nutty aroma very similar to that of *usli ghee*. This resemblance is no accident, for Indian vegetable shortening has been created as an inexpensive substitute for *usli ghee*, which is very expensive. Hindu Brahmins and Jains consider this shortening an imposter and scorn the mere thought of eating it.

They seriously believe that India's problems today are due to all the adulterated fat (another name for vegetable shortening used primarily by *usli ghee* eaters) consumed by the masses.

I like the flavour of both *usli ghee* and Indian vegetable shortening in specific lentil dishes and breads. Indian vegetable shortening is available in Indian grocers. For those who would like to make it at home, here is my technique, which produces, I think, very good results. To make about 1 lb/500 g of shortening:

1 lb/500 g shortening (supermarket variety)
1 oz/30 g dry milk powder
2 oz/60 g plain flour
Plain yogurt

Melt the shortening in a shallow pan over low heat (300°F/150°C). While the fat is heating, mix the milk powder, flour, and enough yogurt to make a soft dough. When the shortening has melted and is heated, pinch off little portions of dough, roll them into rough balls, and drop into the oil. Fry the balls in oil until they turn dark brown (about 15 minutes). Remove the balls with a slotted spoon and discard. When the fat is cool enough to handle, strain and transfer it to a container. When it is completely cool, the fat or shortening will develop a creamy colour, a grainy texture, and a distinct characteristic flavour very much like authentic Indian vegetable shortening.

SPICES AND HERBS

◆

Spices are sensuous flavourings experienced by all the senses. Most of them are aromatics that are best enjoyed in their fullest fragrance when they are slightly crushed. In this form they can be inhaled like a delicate perfume. In addition to the aromatic spices, there are some that are used in Indian cooking just for the purpose of lending visual appeal – brilliant colour or breathtaking texture. Spices are organic substances that are often difficult to eat in their raw form. They must be treated as a food ingredient and thoroughly cooked, either prior to being added to the food or added and cooked with the rest of the food in the preparation of a dish.

Spices and herbs have many essential medicinal properties. They are the foundation of the five-thousand-year-old Indian herbal medicine, *Ayur Veda*, which is practised even today.

A full discussion of this subject is beyond the scope of this book. What you need to know, however, is that spices are important and good for your body, mind, and soul. You also need to know their properties, that is, what they do to food, and gradually become familiar with them. You will then be able to venture far beyond the recipes in this book and begin creating your own flavourings and expressing your preferences, which is the true art of Indian cooking.

◆

ANISE AND STAR ANISE *Saunf aur Badayan*

The tiny oval seeds of anise, both *Anisum vulgare* and *Anisum officinalis*, are known as *vilayati saunf* (meaning 'foreign fennel') in India because the original true *saunf* is fennel (*Foeniculum vulgare*). Anise, because of its delicate flavour, is valued more and therefore preferred.

Star anise (*Illicium verum*) is a similar-smelling spice, but a little stronger and sweeter. Star anise is mainly imported from China to India and used in the Bombay region by the Parsis in their pilafs and braised dishes. Star anise, called *badayan* is an important spice in the multi-purpose Parsi spice blend *dhanajeera*. Star anise costs far less than 'true' anise, hence is extensively used in restaurants and commercial food establishments throughout India.

ASAFETIDA *Heeng*

Asafetida is the dried gum exuded from the living rhizome of several species of *Ferula* growing in India along the slopes of Kashmir and in Afghanistan and Iran.

It is sold commercially in lump or powder form. In lumps, brownish black in colour, it is in its purest form, and virtually odourless until it is powdered. Then it releases its characteristic aroma that may take over the entire kitchen and linger on. When it is sold commercially, ground asafetida is always combined with rice powder to prevent it from lumping. It is also almost always adulterated with gum arabic, barley, or wheat flour, and sometimes even chalk and red clay! I therefore strongly recommend using asafetida in lump form, although most urban Indians have started buying asafetida powder for convenience. You can store the lumps of asafetida and grind one whenever you need it. Or you can make a powder of the entire lump and then store it. If, however, you decide to purchase ground asafetida powder, remember to use double the amount called for in the recipe.

Asafetida is the most favoured spice of vegetarians because when it is exposed to heat it exudes an onion-like aroma, a vegetable usually prohibited to Hindu Brahmins and Jains. The onion smell, incidentally, is due to the sulphur compounds present in the volatile oil in asafetida.

◆

BASIL *Tulsi*

Mention *tulsi* and a Hindu will immediately fold his hands in the eternal worship gesture. This religious association with basil dates back to the Vedic period. Today a Hindu home is considered impure without a *tulsi* plant growing at the entrance.

In Indian cooking basil is used sparingly for two reasons: first, most varieties of basil cultivated in India are quite aromatic and sharp and hence are used only with certain foods and preparations. Examples include holy basil tea made with ginger essence and honey; and camphor- or basil-laced pea and pumpkin stew. Second, the long and deeply sacred association of basil with the supreme god of creation Vishnu has been a constant deterrent to its use in cooking.

The chief kinds of basil cultivated in India are holy basil (*Ocimum sanctum*, known as *Vishnu tulsi*), white basil (*Ocimum album*, or *biswa tulsi*, and camphor basil (*Ocimum kilimandscharicum*, or *kapoor tulsi*).

Camphor basil and holy basil are not available fresh here; they are, I think, useless dried. Sweet basil makes an acceptable substitute for holy basil when combined with a few leaves of peppermint, and for camphor basil when it is combined with a few pieces of star anise.

◆

BAY LEAF, INDIAN *Tej Patta*

Indian bay leaf, spicy but mellow tasting, is the leaf of the cassia tree (*Cinnamomum cassia*), native to India and most of eastern Asia. Bay leaves are used extensively in the cooking of northern India, particularly in the northeastern regions, where they are grown in their natural habitat. Bay laurel leaves may be substituted, except they have a more pungent, lemony aroma.

◆

BLACK ONION SEED OR NIGELLA *Kalaunji*

Black onion seeds, also called nigella, are tiny satiny seeds of the plant *Nigella sativa*. Black onion has no connection whatsoever with the onion plant, but the seeds resemble onion seeds, hence the name. Nigella grows wild throughout all of north India. It is used extensively in eastern regional cooking. There, these seeds, because of their shape and colour, are called *kala jeera* (meaning black cumin) and the actual black cumin or royal cumin are called *shahi jeera* (i.e. just royal cumin). The confusion begins when people move out of the region and refer to spices by their regional names. Unless one has a full knowledge of these differences, the wrong cumin (or spice) can very easily be added, thus changing the flavour of the dish.

Black onion seeds are extensively used in stir-fried vegetable dishes, in flavouring pulses (*dal*), and in pickles.

◆

CARAWAY *Gunyan*

Caraway, the seeds of the plant *Carum carvi* or *Carum bulbocastanum*, grows wild in the hills of Kashmir, the northernmost state of India. Caraway, called *gunyan* in Kashmir, is essentially used in Kashmiri cooking to flavour breads and pastries and to create mock meat dishes.

CARDAMOM *Elaichi*

Cardamom, the fruit of the plant *Elettaria cardamomum*, is native to southern India and Sri Lanka. The seeds contained inside the pods hold the fragrance. In dishes that call for a milder spice flavour, such as pilafs, whole cardamom pods are used. For a more aromatic effect, as in puddings and sweetmeats, ground or crushed cardamom is preferred. Either the whole pod or just the seeds may be ground. Naturally the seeds without their skins will give you a more strongly flavourful batch of ground cardamom. Cardamom comes in three colours: green, white, and black (which is also larger). The white cardamom pod is really a bleached variety of the green. Natural green is always preferred, if you can get it, because it has more flavour. Black cardamom is mellower and only slightly spicy as compared to the highly aromatic sweet green pods. The general rule is to add green cardamom to sweets and puddings, and black to all pilafs and savoury dishes, although green works well for all kinds of dishes.

◆

CAROM OR AJOWAN *Ajwain ya Omum*

Carom, also known as ajowan or bishop's weed, are the tiny poppy-seed-like spice of the plant *Carum copticum*, cultivated in south-western Asia, including India. Carom has a distinct pungent aroma and a sharp taste, hence it must be used in moderation. It is a well-known medicine in India prescribed for flatulence and grippe. For this reason and for its natural affinity to starch, carom is used in snacks like rich pastries, breads, and biscuits, and with beans and starchy roots.

Thyme (*Thymus vulgaris*) makes a good substitute for carom. Both contain the volatile oil *thymol*, which is what imparts its unique aroma. Lovage also makes a fine substitute, as its volatile oil, *lovage oil*, is similar to thymol oil.

◆

CINNAMON *Dalchini*

The cinnamon used in Indian cooking is the bark of the cassia tree (*Cinnamomum cassia*). It is a more intensely flavoured spice than the bark of the other cinnamon (known as sweet or true cinnamon) tree,

Cinnamomum zylanicum. Cinnamon, grown in the eastern regions of India, is an important spice there. It is also an essential spice of Moghul cooking and of the spice blend, *garam masala.* Depending upon the intensity of flavouring required in a dish, cinnamon is used as whole sticks, crushed, or ground.

◆

CLOVE *Laung*

Cloves are the dried buds of the plant *Syzygium aromaticum,* native to the Molucca Islands in eastern Indonesia. Clove, fragrant and pungent, is an essential spice in Moghul cooking and eastern regional cooking. It is used extensively in pilafs, braised dishes that have rich onion-tomato sauces, and for perfuming oil to cook vegetables.

◆

COCONUT FLAKES, DESICCATED *Khopra*

Khopra, or desiccated coconut flakes, used as a spicy flavouring in Indian cooking, is not to be confused with fresh fruit coconut (*narial*) (see p. 83).

The coconut fruit, when left on the tree to mature fully, then plucked and sun-dried, yields a product called *khopra.* In India *khopra* is sold whole. There the cook breaks off a small piece and grates it. Here *khopra* is sold only in grated form, also called *flaked* or *desiccated* coconut. Since *khopra* contains a large amount of oil, you must store it in a cool place or it will become rancid.

◆

CORIANDER *Dhania*

The plant *Coriandrum sativum* yields both the pungent-smelling, white-pepper-like spice known as coriander seeds and the highly aromatic herb known as coriander leaves. Coriander seeds, the most extensively used spice in all of Indian cooking, are the primary ingredient in curry powder and in the northern Moghul spice blend *garam masala.* In Indian cooking coriander seeds are generally ground and then added to hot oil and fried to flavour vegetables and pulses.

CUMIN, ROYAL OR BLACK *Shahi Jeera ya Kala Jeera*

Black cumin (*Cuminum nigrum*) is a rare variety of cumin that grows wild in the southeast part of Iran and along the valleys of Kashmir. It has a mellow, sweet taste. Black cumin seeds, when crushed, smell faintly like white cumin but more like black truffles from Perigord. Black cumin is more herbal and therefore it is much sought after for the delicate pilafs of Kashmir and for dishes of Moghul origin.

Black cumin, known as *shahi jeera* or *kala jeera*, is not to be confused with caraway seeds (*gunyan*) or black onion seeds (*kalaunji*), both of which are often mistakenly referred to as black cumin.

◆

CUMIN, WHITE OR GREEN *Jeera*

Greenish yellow cumin seeds (*Cuminum cyminum*) resemble caraway and are another of the most important spices used in Indian cooking. They are put in appetizers, snacks and main dishes, yogurt salads, and pickles. Cumin seeds have been an integral part of Indian cooking since time immemorial. Cumin is an important spice in the northern Moghul spice blend *garam masala*, as well as in the eastern five-spice mixture *panch phoron*. The combination of roasted cumin and freshly chopped coriander leaves is what imbues a dish with the aroma associated with Indian food.

◆

CURRY LEAF *Meetha Neem*

This is the flavouring, referred to as a spice or a herb interchangeably, that is the cause of much confusion in the West. It is the aromatic leaf of the plant *Murraya koenigii*. In Indian cooking the small leaves, 1 in/2.5 cm long and ¼ in/5 mm to ¾ in/2 cm wide, are used whole, usually several of them attached to the stem, to lend a dish the distinct aroma of the plant. The curry (or *kari* as it is pronounced in India) has been grown for use since ancient times.

Fresh curry leaves keep well in the refrigerator for up to two weeks. Dry leaves make reasonable substitutes, except you will need to use more of them (two to three times more), as they unfortunately have little fragrance.

DILL *Sowa*

Indian dill (*Anethum sowa*), both wild and cultivated varieties, is somewhat similar to European dill. Indian dill weeds are longer, lighter in colour, and less fragrant. They appear mostly in winter in the markets in India. In Gujarat, the western state of India, wonderful stews of whole green lentils (grandalas) are prepared with dill weeds as the vegetable greens. Gujaratis also dry the dill seeds (these are much larger than European dill seeds) and enjoy them as after-dinner digestives, as these seeds are aromatic and carminative.

◆

FENNEL *Saunf*

The greenish yellow seeds of fennel resemble cumin, except these are fatter and larger. The fennel plant (*Foeniculum vulgare*), which yields the aromatic liquorice-tasting bulb *finocchio* much loved by Italians, also yields the seeds used as a spice. Fennel has a natural affinity to vegetables and is therefore often used whole to scent stir-fried vegetables. It is an important spice for flavouring braised okra, and one of the five spices in the eastern spice blend *panch phoron*. Fennel is also used in flavouring drinks, sweets, and pastries.

Fennel is considered one of the most effective digestives, so it is often lightly toasted and candied (by coating it with a thin syrup) and served as an after-dinner mint in Indian homes and restaurants. For this preparation a finer grade of fennel from the city of Lucknow, called *Lakhnawi saunf*, is preferred.

◆

FENUGREEK *Methi*

The fenugreek seed, rectangular and brownish yellow in colour, is actually a pulse like a mung bean, but because of its intense aroma and bitter taste, it is used as a spice. Fenugreek seeds come from the plant *Trigonella foenum-graecum* that yields the edible leaves fenugreek greens (p. 23). Fenugreek, cultivated since prehistoric times, is one of the most important spices of vegetarian cooking and pickling in India. To mask or mellow its bitter taste, it is always used in moderation, and generally fried or toasted first.

GINGER *Adrak*

Fresh ginger is the pungent aromatic rhizome of the tropical plant *Zingiber officinale,* a much relished seasoning throughout all of India and the Orient. It is usually peeled before being used for cooking.

◆

CAMPHOR GINGER *Karpoora Injee*

Another variety of rhizome is camphor ginger; it has the unique aroma of raw camphor. It grows wild in the lower hills of the Himalayas and southern regions of India. Camphor ginger (*Zingiber zerumbet*) possesses innumerable medicinal properties; therefore it is frequently eaten raw in salads, relishes, or cold appetizers. Since camphor ginger has a slightly bitter taste, Indians often combine it with regular fresh ginger or mango ginger in cooking.

Camphor ginger is difficult to obtain, but regular ginger combined with a little ground anise and a drop of peppermint essence produces a good substitute.

◆

MANGO GINGER *Amada*

This is a special variety of rhizome that gives off the aroma of unripe mangoes. Actually mango ginger is not really ginger at all but a member of the turmeric family that has a texture and flavour that resemble ginger. It generally grows wild and is available in markets in the summer in the southern and eastern regions of India. Mango ginger (*Curcuma amada*), also known as *manga ingee,* is chiefly used to make fresh relish, soups, and yogurt salads. If mango ginger is not available, use fresh ginger combined with unripe mangoes.

◆

LEMON CRYSTALS OR CITRIC ACID *Nimboo ka Sat*

Lemon crystals, called *nimboo ka sat* in India, are a popular souring agent among the Gujarati. Lemon crystals are preferred over all other souring agents in dishes in which moist seasonings are avoided, such as in *dhokla* (p. 112). Lemon crystals are available at any chemist under the name citric acid.

MACE *Javitri*

Mace is the brilliant red, netty membrane that covers the nut (nutmeg) of the tree *Myristica fragrans*, native to Molucca. Mace, sold as blades or ground powder, has a wonderful sweet aroma and a slightly bitter taste. It is generally used in making the northern spice blend *garam masala* and in chutneys.

◆

MANGO POWDER *Amchoor*

Amchoor, tan-coloured sour-tasting mango powder, is made by sun-drying and grinding peeled slices of very tart varieties of unripe mangoes to a fine powder. Mango powder is used throughout all of north India to impart a sour taste to food. It is inexpensive and plentiful, hence much loved by people living in rural areas, particularly vegetarians, to flavour stir-fried vegetables, stuffings for bread, and savoury pastries and drinks.

◆

MANGOSTEEN *Kokum*

Mangosteen, or *kokum* as it is called in India, is the fruit of the tree *Garcinia india* (which is not to be confused with the Malaysian mango-steen, *Garcinia mangostana*, which produces edible fruit). The Indian mangosteen, grown mainly along the western coast from Sindh to Konkan, is a tart fruit about the size of a small plum. It is used mainly to give a piquant taste to food. Maharashtrians and Coorgis adore its flavour and use it in place of tamarind in many of their dishes.

◆

MARJORAM, INDIAN *Mirzan josh*

Indian marjoram or wild marjoram (*Origanum vulgare*) is a highly aromatic herb similar to thyme. It grows wild in the hills of the Himalayas, all the way to Sikkim. This herb is used as a vegetable by the farmers of Punjab. The mountain people in Simla in the Himachal province and in the Kashmir valley add marjoram to hearty chick-pea stews and roasted vegetable purées. Fresh thyme makes a good substitute.

MINT *Podina*

Mint (*Mentha spicata*) is used extensively in Indian cooking for flavouring yogurt salads, pilafs, cold appetizers called *chat*, and in making the wonderful cumin drink *jal jeera*. In an emergency, dried mint leaves may be substituted.

◆

MUSTARD *Rai*

The same mustard plant (*Brassica*) that yields succulent leaves also yields seeds that are one of the most important spices in Indian cooking. Mustard seeds are used to flavour just about every savoury preparation in the southern, southwestern, and eastern regions. It is to the south what cumin seeds are to the north. Mustard paste is a prized flavouring in the cooking of Bengal. Mustard seeds, because of their preservative properties, are used extensively in pickling. The seed of certain plants that contain high amounts of volatile oil are pressed to yield the wonderfully fragrant oil called mustard oil (p. 56).

◆

NUTMEG *Javitri*

Nutmeg, the aromatic nut of the tree *Myristica fragrans*, is used mostly in chutneys, fruit conserves, and sweetmeats. It is an important spice in the spice blend *garam masala*, used in Moghul cooking. In the western state of Gujarat, nutmeg is also used in puddings and yogurt desserts, often in combination with cardamom.

◆

PEPPER *Mirch*

Indians are crazy about peppers – they adore every aspect of their peppery taste, spicy aroma, and sheer visual appeal. The mere mention of chili-laced food starts Indians salivating. To some Indians the most severe punishment is to eat a meal devoid of any form of pepper.

GREEN CHILI PEPPERS *Hari Mirch*

Green chilies are the fresh unripe pods of the plant *Capsicum*. Many varieties of chilies are grown in different parts of India. They range from mild 7 in/17.5 cm long pods to tiny 1 in/2.5 cm capsules that are devilishly hot. The most common variety grown throughout India is 3 in/7.5 cm long and ⅜ in/1 cm thick, and intensely flavoured. Indian grocers carry a variety of green chilies similar to the common Indian type.

◆

HOT RED PEPPER *Lal Mirch*

The red pepper is the ripe, sun-dried pod of the same plant, *Capsicum*, as the green chili. Chili peppers used as dry chili pods and red peppers are selected because they have a high pungency, thin skins, and very few seeds. Red pepper comes in two forms commercially: whole pods, or a powder called red pepper or cayenne pepper. (Cayenne pepper is a generic term for an extremely fiery variety of peppers called 'bird chilies', which are also used in making tabasco sauce. Cayenne pepper is always sold ground commercially. Because true cayenne is in limited supply in the world, highly pungent red pepper is often given the generic name cayenne.) Red pepper is more suited for Indian cooking.

◆

SWEET RED PEPPER OR PAPRIKA *Deghi Mirch*

Indian paprika is made from a very mild variety of red pepper that is sun-dried and ground to a fine powder. Indian paprika grows mainly in Kashmir. It has the distinct red pepper's pungent aroma but a very sweet taste. *Deghi mirch* is used to lend brilliant red colour to food. It is this spice combined with turmeric that lends Indian sauces their characteristic red-orange colour.

◆

LONG PEPPER *Pipal*

Another pepper popular in Indian regional cooking and herbal medicine is *pipal*, the long pepper of the plant *Piper longum*. The cylindrical fruits, 1 in/2.5 cm long and ⅛ in/3 mm thick, growing like spikes from the stem, are dried to yield this pepper. Long pepper is a spicy black pepper with a gingerlike aroma and taste. Long pepper is ground and used in pickles, chutneys, and certain breads.

◆

POMEGRANATE SEEDS *Anardana*

Pomegranate seeds, called *anardana* in India, are the sun-dried fruit kernels of the plant *Punica granatum*. In northern and northwestern regional cooking, the seeds are ground and used extensively in vegetarian cooking to impart a piquant flavour to braised vegetables, beans, stir-fried dishes, and pastry fillings. Since the acidity is of prime importance, the seeds of the sweet cultivated pomegranate fruit are not an acceptable substitute. Instead, the wild variety, which grows along the lower hills of the Himalayas is used.

◆

POPPY SEEDS *Khas Khas*

White poppy seeds, called *khas khas* in India, are the seeds of the white poppy plant *Papaver somniferum*, variety album, which has been growing in India since ancient times. White poppy seeds are generally ground with wet seasonings (such as ginger and garlic) and fried or roasted before they are added to other ingredients. In ground form, poppy seeds act as thickeners and binders in sauces. Frying or roasting intensifies their flavour. In dishes where colour is not important, the common black poppy seeds may be substituted, although there is a slight variation in the flavour.

◆

SAFFRON *Kesar*

Saffron is the most expensive spice in the world, for 1 lb/500 g of saffron is made of dried stigmas from some 250,000 flowers of the plant *Crocus sativus*. It is one of the most prized spices of the Moghuls and in the southern and southwestern regions of India, where almost all religious festival sweets and puddings are laced with saffron. It is essential in saffron pilaf, almond *halwa*, and the sweet *laddoo*, a must at all Indian wedding ceremonies. Saffron is available in thread or ground form. Threads are preferred for purity. Saffron has a sweetish bitter taste but when added to a dish in moderate amounts, lends it a brilliant orange-yellow colour and captivating aroma.

TURMERIC *Haldi*

Turmeric is the magical spice that gives curry powder its characteristic yellow colour. Like ginger, it is a rhizome of the plant *Curuma longa*, growing horizontally underground. The roots are dug up, cleaned, boiled, dried, and powdered to produce a nutty-tasting aromatic yellow powder. Turmeric, the chief spice in vegetarian cooking, lends distinctive colour to many preparations. The lentil purée *dal* is inconceivable without turmeric. Southern vegetarian cooking that relies heavily on lentil stews utilizes turmeric as much as salt!

Turmeric shoots look like tiny fresh gingerroot. If the shoots are not available, substitute the powdered form.

SPECIAL INGREDIENTS AND TECHNIQUES

The following ingredients are listed separately because they involve some special techniques for either their preparation or handling.

SPICE BLENDS

MASALA

The word *masala* is known to all Indians. It is the *masala* that gives a dish the characteristic flavour we associate with Indian food. When an Indian requests a recipe, he inevitably asks only one question of the cook: 'What *masala* did you put in?' In that answer lies the secret of Indian vegetarian cooking. The *masala* is understandably the prized possession of an Indian cook. A *masala* can consist of only spices, or spices and herbs, or spices combined with herbs and seasonings (such as onion and garlic). The number of spices and herbs in a *masala* can range from a meagre one to twenty-five or more! Making a *masala* can be a very simple affair or a very lengthy process that requires several days.

The spices and herbs that constitute a *masala* are not always combined in a blend. They can also be added to a dish at different stages of the cooking process. For example, whole spices are added at the beginning and ground spices and seasonings during the actual cooking process, while herbs can be folded in at the end. In other words, the spice/herb/seasoning composition of any Indian dish is the flavouring (or the *masala*) of that dish.

Masala blends can be *whole*, such as pilaf *masalas*; *powdered*, the two most famous regional examples being curry powder from Madras and *garam masala* from Punjab; or *wet*, in the form of a paste, such as the *avial* herb blend from Malabar.

Each region in India has its own combination of spices and herbs with which it flavours its specialities. These local blends are what give regional food its character. Curry powder is the classic *masala* of southern India, while *garam masala* is the classic blend of the north, and *panch phoron* is the east's magical spice mixture.

The following is a selection of the most important *masalas* used in Indian vegetarian cooking. They represent the true style and character of regional foods as they have been interpreted by different religious groups.

Since the ultimate flavour of a *masala* is determined by the individual cook, these recipes reflect my own palate and taste preferences, meaning my fondness for certain spices and the degree of hotness I like a dish to have. The healthy quantities of cumin, mustard, and coriander reflect my liking for them, as they lend a spicy flavour without being overpowering. In all the blends, unless it contains no peppers at all (the *panch phoron*, for example), I use less pepper so the blend will have hotness without being scorchingly hot. This way I get the hot flavour without totally numbing my palate. You can, of course, increase the hotness to any degree you like. All the recipes can be cut in half or reduced to a fraction of the quantity called for. Just be sure you keep the same proportions.

NOTE: The spices you use to prepare blends always have to be roasted, not so much to cook them as to dry them so that they do not rot with keeping. Roasting also makes grinding easier. Certain spices and spice blends, such as cumin, coriander, and *garam masala*, which are frequently sprinkled on a dish at the end of cooking, are roasted and browned to eliminate the raw taste and aroma and make them easy to digest.

THE ORIGINAL VEDIC CURRY POWDER

This curry powder is generally prepared fresh just before the Vedic ceremony to honour the dead (*Shradha*). Because all other blends are considered new and therefore not appropriate for the holy ceremony, it is the only one used at this Hindu ritual. This is a herbal, lightly spiced blend that I find perfect sprinkled on salads.

MAKES ABOUT 4 oz/125 g

2 oz/60 g fresh curry leaves, or 4 tablespoons dried

2 tablespoons white hulled gram beans (urad dal)

2 tablespoons black peppercorns

1 Preheat oven to 350°F/180°C/Gas 4.
2 Spread fresh curry leaves, beans, and peppercorns on a large baking tray in a single layer. Place the tray in the middle of the oven. Roast, uncovered, for 25 minutes, turning the contents once or twice. If you are using dried curry leaves, add them at the last 10 minutes of roasting. At the end of the roasting time the beans should be lightly coloured, the curry leaves dry, and the peppercorns slightly darkened.
3 Remove the sheet from the oven and let the mixture cool completely, then grind it in batches to a powder in a spice mill or a coffee grinder (leave the powder a little coarse to create a nice texture and flavour).
This keeps well for up to 2 weeks at room temperature, covered.

CURRY POWDER MASTER RECIPE

This is the most fragrant curry powder imaginable. Although used extensively in southern India to flavour vegetable dishes that are mostly stir-fried, it is wonderful in any recipe that calls for curry powder because it is so aromatic and not overpowering. This is my own blend, which I make in large batches at Christmas to give to my friends.

MAKES ABOUT 4 oz/125 g

◆

2 oz/60 g coriander seeds
15 dry red chili pods (optional, see Note)
1½ teaspoons cumin seeds
1½ teaspoons mustard seeds
1½ teaspoons fenugreek seeds
1½ teaspoons black peppercorns
15–20 curry leaves (dry or fresh, optional)
3 tablespoons turmeric powder

1 Mix coriander, chili pods, cumin, mustard seeds, fenugreek seeds, and peppercorns in the container of an electric blender or spice mill and grind the spices to a fine powder in several batches. Pour into a bowl and combine well.

2 If you are using fresh curry leaves, dry them briefly (about 4–5 minutes) in an ungreased frying pan over low heat. Grind them in the blender and then add them to the spice powder in the bowl.

3 Stir in the turmeric.

4 Transfer the curry powder to an airtight jar, cover tightly, and store in a cool place for up to three months.

NOTE: For mild-tasting curry powder, reduce or eliminate chili pods.

HYDERABAD CURRY POWDER

◆

This curry powder, popularly known as *Andhra masala*, is essentially a variation on the master recipe.

The addition of cinnamon and cloves reflects the influence of Moslem-Moghul rule in Hyderabad; it imparts a sweet flavour to the blend.

MAKES ABOUT 4 oz/125 g

Follow the instructions given in the Curry Powder Master Recipe, except add 1½ teaspoons ground cinnamon and ¾ teaspoon ground cloves to the mixture. Mix well and store in a cool place, tightly covered, for up to three months.

SAMBAAR POWDER

◆

This is the classic spice blend used by the southern Brahmins primarily to flavour lentil stews, spicy broths, braised dishes, and fiery tamarind-based sauces. In some families no other curry powder blend is ever prepared. *Sambaar* powder has a spicy-nutty, intriguing flavour because of the roasted beans, which also help thicken sauces, giving them a velvety, rich texture. It also lends the dish a beautiful yellow colour, the same way curry powder does. This is hotter than the master recipe for curry powder.

MAKES ABOUT 4 oz/125 g

◆

2 oz/60 g coriander seeds
12–14 whole dry red chili pods
1½ teaspoons cumin seeds
1½ teaspoons black peppercorns
1½ teaspoons fenugreek seeds
1½ teaspoons white split gram beans (urad dal)
1½ teaspoons yellow mung beans (moong dal)
1½ teaspoons yellow split peas (channa dal)
2 tablespoons turmeric

1 Put coriander seeds, chili pods, cumin seeds, black peppercorns, and fenugreek seeds in a large frying pan or *kadhai* and place on medium-high heat. Roast the spices, stirring with a wooden spoon, for 4–6 minutes, until they lose any excess moisture and start to release their aroma. Transfer the spices to a bowl. Cool completely.
2 Put all the pulses into the same frying pan or *kadhai* and roast over medium-high heat, stirring constantly, until they are barely coloured (6–8 minutes). Remove them to the same bowl. Set aside and let the mixture cool completely.
3 Add the turmeric to the same hot frying pan or *kadhai* and stir for a minute or two until it loses its raw aroma. *Do not turn on the burner.* Transfer the turmeric to another bowl. Set aside.
4 Grind the completely cooled spices and pulses to a fine powder,

using a blender or spice mill. Add cooled turmeric to this mixture. Mix well and store in airtight containers in cool, dry place.

Sambaar powder keeps well for up to six months at room temperature, after which time it won't spoil but it will become less and less aromatic.

BESE BELE POWDER

◆

This is an aromatic blend of spices, gently scented with cinnamon and cloves. As the name suggests, its chief use is to perfume the Bangalore speciality *Bese Bele Olianna* (a vegetable, rice, and lentil pilaf with herbs, nuts, and seasonings, p. 224). The people known for making this blend to perfection are the southern Brahmins from Bangalore, who worship Lord Vishnu.

MAKES ABOUT 8 oz/250 g

◆

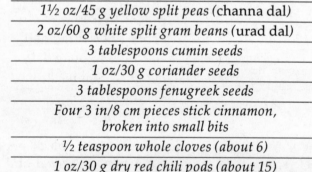

1½ oz/45 g yellow split peas (channa dal)
2 oz/60 g white split gram beans (urad dal)
3 tablespoons cumin seeds
1 oz/30 g coriander seeds
3 tablespoons fenugreek seeds
Four 3 in/8 cm pieces stick cinnamon, broken into small bits
½ teaspoon whole cloves (about 6)
1 oz/30 g dry red chili pods (about 15) or less, to taste, broken into bits
2 tablespoons dry curry leaves, broken up
3 oz/90 g packed desiccated coconut

1 Heat a *kadhai* or a heavy frying pan for 2 minutes over medium-high heat. Add the peas and dry-roast them, stirring and turning them constantly, until they begin to colour (about 5 minutes). Add the beans and continue roasting until both peas and beans smell nicely roasted and turn a light golden brown (12–15 minutes). Transfer them to a plate and cool completely.

2 Add the cumin, coriander, fenugreek, cinnamon, cloves, and chili bits to the same pan. Roast the same way, stirring and turning, until all the ingredients are several shades darker and exude a spicy aroma (10 minutes).

3 Add the curry leaves and coconut and continue roasting for an additional 2–3 minutes. Turn off the heat. Mix all the ingredients with the reserved peas and beans and cool completely.

4 When the pulses and spices have cooled completely, grind them to fine powder, using a blender, spice mill, or coffee grinder. Store in an airtight container in a cool place. *Bese bele* powder will keep fresh for up to three months.

GARAM MASALA

◆

Garam literally translated means 'warm' or 'hot'. *Garam masala* means a blend of hot or warm spices. The terms warm and hot, incidentally, do not mean only spicy hot to the taste. The reference, also, is to the internal heat that these spices generate in one's system. The name also cautions cooks from using this blend too often in warm months.

Garam masala is the basic spice blend of northern India. Just as curry powder varies from one southern region to another, *garam masala* has its own interpretation in every northern state. This spice blend is essentially added at the end of cooking to lace the dish with the gentle aroma of roasted spices.

Garam masala blend is available in most Indian grocers, but it contains *all* the ingredients of *all* the *garam masala* blends: in addition, it is stale and flavourless. To truly enjoy the delicacy of each of these blends, I urge you to make your own from scratch.

PUNJABI *GARAM MASALA* OR *GARAM MASALA*

◆

This *garam masala* is a master recipe, a classic recipe from Punjab and Uttar Pradesh. It is milder tasting than curry or *sambaar* powders, with the flavours of cumin and coriander predominating. It is wonderful in braised *kormas*, in kebabs and vegetable pilafs – all dishes that are of Moghul origin.

MAKES ABOUT 3 oz/90 g

◆

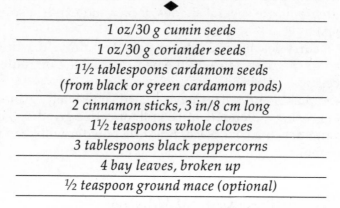

1 oz/30 g cumin seeds
1 oz/30 g coriander seeds
1½ tablespoons cardamom seeds (from black or green cardamom pods)
2 cinnamon sticks, 3 in/8 cm long
1½ teaspoons whole cloves
3 tablespoons black peppercorns
4 bay leaves, broken up
½ teaspoon ground mace (optional)

Heat a *kadhai* or heavy frying pan for 2 minutes over medium-high heat. Combine all the spices except the mace, and add them to the *kadhai*. Dry-roast them, stirring and turning them constantly, until all the spices are several shades darker and exude a spicy aroma (about 10 minutes). Transfer them to a bowl. Let the spices cool completely, then grind them to a fine powder using a blender or spice mill. Add the mace to this mixture, mix well, and store in an airtight container in a cool, dry place for up to three months.

GUJARATI *GARAM MASALA*

◆

This is a Gujarati version of *garam masala* that is popular with the Jains in the western part of India. It is more spicy than the Punjabi blend. The addition of carom (*ajwain*) and fennel gives this blend a very herbal taste. Gujarati *garam masala* is especially good in hearty vegetable and bean casseroles.

MAKES ABOUT 5 oz/150 g

◆

1 oz/30 g cumin seeds
1 oz/30 g coriander seeds
1 oz/30 g black peppercorns
4 dry red chili pods, broken into bits
½ cinnamon stick, 3 in/8 cm long, broken into bits
¾ tablespoon whole cloves
1½ teaspoons cardamom seeds (from black or green cardamom pods)
1½ teaspoons sesame seeds
½ teaspoon fennel seeds
7–8 whole bay leaves
¼ teaspoon carom seeds, or ½ teaspoon dried thyme
½ teaspoon freshly grated nutmeg

Heat a *kadhai* or heavy frying pan for 2 minutes over medium-high heat. Combine all the spices except thyme if you're using it and nutmeg, and add them to the *kadhai*. Dry-roast them, stirring and turning them constantly, until all the spices are several shades darker and excude a spicy aroma (about 10 minutes). Add thyme during the last minute of roasting. Transfer to a bowl and let the spices cool completely, then grind them to a fine powder in a blender or a spice mill. Add the nutmeg to this mixture, mix well, and store in an airtight container in a cool, dry place for up to three months.

MARATHI *GARAM MASALA*

◆

This *garam masala* is a classic example of Marathi cuisine; it reflects the combined influence of Gujarati and Madras flavourings. Even though it is called a *garam masala*, the blend also contains a few of the spices usually reserved only for curry powders, such as fenugreek and chili pods, so this blend is aromatic as well as spicy hot.

MAKES ABOUT 4 oz/125 g

◆

1 oz/30 g coriander seeds
3 tablespoons cumin seeds
2 tablespoons fenugreek seeds
½ teaspoon whole cloves
1½ tablespoons cardamom seeds (green or black)
7–8 bay leaves, broken into small pieces
2 oz/60 g desiccated coconut
7–8 dry red chili pods, broken into bits

Heat a *kadhai* or heavy frying pan for 2 minutes over medium-high heat. Add coriander, cumin, fenugreek, cloves, and cardamom. Roast the spices, turning them constantly, until they look several shades darker and give off a spicy aroma (about 8 minutes). Add bay leaves, coconut, and chili bits. Continue roasting, stirring, for 2–3 additional minutes. Turn off heat. Transfer spices to a plate and let cool completely. Grind to a fine powder, using a blender, spice mill, or coffee grinder. Store in an airtight container in a cool place for up to three months.

PARSI *DHANAJEERA MASALA*

◆

This is a popular spice blend used by the Parsis (a small community of people who worship Zoroaster; they emigrated from Persia to escape religious persecution and are now settled mainly in Bombay). The word *dhanajeera* means coriander-cumin, probably because of the large amounts of these spices in the blend. The addition of star anise and cloves, together with mustard and all the Moghul spices, gives this blend an aroma that can best be compared to the experience of standing in an Indian spice shop. *Dhanajeera* is the primary flavouring of the Parsi special stew called *dhan shak*.

MAKES ABOUT 5 oz/150 g

◆

3 oz/90 g coriander seeds
2 tablespoons cumin seeds
1½ teaspoons mustard seeds
½ teaspoon fennel seeds
1 tablespoon white poppy seeds
1 tablespoon black peppercorns
2-3 pieces star anise
½ teaspoon whole cloves
½ cinnamon stick, 3 in/8cm long, broken up
1 tablespoon whole green cardamom pods
5 bay leaves, broken up
¼–½ teaspoon saffron threads
1 teaspoon nutmeg, freshly grated

1 Preheat the oven to 225°F/105°C/Gas ½.
2 Put all the spices except the saffron and nutmeg in a large roasting tin and spread them to make a single layer.
3 Place the tin on the bottom shelf of the oven and roast for 30 minutes or until the spices are lightly browned. Mix and turn the spices several times during the roasting to ensure that they don't burn. During the last 5 minutes of roasting, sprinkle the saffron and nutmeg on the spices.
4 When the spices are cool, grind them in a spice mill or coffee grinder. Store the *dhanajeera* powder in airtight containers in a cool, dry place, for up to three months.

BENGAL *PANCH PHORON* MIX

◆

A creation of the Bengalis in the eastern part of India, this is a simple blend of five whole spices combined in equal proportions. This particular spice mix is always added to the hot oil at the very beginning of cooking and fried before any other ingredients are added so as to perfume the oil.

Panch phoron is used in flavouring vegetables, *dal*, and bean dishes. Since the spices are left whole, they lend texture and visual appeal.

Cumin seeds
Fennel seeds
Mustard seeds
Fenugreek seeds
Black onion seeds

Combine the spices in equal proportions and keep in an airtight jar for up to a year.

CHAT MASALA

◆

This spice blend is used for flavouring vegetable and fruit salads that are eaten as appetizers and snacks. For the best flavour, *chat masala* must contain several spices, roots, twigs, and seasonings, the preparation of which is time consuming, bothersome, and expensive to do at home. That is why the best *chat masala* blends are commercially made. For those who would like to make the authentic blend at home, this simpler version works very well.

MAKES ABOUT 1½ TABLESPOONS

◆

1 teaspoon ground roasted cumin seeds
½ teaspoon cayenne pepper

¼ teaspoon asafetida powder
¾ teaspoon mango powder
½–¾ teaspoon garam masala (p. 77)
½ teaspoon black salt (kala namak) (p.19–20)
1 teaspoon coarse salt

Mix all the spices and keep in a jar, tightly covered, in a cool place.

COCONUT

NARIAL

◆

The coconut palm (*Cocos nucifera*) dots the entire southern coastline of India from Gujarat to Bengal. It is one of the most important ingredients of vegetarian cooking in all these regions. It is also an integral part of all Hindu Brahmin rituals. Almost no auspicious event begins without breaking a coconut before Lord Ganesha, the elephant-headed god, remover of all obstacles.

In Indian cooking coconut is used in three forms – sliced, grated, and liquid – each one lending distinctly different texture and flavour to the food.

When buying a coconut, you must be careful to choose one that has no cracks on the skull and whose three eyes at one end are free of all greenish grey mould (a sign of rotting). A very fresh coconut is usually heavy because of the liquid inside it; therefore, shake your coconut before you buy it.

To crack a coconut, hold it over the kitchen sink. With a hammer or cleaver in the other hand, whack it until the shell cracks. As soon as the water inside the coconut begins to ooze out, hold a small dish underneath to collect it. You should drink or at least taste the water. If it tastes sweet and fragrant, the coconut is fresh. If, on the other hand, it tastes oily and sour, the coconut is rancid and must be thrown away. Using a sharp paring knife, cut away the flesh from the shell and peel the brown skin off.

Alternatively, you can crack a coconut by placing it in a preheated 375°F/190°C/Gas 5 oven for 25 minutes. Before putting it in the oven, drain the coconut of all the water by piercing the eyes with a skewer.

To release the flesh from the shell, whack it gently with the hammer, then hit it hard to crack open the shell. Peel the skin off the flesh, using a paring knife.

Now that you have peeled the coconut, it may be prepared in any of the following three ways.

SLICED COCONUT
◆

To make thinly sliced coconut, hold a large piece of peeled coconut firmly in one hand and slice it on the potato-slicing side of a grater, or use the slicing attachment on your processor.

Lightly toasted sliced coconut is delicious folded into braised vegetable dishes and sprinkled over fresh fruit. It is also heavenly eaten plain, in combination with jaggery and toasted unsalted peanuts as a snack.

FRESH FLAKED OR GRATED COCONUT
◆

Coconut may be flaked or grated in one of two ways: either by using an Indian coconut grater (p. 95) or in a food processor or blender. There is, however, one important point to remember. If you want to flake coconut Indian-style, you must plan the procedure well in advance. To flake it the authentic Indian way, you must crack the coconut by hand into two neat hemispheres, because only in this form will the coconut halves fit into the Indian implement.

To flake coconut in a food processor or blender, put about 3 oz/90 g of coconut flesh cut into 1 in/2.5 cm pieces into the container of the processor or blender and process until the contents are reduced to a fine, moist mass.

Ideally, coconut flakes should be made only by scraping the flesh very carefully from the shell, using a coconut grater from India or southeast Asia. This way the fibres containing the fat are not destroyed. The flaked coconut that emerges is fluffier, resembling a mass of flower petals, and more moist and fragrant than other kinds. Food processors and blenders tend to crush the coconut which releases the moisture and fat present, producing coconut shreds that are somewhat lumpy and greasy.

COCONUT MILK

◆

The difference in flaked coconut obtained when using a processor or blender is not of any importance when you are making coconut milk, as the grated coconut is ground up anyway. Coconut milk is the essence of moisture contained within the fibres of flaked coconut. (This is not to be confused with the water contained inside the coconut fruit itself, which is called coconut water.) In the Polynesian Islands and in Malabar, India, where coconuts are plentiful, the scraped shreds of the coconut are gathered between one's hands and then squeezed to release the juice (or milk, as it is popularly called because of its pure white colour). This process requires some half-dozen coconuts to yield a mere 4 fl oz/125 ml. Therefore, modern homes all over the world have adopted a process that makes a lot more sense. The grated coconut is combined with boiling water (equal volume of water to coconut), and the mixture is allowed to rest for a while (a minimum of 15 minutes) so that more flavour is released into the liquid. The pulp, along with the liquid, is then puréed in a blender or food processor in batches and strained through a double layer of muslin, squeezing as much juice out of the pulp as possible. This yields a very flavourful coconut milk – not, of course, as rich as the classic technique but awfully good.

Both flaked coconut and coconut milk freeze beautifully for several months without suffering any significant change in flavour or texture. Since they are time-consuming to make, I suggest that you regularly stock your freezer.

Under no circumstances substitute sweetened desiccated coconut or tinned sweetened coconut cream in recipes that call for fresh flaked coconut.

TAMARIND

IMLI

◆

Tamarind, the pulpy pod of the tropical plant *Tamarindus indica*, native to India, tastes like sour prunes. It is essentially used to lend a sweetish-sour taste to food. Tamarind is used extensively throughout India for its piquancy as well as for its distinct flavour. Tamarind is available in Indian grocers in 1 lb/500 g cakes (peeled, pitted, and commercially pressed tamarind pulp) called tamarind pulp, or as tamarind paste (made by extracting the tamarind flesh from the fibrous residue and concentrating it into a thick mass). In Indian cooking both are acceptable, although tamarind pulp has more herbal flavour.

To make tamarind paste at home, put a 1 lb/500 g cake of tamarind in a large nonmetallic bowl. Add 1½ pints/800 ml of boiling water and let the tamarind soak in it until the water has cooled to room temperature. Using your fingers or a fork, loosen the tamarind pulp into several small lumps. Cover with cling film and let the tamarind lumps soak in the water for 8 hours or overnight. With a fork mash the pulp again, squeezing out as much juice as you can. Strain the juice through a sieve, and throw out the fibrous tamarind residue. Pour the tamarind juice into ice cube trays and freeze, uncovered. When frozen, put the cubes into a plastic bag and seal it tightly. Defrost the cubes as you need them or add them directly to cooking sauces and stews. Three standard-size frozen cubes of tamarind paste are equivalent to about a 1 in/2.5 cm round of tamarind pulp (about 2 oz/ 60 g). This recipe makes about 2 dozen cubes of tamarind paste.

JAGGERY OR UNREFINED LUMP SUGAR

GOODH

◆

Jaggery, or _goodh_ as it is called in India, is lump sugar (almost pasty at times) that has a brownish colour and a maple-sugar-like flavour. Many of the world-renowned Indian delicacies – the desserts of Bengal in the eastern region, the sweetmeats of Rajasthan and Gujarat in the west, and the candies of southern India – are created with jaggery. Some of these desserts are so delicate that substituting ordinary sugar in place of jaggery changes the flavour totally.

Jaggery, or _goodh_, is made from the juices of sugar cane or palm. Cane sugar jaggery, the kind most commonly available, is produced throughout India. Palm sugar jaggery, more aromatic and nutritive, is produced along the coastal areas of India, namely Madras and Bengal, where certain species of palm yielding sweet sap thrive. Its unique flavour and aroma are highly prized in the confectionery industry. Because of its limited supply and high demand, palm jaggery almost never leaves the area in which it is produced. The jaggery you see in this country is most likely to be cane sugar jaggery.

Jaggery is prepared from the processed juices of sugar cane or the sap collected from palm. The juices are boiled down to a very thick, viscous mass, which is then poured into moulds and allowed to set. This unrefined sweet lump is called jaggery or *goodh*. Sometimes, just before the reduction process is completed, part of the syrup is taken out. This syrup, called jaggery syrup, is a delicacy in the southern and eastern regions of India, where it is served with griddle cakes and pancakes.

Soft brown sugar is an acceptable substitute.

SPROUTED BEANS

UGADELA KATHAR

◆

Sprouting beans for cooking is common in Maharashtra, Gujarat, and Andhra Pradesh; this process makes them easily digestible as well as more nutritive. Indian sprouted beans are, however, very different from Oriental bean sprouts. Indians sprout the beans only enough to begin their germination; thus they look exactly like whole beans except for being puffed and featuring a tiny white sprout. These are crunchier than the Chinese kind and more substantial.

In Indian vegetarian cooking sprouted beans are used to make lovely salads, appetizers, snacks, and many main dish entrées.

To sprout mung beans, rinse the beans in running warm water. Put the beans in a bowl and add enough warm water to cover the beans by at least 2 in/5 cm. Soak the beans for 8 hours or overnight. Drain and rinse the beans thoroughly in warm water. Drain again. Line a wicker basket with a damp tea towel and put the beans in it. Cover loosely with another damp tea towel. Place the basket in a warm place (75–90°F/24–32°C) for 8–24 hours or until the beans are cracked and tiny white sprouts start to appear. During sprouting, sprinkle with a little water once or twice to ensure that the towel is kept moist. Rinse the sprouted beans in cold running water, drain thoroughly, and use immediately or wrap in a moist tea towel and refrigerate until needed.

Sprouted beans will keep for two days in the refrigerator, after which time they will begin to turn musty.

INDIAN NOODLES

SEVIAN, PHALOODA AUR SEVAI

◆

Most people associate noodles with Oriental, Italian, and possibly Hungarian cooking. It is always a matter of astonishment when I mention the wonderful steamed noodle dishes of southern India or the transparent noodle threads used on desserts in northern India. The Indian familiarity with noodles dates back several centuries. Indians make noodles from unusual grains and use unique techniques to yield distinct types of products. Indian noodles can be classified into three broad categories.

◆

RICE NOODLES *Sevai*

Rice noodles are a speciality of the southern regions of India. They date much further back than noodles made with wheat. Rice noodles are made by cooking rice flour with water (equal volumes of water to rice flour, and a little oil to prevent the cooked dough from sticking) to form a firm dough. When slightly cool, the dough is pressed through a noodle press, which has a perforated disc attached directly to the lined *idlee* steamer racks (p. 94) and steamed. The noodles take about 10 minutes to steam; then they are unmoulded and cooled before being stir-fried. These noodles are always broken into pieces, because Indians traditionally eat with their hands, and eating long strands of noodles would be unsightly and messy.

◆

WHEAT NOODLES *Sevian*

These noodles are made with hard durum wheat. They are as thin as angel hair and are always made commercially. *Sevian* are primarily used to make puddings with milk. Sevian cooking, although a speciality of the Moslems of Hyderabad, Kutch, and Uttar Pradesh, is enjoyed by Indians of all religious persuasions. Some of the outstanding examples of sevian cooking are sevian pudding, which the people of Bangladesh eat at breakfast with *paratha*; and *sheer korma*, a rich noodle dessert made with butter, dried nuts, and fruits eaten by the people of Hyderabad and Kashmir.

WHEAT CELLOPHANE THREADS *Phalooda*

These transparent noodle-like threads are made from the starch of wheat berries. The wheat berries are soaked and ground with water to yield a milky liquid called *nishasta*, which is then cooked to a glutinous mass. The warm dough is then put through a noodle press and the threads fall directly into a bowl of ice-cold water. The soft, transparent threads become firm and turn opaque immediately upon coming into contact with the water. At this stage pine or rose essence is added to the water to give the wheat threads more character. These wheat threads are a prized delicacy in northern India, where they are served chilled as a dessert in their own right. Sometimes Indians pour a sweet sugar syrup over them. *Phalooda* are also the classic garnish for Indian ice cream (*kulfi*).

ESSENCES

RUH

◆

For centuries Indians have been lacing their desserts and sweetmeats, such as *halwa* and *barfi*, with the fragrance of flowers, wood barks, and leaves, much the same way we use vanilla or almond essence. Not all regions use all these essences; much depends upon availability. Of the innumerable locally used essences, four are important in Indian dessert making: rose, screw pine, sandalwood, and camphor.

◆

ROSE ESSENCE *Ruh Gulab*

Rose essence (*ruh gulab*), which also comes in the form of rose water (*gulab jal*), was developed in India in the sixteenth century when the intensely fragrant damask rose (*Rosa damascena*), known locally as *barwana*, was introduced from Asia Minor by the Moghuls. Today this rose and another cross-bred variety, the Edward rose (*Rosa bourboniana*), known locally as *baramasi*, are primarily grown for their essences. In India rose essence is extracted by a water distillation process that yields a mellow, gentler product than the kind produced by distilling essences with steam. That is why Indian rose essence and rose water never overpower the dish they are added to.

Rose essence is used primarily in New Delhi, Uttar Pradesh, and

Punjab. It is the primary essence in flavouring the yogurt drink *lassi*, puddings, fudge, and sweetmeats. Indians also sprinkle it around a room as an air freshener during weddings and religious festivals.

◆

SANDALWOOD *Ruh Chandan*

The sandalwood tree has been growing in India since Vedic times, mainly south of the Vindhya Mountains in Mysore and Tamil Nadu. Today it is also cultivated in sections of Orissa and Uttar Pradesh. Because of its long association with Hindu Brahmin culture, sandalwood cream is used in all religious functions (monks and priests paint it on their faces and bodies as a decoration). The most popular culinary use of sandalwood essence is in making a refreshing punch, *sandal sharbat*, known for its great cooling effect. Sandalwood essence (or water) is made by soaking sandalwood chips in water, then heating them and condensing the vapours.

◆

SCREW PINE ESSENCE *Ruh Kewra*

Screw pine, called *kewra* in India, is a special pine shrub with thick, leathery leaves that resemble petals. These pale yellow leaves hold a hypnotically fragrant smell, the Indian fondness for which dates back to Vedic times. Screw pine (*Pandanus tectorius*), although originally found growing in southern India, is grown in the eastern and northern regions as well. *Kewra* essence and *kewra* water are extensively used in Indian cooking to flavour sweets and sweetmeats, especially those made with milk, such as *ras gulla* (p. 341). In southern India fresh *kewra* petals, called *tayai*, are woven into a young girl's braids both for decoration and fragrance.

SILVER OR GOLD FOIL

VARK

◆

Vark, the pure sterling silver or gold foil, thinner than tissue paper, was used along with crushed mother-of-pearl and star ruby emulsions by the Moghuls to adorn the elaborate food of their splendrous court.

Today Indians use it on occasions such as weddings and religious festivals to decorate special pilafs and sweetmeats.

Vark is made by compressing the moist dust of silver or gold between layers of thin paper. The result is a tasteless and odourless shimmering foil whose sole purpose is to lend visual appeal and elegance to food. *Vark* is perfectly safe to eat. In fact, in the ancient *Unani* (Greek) and *Ayurvedic* (Hindu) medicine in India, the *bhasma* (reduced, precious metal) preparation was and still is today recommended as the sovereign remedy in several chronic illnesses, such as heart disease.

To place vark *on food*, peel the top sheet of paper off the *vark*. Gently invert and place the bottom sheet of paper with the *vark* stuck to it on the food. The *vark* will adhere to the food in a few seconds. When it does, lift off the layer of paper.

SPECIAL EQUIPMENT

◆

The tools and equipment found in the average British kitchen are more than adequate to perform most of the tasks required in the preparation of Indian vegetarian cooking. There are, however, certain dishes that are prepared by specific techniques for which special tools and equipment are needed. They are essential to the proper execution of the dish, lending it the desired look and the correct flavour and texture. In an emergency, obviously, substitutions with make-do equipment can be made, but bear in mind that the dish will not have its true Indian character. The following tools and equipment are worth considering buying.

POTS AND PANS

◆

Kitchen utensils reflect the evolution of any culture. The shapes and materials depend largely on the kinds of fuel and food available.

Indian households have traditionally used wood-burning or charcoal-burning stoves for cooking food. These stoves, which are shaped like a miniature barbecue pit with a small opening on the top, can only accommodate round-bottomed pans that fit snugly without wobbling. These pans come in a variety of sizes, ranging from the small ones used in homes to the kind used for large-quantity cooking such as in restaurants. Originally all Indian pans were made of clay or iron, but today they are manufactured in different materials, the most popular being tin-lined copper and brass. In many regions these pans are beautifully ornate, featuring masterful carving, welding, and painting that gives them individuality and character. The pans used for general cooking – braising, stewing, preparing rice and lentil purée (*dal*) – are shaped like a jug, to hold flavour and moisture. They are called *handi* in the northern parts of India and *panai* or *shomboo* in the southern states.

For frying and sautéing, Indians use a pan with a broad, round bottom and a wide opening at the top to provide maximum evaporation. This is called a *kadhai* or an Indian wok.

Breads are baked flat on flat round griddles made of either heavy stone or iron, thus staying secure over the stove. These griddles are called *tava* in the north and *kallu* in the south of India.

Most Western-style pots and pans do the job in Indian cooking very well. Some are, in fact, far better.

I prefer to use pots with non-stick surfaces as well as well-seasoned, heavy-bottomed sauté pans and sauce pots for most cooking. Sauté pans and frying pans with covers are good for the dry cooking of vegetables and pulses. Breads are best baked on cast-iron griddles or heavy-bottomed large frying pans.

For frying (deep-, shallow- and turn- or stir-frying), you should seriously consider acquiring a *kadhai*, the Indian-style wok. The process of turn-frying is easy and effortless in a *kadhai*, and it takes much less oil to deep-fry in a *kadhai*.

This implement is simple in design and comes in a variety of sizes and materials: brass, iron, stainless steel, tin, and copper. Treated cast-iron is best suited for this purpose; it holds heat longer and its weight guarantees that it will stay securely over the stove without your having to buy a wok ring.

A *kadhai* must be seasoned before you use it. To season a *kadhai*, coat the inside with about 1–2 tablespoons oil and heat it over a high flame. When the oil smokes, sprinkle 2–3 tablespoons salt all over the inside surface and turn off the heat. When the *kadhai* is cool enough to handle, scrub the inside well with kitchen paper. Rinse with soap and water, then oil, and repeat the process. The *kadhai* is now ready for use. It will never need further seasoning or special care. After each use, rinse (do not scour) your *kadhai* with soap and water, and wipe it completely dry with kitchen paper.

STEAMERS
◆

Steam cooking is the speciality of the southern regions of India. Southern Indians have been steaming their dumplings, noodles, cakes and lentils for many centuries. In most instances the food is shaped into special forms, then placed into a pan and steamed. In others, however, special steaming apparatus is required because the batter is poured into moulds that fit the apparatus and is then steam cooked.

Every region in the south has its own vegetarian speciality that is cooked in a special steamer. In Indian vegetarian cooking two steamers are the most popular and the most important: the *idlee*, required to make the pillow-shaped rice-and-bean dumplings from Madras; and the *dhokla*, used to make the split pea bread-like cakes from Gujarat.

DHOKLA STEAMER

The *dhokla* steamer is similar to the *idlee* steamer, but the trays look like flat 7½ in/19 cm round shallow cake pans. The batter is poured into the trays and steamed. The cooked cakes are unmoulded, cut into diamond shapes, and seasoned before serving.

Any pie plate or round cake tin with an 8–9 in/20–23 cm diameter makes a good substitute.

◆

IDLEE STEAMER

This steamer, called *idlee panai* in the Madras region, consists of an aluminium or stainless-steel post to which three or four circular trays with indentations ½ in/1 cm deep and 3 in/8 cm in diameter are attached. The trays are lined with muslin and filled with batter. The entire apparatus is placed in a large pot containing water, covered, and then steamed. The tiny perforations in the tray, particularly on the indented part, enable the steam to travel through the container freely and evenly, thereby producing fluffy dumplings.

If you do not have an *idlee* steamer, an egg poacher can be used as a substitute, but remember your dumplings will not be as light as is traditional.

The *idlee* steamer is also used to make rice noodles. The thick cooked dough is put into a noodle maker, then pressed onto muslin-lined racks, then steamed. The freshly cooked and formed noodles are seasoned before serving.

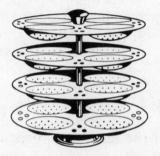 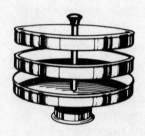

OTHER EQUIPMENT

◆

COCONUT GRATER *Narial Kas*

This implement should really be called a coconut flaker or scraper, as the fine teeth of the rotating circular blades scrape the flesh into moist flakes. In fact, this is the right way to grate coconut, as the cream and fat present in the flesh do not separate from the fibre of the tissue and make it look greasy. The grating device, consisting of circular blades that are moved by a hand crank, is held vertical with a steel post attached to a flat wooden board. To grate coconut, the implement is placed over a tea towel on the ground. The half shell of coconut (with the flesh attached on the inside) is held against the blades, which are moved by rotating the handle.

◆

FOOD PROCESSOR

This is one machine I have almost become addicted to. For Indian cooking it's a blessing. There is almost nothing that this machine cannot do. For most dishes it can chop, mince, and grind all seasonings and herbs. It is perfect for powdering nuts, puréeing vegetables, and making smooth batters. And, to everyone's delight, this machine also kneads dough for Indian breads to perfection.

◆

INDIAN ICE CREAM MOULD *Kulfi ka Sancha*

Kulfi moulds are 3 in/8 cm long, cone-shaped moulds used just for making *kulfi*, the frozen Indian dessert that somewhat resembles our ice cream. The milk mixture, with nuts and flavourings, is poured into these moulds and frozen. *Kulfi* moulds come in two materials –

aluminium and stainless steel. Aluminium moulds are better, because the *kulfi* freezes better and faster in them.

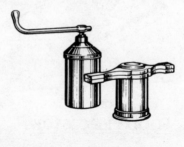

NOODLE PRESS *Morokoo*

This classic noodle press is common throughout India. It is somewhat similiar in design to a biscuit press, except that the top part of the tool that presses the dough through the perforation is designed differently. This tool is used for making noodles – steamed and dried as well as fried. For making fried noodles the dough is pressed quickly and directly into the hot oil and cooked until crisp and brown. For steamed noodles the dough is pressed onto lined racks of *idlee* steamers and steamed. For dried noodles, the kind that are fried later and enjoyed as a snack, the dough is pressed onto clean towels and dried either under the sun or in mechanical dryers.

◆

PERFORATED SPOON *Jaleedar Karchi*

In Indian cooking the perforated spoon is used to lift out fried food so the excess oil may drain away, and also to turn-fry vegetables and to make fudge and sweetmeats. Another important use of this spoon is in the preparation of tiny crisp puffs made of chick-peas. The batter is pressed through the perforations to form tiny ⅛ in/3 mm round balls that drop into hot oil to be fried. Sifters and sieves, incidentally, do not work as well for this purpose.

SIFTER/SIEVE *Chalni*

The Indian sifter/sieve is unique in its design. This lightweight aluminium implement, *chalni*, consists of a 7–9 in/18–23 cm ring with 2 in/5 cm high sides and has three interchangeable sifting discs with meshes of different gauges. The choice of disc depends upon the ingredient to be sifted, such as removing excess bran from Indian flour (*atta*), the ground whole wheat berries used for making the basic Indian bread. Various other flours, such as chick-pea, mung bean, chestnut, and rice, which have a tendency to lump, are also sifted in a *chalni*.

◆

SPICE AND OTHER GRINDERS

In India spices, herbs, and seasonings are always ground on a stone grinder called *sil-batta*. It consists of a flat stone on which the herbs and spices are placed. The grinding stone, designed like a cylinder or a triangle that is about 2 in/5 cm thick, is moved back and forth to crush the ingredients. This *sil-batta* can weigh anywhere from 60 lb/ 132 kg to a staggering 250 lb/550 kg.

You can, however, get fairly good results using several different tools and electric appliances. The simplest, of course, is a mortar and pestle for pulverizing small quantities of spices. A spice mill or coffee grinder is good for grinding large batches of spices. An electric blender is good for puréeing sauces and gravies, although a food processor can do the job as well. A blender, however, grinds beans for pancakes and dumplings to velvety smooth purées far faster than the food processor, because the blades rotate at a higher rate.

◆

VEGETABLE GRATER *Kaddoo Kas*

Indian graters are designed to accommodate the traditional Indian style of cooking, which is usually done squatting on the floor. The grating surface is therefore parallel to the floor (as compared to the vertical ones used in Western graters) to allow maximum exertion of pressure. Surprisingly, Indian vegetable graters work excellently on kitchen countertops.

Indian vegetable graters come in many designs and two materials:

brass or stainless steel. My preference is for the rectangular grater that is 7 in/18 cm long, 5 in/13 cm wide, and 2 in/5 cm high, made of stainless steel, which produces beautiful long shreds and is easy to clean.

PLANNING
AND SERVING
INDIAN
VEGETARIAN
MEALS

Planning a Western meal is, in my opinion, a simple, straightforward task. It has a few clearly defined components that fit into place like pieces of a puzzle. Western meals generally consist of three or more distinctly separate courses: an appetizer or soup accompanied by bread as the first course, the main or second course, and finally dessert. The main course can be expected to include an entrée, a vegetable, and some form of starch, possibly accompanied by a salad.

An Indian vegetarian meal, on the other hand, features many elements, all of which are grouped according to religious taboos, regional needs, and cultural beliefs. In addition the meal, instead of being served in stages, is served all at once.

At an Indian meal the various preparations, including the dessert, are spooned into small cups called *katoori* and placed on a single large-rimmed circular tray, called a *thali*. In the *katooris* are placed all the dishes to be served at the meal, including the appetizer, wafer, pickle and chutney, relish, and condiments, staples (rice and/or bread), sweetmeat, salt, and chilies. In India presenting the entire meal all at once from the appetizer to the sweetmeats is called the *thali* style of serving.

To enjoy an Indian vegetarian meal it is not essential, of course, that you serve it in the traditional *thali* style. You could put all the dishes at the centre of the table and let your family or guests help themselves. If you choose to present an Indian vegetarian meal this way, it would be wise to serve the appetizer and soup as a separate first course before the main dish and accompaniments, and then bring out the dessert at the end of the meal. Beverages and sweets are best served together as a grand finale.

An Indian vegetarian meal, no matter which region it comes from, is generally composed of the following dishes:

◆ A main dish, which may consist of vegetables with pulses; vegetables with a dairy product; or vegetables with pulses, dairy, and grains. These dishes usually have sauces and frequently require special preparation. Some of these dishes are expressly created to resemble a meat dish that is a classic in Moghul cuisine.

◆ Several side dishes, including a simple vegetable preparation, usually stir-fried or steamed with a minimum of effort and seasonings; a purée of lentils called *dal*, flavoured with spiced perfumed butter (*dal* is included in a meal for two reasons: first, to add additional protein; and second, to provide sauce and moisture in the event the main dish is dry); a vegetable salad, to add a fresh uncooked crunch and a herbal aroma to the meal; and a yogurt salad, to guarantee that the meal has protein as well as a cool, soothing sensation to rescue one's stomach, should the curries attack too severely.

◆ The accompanying staples, bread and rice, are essential to an Indian vegetarian meal. This is because many of the vegetarian dishes are fiery and soupy. Without a bland rice or bread they would be too difficult to eat. In fact, many of these dishes were conceived and created by generations of Indian cooks with a staple in mind. You cannot do full justice to their wonderful flavours until you eat them with bread or rice. Rice acts as a sponge to soak up the sauce in a dish, making eating with your fingers a delicious treat, while the supple Indian breads act as a scoop for the drier curries.

◆ An Indian vegetarian meal, without exception, includes certain accompaniments: relishes, wafers, chutneys, and pickles. They are essentially present to add a herbal scent, a crunchy texture, a sweet or tart flavour, and additional peppery punch.

◆ Often a meal may include special sauces, spreads, and spice powders that are intended to be served with specific dishes. Of course, there is no strict rule that all these dishes be served at all the meals, as long as you make sure that you serve a healthy and nutritionally balanced meal.

Indians have traditionally preferred to eat with their fingers instead of using tools such as spoon, fork, or chopsticks. First, the touching and brushing of fingers against the lips – tasting, smelling, and licking – is a highly sensual experience regarded as very important by Indians and is an integral part of enjoying the meal.

Second, although one can argue against eating rice with the fingers, particularly with wet, saucy dishes, since it can be tricky and messy, there is no question that breads are best eaten with the hand. Indian breads are highly pliable, are easy to tear into pieces and can be used as a scoop for curries or for wrapping pieces of stuffed vegetables.

While planning a vegetarian meal, one factor must be borne in mind all the time and that is that it should be a healthy, nutritionally balanced meal. It must be so composed as to include adequate protein and fat in the form of cheese, yogurt, milk, soya, pulses, seeds and nuts, fresh vegetables for vitamins, minerals, and grains for fibre and carbohydrates.

WHAT TO DRINK WITH AN INDIAN VEGETARIAN MEAL

◆

Most Westerners, in my experience, usually assume that beer, particularly Indian or English beer, is the obvious drink to accompany an Indian meal, whether it is vegetarian or not. Beer certainly does have its role in Indian life and cuisine, but it is by no means the only choice. A considerable majority of Indians, whether Moslem, Hindu, Jain, or Sikh, are teetotallers and for religious reasons consume no alcohol at all, so a great variety of non-alcoholic beverages are served with meals in India. These include the various *lassis* and *sharbats*, usually made with fruits, as well as a great variety of teas, both plain and herbal. Wine, although it is neither produced nor widely consumed in India, can accompany any Indian meal, as long as the wine selected can hold its own against the spiciness and hotness of the food. The best choices are wines that have a strong character and are robust enough to stand up against the intensely flavoured and highly spiced food.

In white wines, the dry but spicy Gewürztraminer of Alsace can be an excellent choice. Both Hugel and Trimbach produce good examples. The somewhat less dry, fruity Rieslings or Sylvaners of Alsace can also be recommended.

Good choices in red wines include the hearty wines of the Côte du Rhône, and the somewhat tannic reds of southern and southwest France. Oddly enough, a good Beaujolais can also be most appropriate.

If rosé is to your liking, the rosés of Provence are to be preferred since they have more character than those of the Loire and are better able to stand up to Indian food.

Above all, keep in mind, no matter what your choice of drink, alcoholic or not, to augment it with a tall glass of iced water. A good healthy swallow of water followed by a mouthful of rice or other starch can extinguish the hottest of conflagrations!

BREAKFAST AND LIGHT MEALS (TIFFIN)

Breakfast is the simplest of all Indian meals. It can be as basic as a piece of *paratha* smeared with sour butter and washed down with a cup of cardamom-scented tea. Or it could be interpreted differently from region to region. In Bengal it would be vermicelli pudding with cardamom-scented bread. In Gujarat, green chili-laced millet bread with garlic chutney would be perfect to start the farmer's day, while Kashmiris savour juicy berries and fennel-laced shortbread with their morning brew of green tea. Silky pancakes and spongy dumplings are devoured by southern Indians with fiery sauces and chutney to perk up their lethargic appetites in their extremely tropical climate. Southerners also enjoy coffee made from local beans, in contrast to the tea that northerners prefer.

Most of these preparations are extremely versatile and thus can be served without modification at any time of the day, as a snack or a light meal. In fact, in southern Indian households, where lunch is traditionally eaten at 9.00 am (meaning there is no breakfast in the morning), these dishes are served in the afternoon or at around lunchtime (12 noon to 3.00 pm) as *tiffin*. In the south of India, tiffin is therefore a very important meal, frequently becoming very fancy and elaborate to suit the occasion. Most entertaining in the south is done at tiffin. Tiffins are classic south Indian preparations. Although they are very tasty and interesting dishes, they are rich in carbohydrates. This is because tiffins are generally made with different grains (high in starches) and contain very few vegetables (sometimes none at all), and practically no milk or dairy products (this is true of much southern food – a reflection of the scarcity of nutritious food ingredients). Therefore, to serve these delicious tiffins in a healthy, balanced meal, I recommend that you either combine them with vegetables and salads as a main course or serve them in small portions as a first course or as appetizers with a meal.

CRACKED WHEAT PORRIDGE WITH ALMONDS AND APRICOTS

DALIA

◆

A speciality of the northwest frontier region (an area now within Pakistan), *dalia*, the cracked wheat porridge, is a delicious breakfast treat. Studded with fruits and nuts, *dalia* is particularly welcomed on a wintery morning. In India *dalia* is made with untreated cracked wheat, which takes a long time to soften. I have substituted bulgur (treated cracked wheat) here, thus reducing the cooking time from two hours to fifteen minutes. The results are excellent.

FOR 8 PERSONS

◆

2 tablespoons unsalted butter
6 oz/175 g cracked wheat (bulgur)
1½ pints/800 ml milk
¾ pint/450 ml water
3 oz/90 g dried apricots cut into tiny bits
3 tablespoons jaggery or honey
3 oz/90 g blanched toasted sliced almonds
Scalded milk and jaggery or honey

1 Put the butter in a medium saucepan and place it over low heat until it melts completely. Add the cracked wheat and increase the heat to medium high. Fry the wheat, stirring often, until it turns brown (about 10 minutes).
2 Add ¾ pint/450 ml of the milk, the water, and the dried apricots; mix well and bring to the boil. Lower the heat to keep the liquid at a gentle boil and cook uncovered, stirring frequently to prevent sticking, for 15 minutes or until the moisture is absorbed into the wheat. Turn off heat. Cover the pot and let rest for 10 minutes.
3 Add the remaining milk, the jaggery or honey, and mix well. Over low heat warm the cereal thoroughly. Serve in individual bowls sprinkled with toasted nuts. Pass scalded milk and additional jaggery or honey on the side.

INDIAN CHEESE AND CUCUMBER IN BLACK PEPPER-LEMON DRESSING

KHEERA-PANEER

◆

Freshly prepared Indian cheese (*paneer*) is a delicacy. Dressed with lemon juice, salt, and black pepper, it turns into a soothing preparation commonly enjoyed at breakfast by the Brahmins of northern India. It is also very nutritious, because it has a high protein content and hardly any fat.

FOR 2 PERSONS

◆

Indian cheese (paneer) made with 3 pints/2 litres milk (p. 52)
1 tablespoon honey or sugar
3 medium cucumbers, peeled, seeded, and grated
Coarse salt, to taste
Freshly ground black pepper
Juice of 1 lemon

1 Put the freshly made warm cheese in a bowl and use a fork to break it into small lumps. Add the honey or sugar; mix it in, being careful not to overblend and destroy the texture of the cheese.

2 Put the grated cucumber in another bowl. Add salt, pepper, and lemon juice. Toss well.

To serve, divide the cucumber on two plates and spread into a 5 in/ 12.5 cm circle on each. Place a portion of the cheese neatly in the centre. (This is best done with a small ice cream scoop.) Sprinkle a little freshly ground black pepper on the cheese.

HERB-LACED YOGURT CHEESE SPREAD

KHADI DAHI

◆

In Hindi *khadi dahi* literally means 'strangled yogurt'. In fact, that's what this dish is. It is made by hanging and draining plain yogurt of most of its moisture until it resembles soft, creamy cheese. A speciality of Gujarat, no other people on earth know the art of making or flavouring this wonderful product the way the Gujarati Jains do.

Mixed with herbs and seasonings, this spread is popularly eaten on delicious home-made millet bread. Try it as a fragrant dip with crudités and crackers.

MAKES 1 PINT/600 ML

◆

Hung yogurt cheese made with 1¼ pints/700 ml milk and ½ pint/300 ml double cream (p. 50)
1 small red onion, minced
4 green chilies, minced
4 tablespoons chopped fresh dill weed
4 tablespoons chopped fresh coriander
2 tablespoons finely chopped green garlic shoots (or chives or green parts of spring onions)
Coarse salt, to taste (optional)
Lemon juice, to taste

Put all the ingredients in a bowl and mix well with a wooden spoon. Transfer to a ceramic or glass dish, cover tightly with cling film, and refrigerate for at least an hour to blend the flavours. It is wonderful with barley bread, p. 318. Since this cheese contains no preservatives and is very moist, it is quite perishable. Store in the refrigerator no longer than two days.

GARLIC AND ROASTED CHILI-LACED CHEESE SPREAD

KHADI MASALA DAHI

◆

Here is yet another very popular Indian dish made with hung yogurt cheese. For a variation try the yogurt cheese with any simple pilaf like Tomato Pilaf (p. 326). This spread is simply too delicious to serve by itself with crackers for cocktails.

For best flavour make the yogurt cheese just a few hours prior to serving.

MAKES 1 PINT/600 ML

◆

Hung yogurt cheese made with 1¼ pints/700 ml milk and ½ pint/300 ml double cream (p. 50)
8 oz/250 g mashed potatoes
4 dry red chili pods, broken into bits, seeds discarded
1 tablespoon light sesame or light vegetable oil
1 large clove garlic, peeled and diced
1 small red onion, minced
4 tablespoons coarsely chopped fresh coriander
Coarse salt, to taste

1 Put the cheese and the mashed potatoes in a bowl and mix thoroughly with a wooden spoon.

2 Heat a *kadhai* or a small frying pan over high heat. When it is hot, add the chili pieces and roast them until they turn dark. Take the pan off the heat and transfer the chili pieces at once to a small plate and let them cool.

3 Wipe the pan, return it to the heat, and add oil. When the oil is hot, add the garlic pieces and fry until they turn golden brown and crisp. Add the minced onion and turn off the heat. Mix the onions to coat them well with the flavoured oil. Transfer the onion-garlic mixture to another plate and allow to cool thoroughly.

4 Add the roasted chili peppers and onion mixture to the yogurt cheese along with the coriander and salt. Mix well and serve immediately.

EGGLESS SCRAMBLED EGGS

CHENNA BHORJI

◆

This 'scramble' is an example of the vegetarians' ingenuity in making a meatless dish resemble a classic meat preparation. It has a wonderful fresh taste that comes from doing very little to it. To enjoy the dish in classic Indian vegetarian style, serve it with flaky bread (*paratha*) and a cup of spiced Indian tea.

FOR 4 PERSONS

◆

Indian cheese (chenna) *made with 3 pints/2 litres milk (p. 52)*
2–3 tablespoons usli ghee *(p.57) or light vegetable oil*
1 medium onion, chopped
⅛ teaspoon turmeric dissolved in 2 teaspoons water
2–4 hot green chilies, chopped
1 medium tomato, chopped
Coarse salt, to taste
½ teaspoon crushed roasted cumin seeds
1 tablespoon chopped fresh coriander

1 Put the cheese on a plate and pat into a circle about ½ in/1 cm thick. Set aside until needed.
2 Heat the *usli ghee* or oil in a large frying pan over medium-high heat. When the fat is hot, add the onion and let it cook for 2–3 minutes or until translucent and shiny.
3 While the onion is cooking, sprinkle the turmeric water over the cheese (it will be unevenly distributed).

4 Add the green chilies to the onion and continue cooking for another 2 minutes. Add the chopped tomato and cook 1 minute more.

5 Add the cheese to the vegetables and mix. The mixing should be done by a turn-frying process, as carefully as possible so as to keep the cheese in large lumps. You want it to look like scrambled eggs. This will take anything from 2–5 minutes. Using a non-stick pan and a wide, flat spatula is best here.

To serve, transfer the 'scramble' to a heated platter or individual plates. Sprinkle with roasted cumin and chopped coriander.

NOTE: To reduce the cooking time, roast the cumin seeds well ahead and store.

EGGLESS FRENCH TOAST WITH HERBS

MASALA DABAL ROTI

◆

Like many meat-lookalike Indian vegetarian dishes, this French toast is made without eggs. Chick-pea flour is combined with herbs and bean curd and then used to coat slices of bread.

My reason for including this dish is not so much to give you the Indian vegetarian version of French toast as to offer you a recipe that turns out to be unbelievably delicious. I love this as a snack cut into bite-size pieces.

FOR 2 PERSONS

◆

1½ oz/45 g chick-pea flour (besan)
4 tablespoons coarsely chopped fresh coriander
⅛ in/3 mm thick slice fresh ginger, peeled
2 tablespoons chopped onion
4 tablespoons crushed bean curd or paneer (p. 53)
¼ pint/150 ml water
½ teaspoon coarse salt, or to taste
3–4 tablespoons unsalted butter
4 slices toasting bread, white or wholemeal

1 Put all the ingredients except butter and bread into the container of a food processor or blender and blend until the mixture is thoroughly combined and the herbs are finely minced. (Do not worry if the chilies and the coriander are not evenly mixed. The coarse texture will add character to the toast.) Pour the batter into a large shallow dish. It can be made several hours ahead and even kept refrigerated for three days, covered.

2 When you are ready to cook the toast, heat a large griddle or frying pan over high heat until it is very hot. Reduce the heat to medium, add 3 tablespoons butter and quickly spread, using a spatula, to coat the entire surface. Dip the slices of bread into the batter one at a time, being sure to coat them thoroughly, and place on the griddle. When the bottom is nicely browned (about 2 minutes), turn and cook the other side for a minute or so until browned. Add the remaining tablespoon of butter if necessary while cooking the second side. Also, regulate the heat between medium-low and medium-high. Serve immediately.

STEAMED SOURDOUGH SPLIT PEA CAKES WITH SESAME AND CORIANDER

KHAMAN DHOKLA

◆

Every southern state in India can boast of a prized steamed delicacy. In Gujarat it is *dhokla*. And the people of the city of Surat demonstrate the art of making them to perfection. *Dhokla* are made by grinding and mixing a soaked pulse with several other ingredients, including yogurt, fresh ginger, and spices. The special steaming equipment used is called a *dhokla* steamer (see p. 94). The cakes that result are neatly cut into diamond-shaped pieces and once again flavoured with coriander, sesame, and mustard seeds before they are served.

FOR 6 PERSONS

◆

10 oz/300 g yellow split peas (channa dal)
1½ oz/45 g long-grain rice
4 oz/125 g plain yogurt
4 hot green chilies, minced
1 tablespoon crushed or grated fresh ginger
⅛ teaspoon turmeric (optional)
1½ teaspoons coarse salt, or to taste
¾ teaspoon citric acid (nimboo ka sat) *or 3 tablespoons lemon juice*
½ pint/300 ml water
1 teaspoon bicarbonate of soda
4 tablespoons light sesame or light vegetable oil
1 teaspoon black mustard seeds

1½ teaspoons sesame seeds
4 tablespoons fresh flaked coconut
4 tablespoons chopped coriander
Red pepper or paprika

1 Put the split peas and rice in separate bowls. Wash in several changes of water. Add enough water to cover by at least 1½ in/4 cm, and let soak for 8 hours or overnight. Drain, rinse, and drain again.

2 Put the rice into the container of a food processor or blender and purée. If needed, use a little (4 to 5 tablespoons) yogurt to make the puréeing easier. Now add the peas all at once and continue puréeing until you have a mixture that is slightly textured and not a complete paste. It should look somewhat lumpy and coarse.

3 Transfer the mixture to a bowl. Add the remaining yogurt, chilies, ginger, turmeric, salt, citric acid, and water. Mix thoroughly.

4 Bring water to the boil in a *dhokla* steamer, a pressure cooker, or a 10–12 pint/6–7 litre sauce pot in which the *dhokla* racks fit. Stir the bicarbonate of soda into the batter and spoon it into oiled *dhokla* racks or pie plates and, if using *dhokla* racks, attach them and place in the steamer. Steam for 10 minutes. Take out the racks or pie plates with *dhokla* and let them cool for 10 minutes. Cut the *dhokla* rounds into neat diamond-shaped pieces or wedges. Cover and set aside for several hours at room temperature.

5 When you are ready to serve the *dhokla*, steam them briefly (about 5 minutes) to warm thoroughly. Arrange the pieces neatly on a serving platter.

6 Measure out the spices and place them right next to the stove in separate piles. Heat the oil in a small frying pan over low heat. When it is very hot, add the mustard seeds. Keep a lid handy, because the seeds may spatter. When they stop spattering, add the sesame seeds and continue frying until the seeds are a pale golden colour. Pour the entire contents of the pan over the *dhokla* pieces at once, distributing evenly. Sprinkle with coconut, coriander, and a little red pepper or paprika. Serve immediately.

FOAMY WHITE STEAMED RICE AND BEAN DUMPLINGS

IDLEE

◆

Idlee is the world-famous south Indian breakfast or tiffin treat. It is made with a fermented batter containing soaked black gram bean paste and rice semolina. The batter is poured into the depressions in the *idlee* moulds and steamed to yield porous, spongy cushions called *idlee*. The proportion of beans to rice is the most crucial element in making light and airy *idlees*: the rice is always twice the quantity of beans. The dumplings expand when they are steamed, and their nutritional value goes up with fermentation of the batter; they become rich in proteins that are easily digestible.

These dumplings are traditionally served with coconut chutney (p. 294). Children usually like to eat them with palm jaggery syrup, which is somewhat difficult to find in Britain. However, molasses, natural honey, and maple syrup make good subsititutes. For a heartier dish you may wish to serve a lentil vegetable stew called *Muttakos Sambaar* (p. 192).

The best way to keep the dumplings warm is to put them in another steamer over hot (not boiling) water. You may use any kind you want as long as the steamer is large enough to accommodate all the dumplings without crushing them.

MAKES TWENTY-EIGHT TO THIRTY 2½ IN/16 CM ROUND DUMPLINGS

◆

10 oz/300 g white split gram beans (urad dal)
½ pint/300 ml water
10 oz/300 g rice semolina
1 teaspoon coarse salt, or to taste (optional)
¼ teaspoon baking soda
¼ pint/150 ml light sesame oil or light vegetable oil

1 Pick clean and wash the beans. Put them in a bowl and add water to cover by at least 2 in/5 cm, and let them soak for 8 hours. Drain and rinse the beans.

2 Put the beans and water into the container of a food processor or blender and purée them. The purée should be extremely smooth, light, and fluffy. Transfer to a large bowl.

3 Line a sieve with a double layer of muslin and put the semolina in it. Hold the sieve under cold running water and rinse the cereal until no clinging starch remains and the water begins to run clear through the muslin. Squeeze the semolina thoroughly to remove all moisture and add it to the bean paste. Beat the bean and rice mixture thoroughly. Add salt if desired. Cover the bowl with a kitchen towel or cling film and place it in a warm place for 8 to 12 hours to ferment the batter.

4 When you are ready to make the dumplings, stir the baking soda gently into the batter, using a rubber spatula. (Do not overblend as the batter must remain foamy and airy for the dumplings to come out light.) Let the batter rest for 4 to 5 minutes.

5 While the batter is resting, cut pieces of muslin into neat rounds or squares to fit the depressions of the *idlee* dumpling racks. Each piece of lining can be used twice, so you will need half as many pieces for lining as the number of dumplings. The muslin pieces should be slightly larger than the depressions so that they overhang by about ½ in/1 cm.

6 Line the dumpling racks with the pieces of muslin. Brush them lightly with oil. Bring water to the boil in the *idlee* steamer, a pressure cooker, or a large pan in which *idlee* racks fit.

7 Spoon some batter into each lined depression of the rack. Attach the racks and place in the steamer.

8 Steam the dumplings for 12 to 15 minutes or until a toothpick inserted into them comes out clean. Remove the racks from the steamer apparatus and separate the dumpling racks. Pick up each dumpling with the cloth and gently peel away the muslin. Place the steamed dumplings in another steamer or a covered dish to keep warm.

9 Turn the muslin pieces over and line the racks with the smooth reverse side up. Brush lightly with oil. Proceed with the remaining batter the same way.

To serve, place the dumplings (2 per person) in a rimmed soup plate or a shallow bowl. Make an indentation in the centre of the dumpling with your index finger or with the back of a wooden spoon. Pour about 1 to 1½ teaspoons sesame oil in the depressions and over the dumplings.

STEAMED RICE AND BEAN DUMPLINGS IN SPICY LENTIL AND RADISH SAUCE

IDLEE SAMBAAR

◆

Idlee sambaar is one of the great classic dishes of Indian vegetarian cooking. The dish consists of split peas in a spicy vegetable sauce that is a slightly milder version of the lentil and vegetable stew called *sambaar*. Radish and onion are the primary vegetables used to make this sauce because their distinct fragrance provides a marvellous contrast to the dumplings. *Idlee sambaar* are traditionally served in a generous amount of sauce in individual soup plates. Accompaniments, such as coconut chutney (p. 294), and hot-spicy pickles are also traditional. In India *idlee sambar* are always served at tiffin or brunch.

FOR 8 PERSONS

◆

1 recipe Steamed Rice and Bean Dumplings (p. 114)
1 recipe Spicy Lentil and Radish Sauce (follows)
12 oz/375 g yellow split peas
¼ teaspoon turmeric
1¾ pints/1 litre water
1 tablespoon sambaar powder (homemade, p. 75 or bought)
1 tablespoon ground coriander
½ teaspoon minced garlic
2 medium onions sliced
1 medium daikon radish, thinly sliced
2 medium tomatoes (fresh or canned), puréed with skin or finely chopped
1 tablespoon dry fenugreek leaves, powdered, or ⅓ teaspoon ground fenugreek seeds
1½ teaspoons coarse salt, or to taste
2 tablespoons light sesame or light vegetable oil
4 dry red chili pods
1 teaspoon mustard powder
1 tablespoon lemon juice or more, to taste

1 Pick through, clean and wash the split peas. Put in a large saucepan. Add the turmeric and water and bring to the boil. Lower the heat and cook, partially covered for 40 minutes at a low boil. Stir occasionally to make sure the peas don't burn; when the peas are very soft, turn off the heat. Beat the whisk for a minute to purée the peas. In a separate bowl, measure the purée and add enough water to make 2½ pints/ 1.5 litres of brothy purée. Return the purée to the pan.

2 Measure out the spices and place them next to the stove in separate piles. Turn on the heat and bring the purée to the boil. Add the *sambaar* powder, the coriander, and the garlic and continue to boil the purée, partially covered, over medium heat for 8 to 10 minutes. Add the onions, radish, tomatoes, fenugreek leaves (if you are using ground fenugreek seeds, *do not add them now*), and salt, and continue cooking at a low boil for an additional 10 minutes. Turn off the heat.

3 Heat the oil in a small frying pan over medium heat. When it is hot, add the chili pods and fry until they turn dark (about 15–20 seconds). Lift the pan off the heat, add the mustard powder and fenugreek powder if you are using it, and immediately pour the contents of the pan over the *sambaar*. Stir to mix. Cover and let the dish rest a few minutes so all flavours will have time to blend.

To serve, bring the *sambaar* to a vigorous boil, stir in the lemon juice, and pour it into a soup tureen or serve individually in *katoori*. Serve the dumplings, *idlee*, 2 per person, in soup plates. Spoon *sambaar* over the dumplings as desired.

CAULIFLOWER AND SPLIT PEA DUMPLING CAKE IN TOMATO SAUCE

HANDAVO

◆

Handavo, another vegetarian masterpiece from Gujarat, is somewhat similar to *dhokla*, except here some of the pulse batter is replaced with a purée of cooked vegetables. Cauliflower, cabbage, carrots, squash of all kinds, and greens are the vegetables traditionally used. Also the cake is baked instead of steamed, giving the vegetables a roasted flavour.

Handavo is perfect for breakfast or as a snack. It also makes a wonderful first course in an elegant meal.

FOR 8–12 PERSONS

◆

6 oz/175 g yellow split peas (channa dal)
8 oz/250 g plain yogurt (very tart, if possible)
12 oz/375 g cauliflower, cut into florets, cooked and coarsely chopped
2 oz/60 g green peas (fresh or frozen), cooked
3 fl oz/100 ml water
½ tablespoon grated or minced fresh ginger
2–4 hot green chilies, minced
1 teaspoon coarse salt, or to taste
1 teaspoon bicarbonate of soda
¾ teaspoon citric acid (nimboo ka sat) or juice of 1 lemon
6 tablespoons flaked coconut (fresh or unsweetened tinned)
FOR THE TOPPING:
4 tablespoons light sesame or light vegetable oil
½ teaspoon carom seeds (or 1 teaspoon thyme, crushed)
1½ teaspoons sesame seeds

Chopped coriander (about 2 tablespoons)

1½ teaspoons black mustard seeds

1 recipe Tomato Sauce (follows)

1 Pick clean the split peas and put them in a bowl and add enough water to cover by at least 1½ in/4 cm. Let soak for at least 4 hours, preferably 8 hours or overnight. Drain, rinse thoroughly, and drain again.

2 Put the split peas into the container of a blender or food processor. Add half the yogurt, and process until the contents are reduced to a coarse purée. Transfer the purée to a bowl. Stir in all the other batter ingredients. (Instead of chopping the cauliflower separately and folding it in, it can be added to the split peas as large 2 in/5 cm pieces halfway through puréeing.)

3 Preheat the oven to 325°F/165°C/Gas 3.

4 Grease an 8 in/20 cm round cake tin. Pour in the puréed mixture and smooth the top with a spatula.

5 For the topping, measure out the spices and place them right next to the stove in separate piles. Heat the oil in a small frying pan over high heat. When it is very hot, add the mustard seeds. Keep a lid handy because the seeds may spatter. When the spattering subsides, add the carom (do not add the thyme now, if you are using it) and the sesame seeds, and continue frying until the sesame seeds are lightly coloured. Immediately pour the entire contents of the pan over the puréed mixture in the cake tin, distributing evenly. If you are using thyme, sprinkle it on top at this point.

6 Bake the cake uncovered in the middle of the oven for 45 minutes or until a wooden skewer inserted in the centre comes out clean. Remove from the oven and let it rest in the tin for 10 minutes before you turn it out.

7 Run a wet knife around the edges of the cake. Place a serving platter on top of the tin and invert.

8 Sprinkle with chopped coriander and serve hot, sliced in wedges. Pour a little tomato sauce (see overleaf) over each wedge, with extra on the side.

TOMATO SAUCE

MAKES ¾ PINT/450 ML

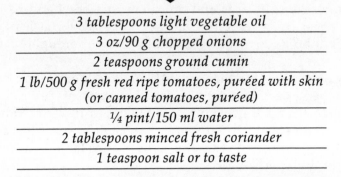

3 tablespoons light vegetable oil
3 oz/90 g chopped onions
2 teaspoons ground cumin
1 lb/500 g fresh red ripe tomatoes, puréed with skin (or canned tomatoes, puréed)
¼ pint/150 ml water
2 tablespoons minced fresh coriander
1 teaspoon salt or to taste

Put the oil in a small pan over high heat. Add the onions and cook, stirring, until they turn light brown (about 8 minutes). Add cumin, stir for a few seconds, and add the tomatoes and the water. Cook the vegetables uncovered for 15 minutes, or until the contents turn to a slightly thick sauce (like Italian tomato sauce for spaghetti). Turn off the heat and stir in the coriander and salt. Serve with the cauliflower and spilt pea dumpling cake.

If the sauce looks too thick or becomes too thick with keeping, stir in 4–6 tablespoons water, heat well, and serve.

RICE NOODLES WITH MUSTARD SEEDS AND COCONUT

IDLEE APPAI

◆

Serving rice noodles for breakfast or tiffin is a tradition in southern India. The rice noodles may be home-made or bought.

In this preparation, steamed (or softened, if they are bought) noodles are stir-fried with green peas, mustard seeds, and coconut and turned into an irresistible snack.

FOR 4–6 PERSONS

◆

8 oz/250 g very thin rice noodles (also known as rice sticks, p. 88)
3 tablespoons light sesame or light vegetable oil
2 teaspoons black mustard seeds
1 tablespoon white split gram beans (urad dal)
1 tablespoon shredded fresh ginger
2–4 hot green chilies, shredded
2 oz/60 g grated carrot
2 oz/60 g cooked green peas (fresh or frozen)
1½ teaspoons coarse salt, or to taste
8 curry leaves, fresh or dried (optional)
2½ oz/75 g fresh grated or shredded coconut

1 Bring 6½ pints/4 litres of water to the boil in a deep pot. Turn off the heat and add the rice noodles. Let them soak for 5 minutes. Drain and rinse immediately in cold water. Transfer the noodles to a plate, spreading them slightly so they do not clump together.

2 Measure out the spices and place them next to the stove in separate piles. Heat the oil in a *kadhai* or large shallow pan over high heat. When the oil is very hot, reduce the heat to medium-high and add the mustard seeds. Keep a lid handy, as the seeds may spatter. When the seeds begin to spatter, add the beans and stir to ensure that they brown evenly. When the beans turn light brown, add the ginger and chilies and let them sizzle for 15 seconds. Add carrot and peas and toss them for 1–2 minutes. Add noodles; sprinkle on salt to taste and curry leaves. Toss all the ingredients to blend, and heat the noodles thoroughly. Sprinkle on a little coconut (reserve some for garnish) and continue tossing for an additional couple of minutes.

To serve, transfer the noodles to a large heated platter or scoop into individual salad plates and garnish with reserved coconut. Accompany with Tomato Sauce (p. 120).

LEMON-FLAVOURED NOODLES WITH RED CHILIES

ELUMBUCHAPAYAM SEVAI

◆

Here is a delicate lemon-coloured version of rice noodles, spiked with a slight bite of hot peppers. In Indian homes both kinds of noodles are prepared separately and served side by side to provide a contrast in flavour and visual appeal.

FOR 4–6 PERSONS

◆

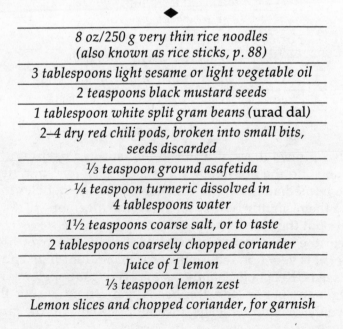

8 oz/250 g very thin rice noodles (also known as rice sticks, p. 88)
3 tablespoons light sesame or light vegetable oil
2 teaspoons black mustard seeds
1 tablespoon white split gram beans (urad dal)
2–4 dry red chili pods, broken into small bits, seeds discarded
⅓ teaspoon ground asafetida
¼ teaspoon turmeric dissolved in 4 tablespoons water
1½ teaspoons coarse salt, or to taste
2 tablespoons coarsely chopped coriander
Juice of 1 lemon
⅓ teaspoon lemon zest
Lemon slices and chopped coriander, for garnish

1 Bring 6½ pints/4 litres of water to the boil in a deep pot. Turn off the heat and add the rice noodles. Let them soak for 5 minutes. Drain and rinse immediately in cold water. Transfer the noodles to a plate, spreading them apart so they do not clump together.

2 Measure out the spices and place them next to the stove in separate piles. Heat the oil in a *kadhai* or large shallow pan over high heat. When the oil is very hot, reduce the heat to medium-high and add the mustard seeds. Keep a lid handy, as the seeds may spatter. As the seeds stop spattering, add the beans. As the beans begin to turn light golden, drop in the chili pods and continue frying until the beans turn light brown (1 minute for the whole process). Add the asafetida, and let the mixture sizzle for a few seconds. Add the noodles, and immediately follow with turmeric water and salt to taste. Toss well to coat noodles evenly with spices. Continue cooking for 5 minutes to heat noodles thoroughly. Turn off the heat and add the coriander, lemon juice, and lemon zest. Toss again.

To serve, transfer to a large heated platter or individual salad plates and serve garnished with a little chopped coriander and lemon slices. Accompany with Tomato-Onion Sauce (*Gozzoo*, p. 287).

SEMOLINA PILAF WITH TOMATO AND SPICES

TAKKALI PAYAM OPMA

Of all the cereal puddings, those made with semolina are the most popular among India's vegetarians because they cook easily and quickly and also because their subtle flavour allows for innumerable variations.

Opma can be made dry like pilaf or moist like pudding, simply by adding less or more water. In either case the semolina is first fried in a little oil before you add the flavours, spices and water. This process ensures a non-lumpy and non-sticky *opma*. This particular *opma* is made with tomatoes. It is tasty and beautiful to look at. It is often served in vegetarian restaurants serving tiffins.

FOR 4 PERSONS

5 tablespoons light sesame or light vegetable oil
3 oz/90 g chopped raw cashew nuts
6 oz/175 g semolina
1¼ teaspoons black mustard seeds
1½ teaspoons yellow split peas (channa dal)
2 teaspoons white split gram beans (urad dal)
1–2 hot green chilies, chopped
⅓ teaspoon ground asafetida (optional)
1 tablespoon chopped fresh ginger
3 oz/90 g chopped onion
3 oz/90 g chopped tomatoes, seeded and drained
1½ teaspoons coarse salt, or to taste
4 oz/125 g plain yogurt mixed with ½ pint/300 ml hot water
1–2 teaspoons lemon juice
Chopped coriander, for garnish

1 Heat a *kadhai* or a large shallow pan over high heat. When it is hot, reduce the heat to medium, add 1 tablespoon oil, and swirl it around to coat the bottom of the pan. Add the cashew nuts and sauté until lightly coloured (4 minutes). Remove with a slotted spoon and transfer to a plate.

2 Add 1 more tablespoon oil to the *kadhai* along with the semolina. Increase the heat to medium-high and fry until the grains of semolina are evenly coated with oil and lightly fried (about 5 minutes). Transfer to a bowl and wipe the pan clean with a paper towel.

3 Measure out the next seven ingredients and place them next to the stove in separate piles. Add the remaining 3 tablespoons oil to the pan and turn the heat to maximum. When the oil is very hot, reduce the heat to medium-low and add the mustard seeds. Keep a lid handy as the seeds may fly all over. As the seeds sputter, add the split peas. When they become lightly coloured (about 1 minute), add the beans. When the beans turn light golden (about 1 minute), add the chili bits and fry until they turn dark (20–30 seconds). Add the asafetida, ginger, and onion and cook for 3 minutes, stirring often.

4 Add the semolina, tomatoes, salt, and yogurt-water mixture and mix all the ingredients thoroughly for 1 minute. It will first look like thick soup. As the semolina cooks, it will get drier and drier, until it becomes a fluffy, pilaf-like, steaming, moist Christmas pudding. During cooking you must stir the *opma* often with a folding motion, the same way you fold egg whites into cake batter, to make sure the vegetables don't become mushy and that the pilaf develops a light, fluffy texture. This will take about 15 minutes. Fold in the cashew nuts, lemon juice, and a little chopped coriander.

To serve, transfer the mixture to a shallow bowl or individual salad plates and garnish with a little chopped coriander. Accompany with Tomato-Onion Sauce (p. 287).

SEMOLINA PILAF WITH AUBERGINE AND GINGER

RAVA OPMA

This version of *opma* is my favourite, because it is bursting with vegetables. It's really a complete meal in itself. In place of aubergine, you can use courgettes, mushrooms, green peppers, or green beans.

FOR 4 PERSONS

5 tablespoons light sesame or light vegetable oil
3 oz/90 g raw unsalted sliced almonds or chopped cashew nuts
6 oz/175 g semolina
1 teaspoon black mustard seeds
3 dry red chili pods, broken into bits, seeds discarded
3 oz/90 g chopped shallots or red onions
1½ teaspoons chopped fresh ginger
6 oz/175 g chopped aubergine, with skin
3 oz/90 g peeled and cubed potatoes
3 oz/90 g green peas (fresh or frozen)
¾ pint/450 ml hot water
1½ teaspoons coarse salt, or to taste
2 teaspoons lemon juice
2–3 tablespoons chopped fresh coriander

1 Have the nuts and vegetables ready and the spices measured out and set next to the stove in separate piles. Heat a *kadhai* or a large shallow pan over high heat. When hot, reduce the heat to medium, add 1 tablespoon oil, and swirl the pan to coat the bottom. Add almonds or cashew nuts and sauté, tossing the nuts until lightly coloured (4 minutes). Remove with a slotted spoon and transfer to a plate. Set aside until needed.

2 Add 1 more tablespoon oil to the *kadhai* along with the semolina. Increase the heat to medium-high and fry until the grains of semolina are evenly coated with oil and lightly cooked (about 5 minutes). Transfer to a bowl. Wipe the *kadhai* clean with a piece of paper towel.

3 Add the remaining 3 tablespoons oil to the *kadhai* and turn the heat to maximum. When the oil sizzles, reduce the heat to medium-low and add the mustard seeds. Keep a lid handy as the seeds may spatter. When the seeds stop spattering, add the chili bits and let them sizzle until they turn dark (about 15 seconds). Add the shallots or onions and ginger and continue cooking for 2 minutes.

4 Add the aubergine and potatoes and fry, turning the vegetables, for 5 minutes or until slightly limp. Add the semolina, peas, water, and salt. Mix well and bring to the boil. The contents of the pan will first look like a thick soup. As the semolina cooks, it will get drier and drier until it resembles a fluffy pilaf – like steaming moist Christmas pudding. During cooking you must stir the *opma* often with a folding motion, the same way you fold egg whites into cake batter, to make sure the vegetables do not become mushy and that the pilaf develops a light, fluffy texture, this will take about 15 minutes. Fold in the lemon juice, the chopped coriander, and the almonds or cashew nuts.

To serve, transfer to a shallow bowl or individual salad plates and garnish with a little more chopped coriander. Accompany with Jaggery (p. 86).

SEMOLINA PANCAKES WITH GREEN CHILIES AND GINGER

RAVA DOSAI

◆

In India semolina pancakes are not much eaten at breakfast because they are a little rich, but at tiffin or at snack time, they closely compete with *masala dosai*. These pancakes are quick to prepare and are absolutely delicious. They look like lace studded with ginger shreds and green chilies. This texture is due to the spices and herbs that are added to the batter. Also the pancake itself is cooked by throwing or splashing the batter onto the griddle, which results in innumerable perforations.

The pancakes are best accompanied by a cup of strong south Indian coffee.

MAKES EIGHT 10 IN/25 CM ROUND PANCAKES

◆

3 oz/90 g semolina
1 oz/30 g plain flour
1 oz/30 g rice flour
½ pint/300 ml water
¼ pint/150 ml light sesame oil or vegetable oil
½ teaspoon black mustard seeds
½ teaspoon cumin seeds
2 dry red chili pods, broken into bits
2 hot green chilies, chopped
1½ teaspoons chopped fresh ginger
4 tablespoons finely chopped onions
1½ teaspoons coarse salt, or to taste

1 Put the semolina and both flours in a large bowl with ¼ pint/150 ml water. Mix well with a whisk or wooden spoon. Cover and let the semolina soak and soften for 1 hour.

2 Heat 2 tablespoons oil in a small frying pan. When it is very hot, add the mustard seeds. Keep a lid handy, as the seeds may fly all over. When the spattering subsides, turn off the heat. Pour the oil with seeds into the flour batter, add all the other ingredients except remaining water, and mix well. Add the remaining water to batter and mix again. The batter will be very thin.

3 When you are ready to make the pancakes, put the remaining oil in a small bowl and keep it handy.

4 Heat a large (12 in/30 cm diameter) non-stick frying pan or griddle over high heat for 3 minutes or until it is very hot. Turn off the heat and let the griddle cool for 15 seconds. Turn on the burner to medium. Stir the batter well, then take about 4 tablespoons of the batter and dribble it on so that it covers the bottom of the pan. (The pancake will have uneven edges and large holes. It will look like lace. If you want a round, even-edged pancake, pour a little batter in one corner of the pan and tilt quickly so that batter runs and forms a border. If necessary, regulate the heat between medium and medium-high.) Dribble about 1 to 2 teaspoons oil around the edges of the pancake and in the holes. Don't try to loosen the pancake from the pan until it browns and turns crackling crisp (about 2 minutes), turn and cook the other side for 2–4 minutes. Transfer to a serving platter and keep warm. Continue with the rest of the batter the same way, stirring well each time.

NOTE: If the batter begins to thicken, add a few tablespoons of water.

RICE PANCAKES WITH CUMIN AND PEPPER FLAKES

ARISI RAVA DOSAI

◆

These pancakes are made very much like semolina pancakes, except they are softer and more spicy because of the addition of pepper flakes.

MAKES 8 PANCAKES

◆

3½ oz/100 g rice flour
6 oz/175 g semolina
¾ pint/450 ml water
2 dry red chili pods, crumbled and seeds discarded
4 tablespoons minced spring onion, including green part
¾ teaspoon cumin seeds, coarsely ground
1½ teaspoons coarse salt, or to taste
¼ pint/150 ml light sesame oil or light vegetable oil

1 Put rice flour, semolina, and half of the water in a bowl. Mix thoroughly, cover, and let soak for 4 hours or overnight at room temperature.

2 Add the remaining water along with all the other ingredients except the oil, and mix well. The batter will be very thin.

3 To make the pancakes, heat a griddle or a large non-stick frying pan over high heat for 3 minutes or until very hot. Brush the griddle lightly with oil. Pour about 4 tablespoons of the batter on the griddle and swirl the pan to coat the bottom completely with the batter. Reduce heat to medium or medium-high and let the pancake cook for 3 minutes.

4 Dribble 1 to 2 teaspoons oil around the edges and continue cooking until the underside is slightly browned (1–2 minutes). Don't try to loosen the pancake from the pan until it browns. Turn and cook the second side for 1 minute. Remove and serve immediately or keep warm while you make more pancakes with the remaining oil.

NOTE: If the batter begins to thicken, add a few tablespoons water to bring it to the right consistency.

CHICK-PEA PANCAKES WITH GINGER AND HOT CHILIES

CHILLA

◆

Chilla is a spicy delicacy, a delightful breakfast treat from the eastern regions of India. Indians also call it an eggless omelette. These pancakes are made with chick-pea flour, and the batter is spiced with fresh ginger and hot chilies, both red and green. For additional flavour and texture I often add a little grated courgette (4 oz/125 g) or some chopped spring onions (4 tablespoons) to the batter.

To enjoy *chilla* best, serve them with a lot of hot steaming tea, Indian-style.

MAKES EIGHT 6 in/15 cm PANCAKES FOR 3–4 PERSONS

◆

4 oz/125 g chick-pea flour
½ pint/300 ml water
1 tablespoon chopped fresh ginger

2 hot green chilies, chopped
⅛ teaspoon red pepper flakes
1 teaspoon coarse salt, or to taste, if desired
2 tablespoons light sesame oil or light vegetable oil
Extra oil for frying

1 Mix the chick-pea flour and water and make a smooth, lump-free batter using a food processor, blender, or wire whisk. Add all the other ingredients except extra oil; mix well.

2 To cook the pancakes, heat a non-stick frying pan (6–8 in/15 cm in diameter) over medium heat until very hot. Then brush the pan lightly with ½ to ¾ teapoon oil.

3 Pour about 4 tablespoons of the batter into the pan. Tilt the pan to coat it evenly with the batter. Cook the pancake until the underside is browned (about 2 minutes). Turn and cook the other side for 30 to 45 seconds. Pour on ½–1 teaspoon oil during cooking to give the pancake a fried taste and texture. Remove and serve immediately or keep warm, while you make more with the remaining batter. For a crispier taste, use 2–2½ teaspoons oil per pancake.

SOURDOUGH PANCAKES WITH SPICY CABBAGE AND CHILIES

MUTTAKOOS UTTAPPAM

◆

These pancakes are quite substantial; they make an excellent entrée at a light lunch or late supper accompanied by a soothing tangy bowl of any vegetable and lentil stew (*sambaar*).

MAKES SIX TO EIGHT 6 in/15 cm PANCAKES

◆

FOR THE BATTER:
2 oz/60 g white split gram bean flour (urad dal atta)
5 oz/150 g rice flour
¾ pint/450 ml water
1 tablespoon semolina
1 tablespoon plain flour
⅛ teaspoon baking powder
1½ teaspoons coarse salt, or to taste
FOR SPICY CABBAGE TOPPING:
2 tablespoons light sesame oil or light vegetable oil
1 teaspoon black mustard seeds
4 hot green chilies, shredded
¼ teaspoon ground asafetida (optional)
1 medium onion, chopped
¼ medium cabbage (about 12 oz/375 g), stem removed and finely chopped
½ teaspoon coarse salt, or to taste
8–10 tablespoons light sesame oil or vegetable oil
More oil for frying

1 Mix the bean flour, the rice flour, and the water in a bowl with a whisk or wooden spoon until it is well blended and you have a lump-free batter. Cover and let the batter rest for 8 hours in a warm place.

2 Add the semolina and the plain flour, and mix thoroughly. Cover and leave at room temperature. Continue fermenting until the batter develops a strong sour taste and aroma (about 8–12 hours).

3 Stir in the baking powder and salt to taste. At this stage the batter should resemble pancake batter. If it appears to be too thick, add 1 or 2 tablespoons water.

4 To make the cabbage topping, measure out all the dry ingredients and set them next to the stove in separate piles. Heat the oil in a large frying pan over high heat. When it is very hot, add the mustard seeds. Keep a lid handy, as the seeds may spatter and fly all over. When the seeds stop spattering, add the chilies and let them sizzle for 15 seconds. Add the asafetida if you are using it, shake the pan for 5 seconds, and then add the onion. Cook the onion, stirring, for 1 minute; then add the cabbage and continue cooking for 3 more minutes. Lower the heat and cook, covered, for 10 minutes or until the cabbage looks cooked and is soft. Add salt to taste and turn off the heat.

5 To make the pancakes, heat a griddle or a large non-stick frying pan over medium-high heat for 3 minutes. Add 1 teaspoon oil, tilt the pan to coat the bottom, and pour about a quarter of the batter in the centre of the pan. Using the back of a spoon, spread the batter into a neat 6 in/15 cm diameter round.

6 Spread about a quarter of the cabbage topping evenly over the pancake, leaving a ½ in/1 cm border all round, pressing it down lightly to make it stick to the batter. Let the pancake cook for 2 minutes. Dribble about 1 tablespoon oil around the edges and continue cooking the pancake for another 2 minutes. When the bottom has browned, sprinkle 1 to 2 teaspoons oil on the pancake and gently flip it. Cook for an additional 2 minutes or until the pancake is browned on the bottom.

Invert the pancake onto a serving platter so that the cabbage and chilies are on the top and serve; or keep it warm, covered, while you make more pancakes with the remaining batter.

CHILI-LACED SPLIT PEA GRIDDLE CAKES

ADAI

◆

This classic griddle cake demonstrates the inventiveness and skill of southern Indian cooks. Simple everyday lentils (*channa dal*) are soaked, ground to a slightly grainy coarseness along with spicy seasonings, and transformed into crisp meaty griddle cakes. They make a good light lunch or late supper, particularly with a glass of wine or a hot cup of coffee.

Indians generally spread *adai* on the griddle with their fingers to give it a distinct rustic look. This can be a little tricky for a beginner. When you start out, you will turn out thick cakes. But as you practise and become experienced, your *adai* will be thin and perfectly round. You can, of course, use a spatula or spoon instead.

MAKES EIGHT 6 in/15 cm PANCAKES

◆

3 oz/90 g yellow split peas (channa dal)
3 oz/90 g yellow lentils (toovar dal)
2 oz/60 g long-grain rice
¼ pint/150 ml water
1 hot green chili, cut into 3 pieces
¼ teaspoon ground asafetida
½ teaspoon red pepper flakes
1 teaspoon coarse salt, or to taste
¼ pint/150 ml light sesame oil or light vegetable oil

1 Pick through and clean the split peas and lentils, put them in a bowl, and wash them in several changes of water until they are free of all impurities. Add enough water to cover them by 1 in/2.5 cm. Put the rice in another bowl and add enough water to cover by 1 in/2.5 cm. Soak both for 8 hours or overnight.
2 Drain pulses and rice in separate bowls. Attach the metal cutting blade to the bowl of the food processor. With the machine running, add the rice through the feed tube and process for 2 minutes or until the rice is finely ground, turning the machine off every 15 seconds to scrape the sides down.

3 Add the drained pulses, water, chili, asafetida, red pepper, and salt and process to a slightly coarse purée, turning off the machine to scrape down the sides of the container. Remove the paste and put into a bowl. The batter should be thick like muffin batter, but not dry. If it is too dry, add 2–4 tablespoons water. The batter may be kept in the refrigerator up to 5 days, or frozen.

4 Heat a griddle or non-stick frying pan over medium to medium-high heat until very hot. Brush the surface very lightly with oil (if necessary, wipe up excess oil with a paper towel, because too much oil will cause the batter to curl), and add about ¼ pint/150 ml batter in the centre of griddle. Spread the batter into a neat 6 in/15 cm round, using your fingers, a spoon, or a spatula. If you are using your fingers, spread the batter in a spiral out from the centre. Make a ½ in/1 cm hole in the middle of the circle, using the back of a spoon. Let the griddle cake cook for 2 minutes. Dribble about 2 teaspoons oil around the edges of the cake and in the hole in the centre. Continue cooking and frying the cake for an additional minute or two, adjusting the heat as necessary, until the underside is nicely browned and crisp. Turn the cake, using a spatula, and cook the other side for 1–2 minutes, or until both sides are golden brown and the griddle cake looks crisply fried.

Serve immediately or keep it warm, covered, while you make the other cakes the same way.

Serve with Jaggery (p. 86) or molasses.

APPETIZERS
FRITTERS
AND
SAVOURIES

Growing up in India, I remember coming home from school and always being welcomed with delicious aromas emanating from our kitchen that meant a fresh savoury or afternoon snack was being prepared. My sisters and I ate them with a cool yogurt drink or fruit punch before vanishing to play.

Indian snacks are well known. They are so delicious one can often make a meal of them. These snacks, called *namkeen*, are sold by street vendors in big cities all over India. They are also served in most Indian restaurants as appetizers, since they are excellent either with cocktails or as a first course.

Indians as a general practice do not include an appetizer or first course with their meal. This is partly due to the fact that food in India is a scarce commodity but mainly, I think, because Indians are simply afraid of filling up too much before the main course.

Today, with so many Indians returning home highly Westernized after staying abroad, eating styles are beginning to change in India. Appetizers, hors d'oeuvres, and cold-salad first courses have gained a place at a typical Indian meal, while crisps, wafers, and other nibbling items accompany cocktails.

I like to start a meal with a little something – to set the mood, perk up my appetite, and to tingle the palate. The appetizer you choose naturally depends upon the occasion. I have included suggestions with each recipe.

The eateries that traditionally serve these delicacies are called *dhaba*. Every neighbourhood has its own *dhaba*, where people who know one another congregate at any time of the day or night – as most *dhabas* are open twenty-four hours a day – to discuss politics. *Dhabas* are the Indian equivalent of the French café. Indians also go to *dhabas* at lunchtime to make a meal of *namkeen*, and at tea break, which Indians happen to take at all times of the day, to nibble on *namkeen* and to sip a sweet hot cup of tea.

APPETIZERS

◆

OLD DELHI FRUIT SALAD

PHALON KI CHAT

◆

Chat is one of the most popular snacks sold on the street in India. It is really a salad, except it is much lighter and spicier, since it contains no oil and is usually flavoured with very aromatic spices such as black salt, roasted cumin, and asefetida. The premixed spice blend, called *chat masala*, is sold in shops or you can make your own (see p. 82).

Chat as a general rule is never chilled for fear that the spices might lose their delicate fragrance when cold.

This *chat* of juicy tropical fruits is the speciality of Nayi Sadak, a street in Old Delhi, that is famous for street snacks. I still remember how often I took the longer bus ride from home just to make a stop and feast on this heavenly combination.

Fruit *chat* is wonderful in a flat serving plate accompanied by toothpicks for easy buffet-style serving at cocktails.

FOR 6–8 PERSONS

◆

2 ripe bananas
1 ripe papaya
2 ripe guavas or pears
1 orange
3 sapotas (chikoo) *or sweet-tasting apples*
2 teaspoons chat masala *(home-made p. 82, or bought)*
2 tablespoons lemon juice
Coarse salt, to taste
Lettuce leaves

1 Peel bananas and cut them into ½ in/1 cm thick slices. Put them into a large bowl. Cut papaya in half and scoop out the pips. Cut each

half into 1 in/2.5 cm wide wedges. Carefully peel the papaya and cut the meat into ½ in/1 cm thick slices. Add this to the bowl.

2 Cut the guavas into quarters. Cut each quarter across into ½ in/ 1 cm thick slices. Add them to the bowl.

3 Peel orange and, if necessary, remove pips, and slice it. Add to the bowl.

4 Finally, peel the sapotas and quarter them. Remove and discard the large black seeds embedded in the flesh. Cut each quarter into two pieces and add these to the bowl also.

5 Sprinkle on the *chat masala*, lemon juice, and salt, toss well and serve over lettuce leaves. This salad is best eaten fresh. With keeping, it tends to lose its marvellous colour.

This refreshing *chat* may precede any main dish except, of course, those containing fruits. I prefer dishes with onion-and-tomato-rich sauces such as Cauliflower, Aubergine, and Potato in Herb Sauce (p. 180) or Courgette *Koftas* in Creamed Tomato Sauce (p. 188).

MULBERRY AND WATER CHESTNUT SALAD

SHAHTOOT AUR SINGHADE KI CHAT

◆

On the upper slopes of the Himalayas under the snow-capped mountains these juicy, tart berries grow. They are often eaten by themselves sprinkled with just a little black salt. Sometimes they are combined with other ingredients and turned into a *chat*.

In India *chat masala* is traditionally added to this salad (about 1 teaspoon for this recipe). I prefer to omit it, for it masks the gentle flavour of the berries and prevents the sweetness of the water chestnuts from emerging. This sweetish tart *chat* is visually stunning arranged on individual plates and served as a first course.

FOR 2–3 PERSONS

◆

12 fresh water chestnuts (singhade)
4 oz/125 g fresh mulberries (or a combination of fresh blackberries and raspberries)
2 oz/60 g fresh cranberries or cherries
¼ teaspoon coarse salt, or to taste
¼ teaspoon black salt (kala namak) (p. 19–20)
½ teaspoon black pepper

1 Wash and then peel the water chestnuts and cut them into ¼ in/ 5 mm thick slices. Put them in a bowl.
2 Rinse the berries, drain, and add to the bowl.
3 Rinse cranberries, chop them finely, and add them to the bowl too (if you are using cherries, pit and chop them).
4 Sprinkle on the two salts and the pepper, toss carefully, and refrigerate until thoroughly chilled.

This *chat* makes an elegant first course followed by a rich lentil and vegetable casserole such as Pumpkin and Split Peas with Camphor Basil (p. 201).

SPICY COURGETTE KOFTAS

GHIA KOFTA

Kofta, a classic dish of Moghul origin, is one of the most important preparations of Indian vegetarian cuisine. It is made by shredding or grating any vegetable, mixing it with spices, herbs, and flour; shaping the mixture into balls (*kofta*), and deep-frying them. Traditionally, koftas are simmered in a delicate sauce and turned into a curried main dish (see recipe p. 188). But since they are so tasty and elegant-looking, not to mention easy to eat, many Indians serve them as hors d'oeuvres.

Ghia kofta, a classic from the holy city of Allahabad, in northern India, is a popular Indian restaurant dish all over the world.

FOR 6 PERSONS; MAKES ABOUT 2 DOZEN 1½ IN/3.5 CM KOFTAS

◆

Peanut oil or corn oil (enough to fill a **kadhai** *or deep fryer to a depth of 2½ in/6 cm*
1½–2 lb/750 g–1 kg grated courgettes
1 medium onion, peeled and grated
3 oz/90 g chick-pea flour
1 tablespoon ground coriander
¾ teaspoon red pepper
2–4 hot green chilies, chopped
3 tablespoons chopped fresh coriander
¼ teaspoon baking powder
¾ teaspoon coarse salt, or to taste (optional)

1 Start heating the oil in a *kadhai* or deep fryer.
2 While the oil is heating, put all the other ingredients in a bowl and mix thoroughly with your hands. When the oil is hot (375°F/190°C), pick up about 1 heaped teaspoon of the vegetable mixture with a spoon or your hands, form it roughly into a ball, and drop it into the hot oil. Fry the *koftas*, stirring and turning, until they are nicely brown all over (about 4 to 6 minutes). Remove and drain on paper towels. Continue

with the remaining mixture the same way, making sure not to over-crowd the koftas in the oil.

NOTE: Since there is no egg used to bind the *kofta* mixture, the balls will be quite fragile. Therefore, be sure to handle them very gently. I recommend using two wide slotted spoons.

3 Serve immediately or set aside, covered, for several hours. To reheat, drop them in hot oil for 1 minute. Drain again before serving.

These vegetarian balls are filling, so be careful not to serve too many of them. A delicate Moghul dish of Sweet Peppers Stuffed with Cheese and Spring Onions in Sauce Afghan (p. 209) would be a most appropriate accompaniment.

VEGETARIAN PATTIES

SABZI KABAB

While *kafta* is the classic vegetable roll (or ball), the *kabab*, made with minced vegetables, peas, or cracked wheat, is a meat-lookalike dish. It is, in fact, even flavoured to taste like meat. (*Kabab*, incidentally, means 'mince' in Hindi, referring to minced meat). Vegetarian patties, a speciality of the Moghul city of Agra, are scrumptious. They are a favourite among all Indian vegetarians, because the dish satisfies their curiosity without getting them into trouble with God or endangering the soul.

MAKES 24 KABABS

FOR COOKING THE PEAS:
9 oz/275 g yellow split peas (channa dal)
3 oz/125 g chopped onion
4 oz/125 g chopped lotus root or mushrooms
1 tablespoon minced garlic
1 tablespoon minced fresh ginger
½ teaspoon ground cardamom
1½ teaspoons ground cumin
½ teaspoon cayenne pepper
Coarse salt to taste
FOR FLAVOURING THE KABAB MIXTURE:
2 tablespoons groundnut oil or corn oil
6 oz/175 g minced onions
4 hot green chilies
½–1 teaspoon black pepper
1½ oz/45 g fresh coriander, packed
2 teaspoons lemon juice
7 oz/200 g breadcrumbs, preferably fresh homemade
Water as needed
About ½ pint/300 ml groundnut oil or corn oil

Cooking the peas:
1 Pick clean the peas, then soak them in enough water to cover by at least 2 in/5 cm, for 2 hours. Drain and rinse the peas.
2 Put them in a pot along with all the ingredients for cooking the peas and 1¼ pints/700 ml water and bring to the boil. Lower the heat to medium and cook, partially covered, for 30 minutes or until the peas are cooked but still hold their shape. The water should be absorbed into the peas. If it is not, increase the heat and boil the mixture until all the water has evaporated. Turn off the heat. Let the mixture cool for a few minutes.

Preparing the kababs:
3 In the meantime, heat the oil in a small frying pan over medium-high heat and add the onions. Fry them, stirring, until they turn caramel brown (about 10 minutes). Turn off the heat.
4 Put the fried onions, chilies, pepper, and coriander in the container of a food processor and process for 30 seconds, turning the machine off every 10 seconds to scrape down the sides. The herbs and seasonings should be evenly chopped and blended. Add the pea mixture and continue processing, turning the machine off to scrape the sides every 10 seconds, for 30 additional seconds or until you have an integrated purée with a little bit of texture.
5 Transfer the mixture to a bowl. Add the lemon juice, breadcrumbs, and a few tablespoons of water so that the purée achieves the consistency of a soft dough.
6 Place a small bowl of water on your work surface. Moistening your fingers occasionally with water, shape the mixture into neat patties, 2 in/5 cm round. Place them on greaseproof paper and set aside while you heat the oil. You should have about 40 patties.
7 Heat 4 tablespoons oil in a large frying pan until it is hot. Put about 8 to 12 patties in the hot oil and sauté, turning them until nicely browned on both sides (about 10 minutes). Remove with a spatula and drain on kitchen paper. Repeat with the remaining patties the same way.

You can follow these patties with any main dish as long as the ingredients in the dish are not minced; you want to be sure to provide a change of texture. For a contrast in flavour, try serving a spicy southern stew such as Madras Fiery Aubergine, Lentil, and Chili Stew (p. 194) or Manali Unripe Peach and Chick-peas with Fennel (p. 200).

SPICY POTATO CROQUETTES IN CHICK-PEA BATTER

BONDA

Bonda is the southern version of vegetarian meatballs (*kofta*), except the resemblance stops at the physical. The filling consists of mashed potatoes curried with mustard seeds, onions, chilies and gram beans. The chick-pea batter coating gives the *bonda* a luscious spiciness to contrast with the fragrant filling.

MAKES 16–20 BONDAS

◆

FOR THE POTATO FILLING:
5 medium potatoes, unpeeled, boiled until very soft
½ teaspoon turmeric
½ teaspoon curry powder   *(home-made p. 00, or bought)*
2–3 tablespoons light sesame oil or vegetable oil
¾ teaspoon black mustard seeds
1½ teaspoons split white gram beans (urad dal)
6 oz/175 g chopped onion
3–5 hot green chilies, chopped
Juice of ½ small lemon
2 teaspoons coarse salt, or to taste
4 tablespoons chopped fresh coriander
FOR THE BATTER:
6 oz/175 g chick-pea flour
2 tablespoons rice flour (or chick-pea flour)
¼ teaspoon cayenne pepper
¾ teaspoon baking powder
¼ teaspoon coarse salt, or to taste
½ pint/300 ml warm water (110°F/43°C),   *or more as needed*
Groundnut oil or corn oil (enough to fill)   *a* kadhai *or a deep fryer to a depth of 3 in/8 cm*

1 Peel the potatoes and crush them, using the back of a spoon, to make coarsely mashed potatoes. Blend in the turmeric and curry powder.

2 Measure out the spices, onion, and chilies and set them next to the stove in separate piles. Heat the oil in a large pan over medium-high heat until it is very hot. When it is hot, add the mustard seeds. Keep a lid handy, as the seeds may spatter. As the seeds are spattering, add the beans and fry, shaking the pan until they turn light golden (about 30 seconds). Add the onion and chilies, and cook until the onions look a little limp and cooked (about 4 minutes).

3 Add the mashed potatoes. Continue cooking, stirring, for 5 minutes or until the potatoes are slightly fried and begin to brown. Turn off the heat and stir in the lemon juice, salt, and coriander. Mix well. When the potato mixture has cooled enough to handle, roll it into balls about 1 in/2.5 cm in diameter. Set aside. You should have about 16–20 *bondas*.

4 To make the batter, mix the chick-pea flour, rice flour, cayenne, bakin powder, salt, and enough warm water to make a thick batter. Set aside, covered.

5 To fry, heat the oil in a *kadhai* or fryer until it is very hot (375°F/190°C). Dip the potato croquettes one at a time in the chick-pea batter to coat completely; shake off excess batter, then drop into the hot oil. Fry just enough croquettes at a time so that they float freely in the oil. Fry them, turning often, until they are golden brown all over (about 3–5 minutes). Remove with a slotted spoon and drain on kitchen paper. Continue with the reamining croquettes the same way.

NOTE: Leftover batter can be used to coat sliced vegetables (such as potatoes, courgette, aubergine, pumpkin) and fried as fritters.

Bonda is quite a substantial appetizer; therefore, to keep the meal reasonably light and well balanced, I prefer to follow them with an Indian cheese dish.

HOT TAPIOCA AND PEANUT CROQUETTES, MAHARASHTRA-STYLE

SAGO VADA

The Brahmin women of Maharashtra are known in India as being the most creative vegetarian cooks. It is therefore not surprising that they would be the ones to create this excellent croquette. Please note that these croquettes are extremely hot – chili hot; therefore be forewarned or cut down the amount of chilies in the recipe.

MAKES TWENTY-FOUR 2 in/5 cm ROUND VADAS

6 tablespoons tapioca
8 hot green chilies, finely chopped
1½ oz/45 g fresh coriander (leaves and stem) finely chopped
2½ oz/75 g roasted plain or salted peanuts, chopped
3 medium-size potatoes (about 12 oz/375 g), boiled, peeled, and coarsely mashed
½ bunch spring onions, green and white parts, chopped
¼ teaspoon ground asafetida or 4 tablespoons finely chopped onion
Groundnut oil or corn oil (enough to fill a kadhai or a deep fryer to a depth of 1½ in/4 cm)

1 Put the tapioca in a colander. Add cold water and drain. Repeat three to four times to wash tapioca of excess starch clinging to the surface. Add enough water to cover the tapioca by 1 in/2.5 cm and let soak for 20 minutes. Drain, rinse, and drain again. Put in a bowl.
2 Add the remaining ingredients except the oil to the tapioca and mix thoroughly, kneading the mixture for a minute. Clean your hands thoroughly.
3 Moisten your hands with a little water (this is to prevent the mixture from sticking to your fingers). Pinch off about 1 in/2.5 cm

round pieces of dough and roll into smooth balls. Press the balls lightly but firmly to flatten them slightly. Set aside. The croquettes may be formed several hours ahead and kept refrigerated, covered with cling film.

4 Heat the oil in a *kadhai* or deep fryer until very hot (375°F/190°C). Add 6–7 croquettes at a time and fry, turning them, until they turn golden brown (about 3 minutes on each side). Drain on kitchen paper and continue with the rest the same way.

To warm the *vadas*, place them on baking trays, uncovered, in a 375°F/190°C) Gas 5 preheated oven for 10–12 minutes.

These croquettes are wonderful but a little starchy; therefore, the best choice of a main dish would be a simple vegetable or Indian cheese preparation such as Stuffed Cauliflower Tart with Tomato-Coriander Sauce (p. 182) or Vegetables Braised in Yogurt and Spices, Patna-style (p. 207).

SPICY SPLIT PEA CROQUETTES

MASALA VADA

◆

In Karnataka, directly south of Maharashtra, a special type of croquette is made by using split peas instead of tapioca. These are laced with green and red chilies, fresh ginger, and coriander. They are mealy and spicy. For variations you can fold in a little chopped sautéed mushroom or aubergine. These are ideal appetizers with cocktails, as tiffin, or at teatime.

MAKES 16 VADAS

◆

6 oz/175 g yellow split peas (channa dal)
2 hot green chilies
4 dry red chili pods, broken and seeded
2 tablespoons water
2 tablespoons chopped fresh ginger
2 tablespoons chopped fresh coriander
2 oz/60 g chopped onion
Coarse salt to taste (about 1 teaspoon)
Groundnut oil or corn oil (enough to fill a kadhai *or a deep fryer to a depth of 1½ in/4 cm)*

1 Pick clean the peas and soak them in 1¼ pints/700 ml water for 4 hours. Drain the peas, rinse well under cold running water, and drain again.
2 Put the peas in the container of a food processor along with the green and red chilies. With the steel blade, process for 1 minute, turning off the machine every 10–15 seconds and scraping down the sides of the container. Add the water during processing. Transfer the mixture, which will be slightly coarse, to a bowl. Stir in all the remaining ingredients except the oil for frying. Mix well.
3 Place a small bowl of water on your work surface. Dip your fingers in the water and then scoop out about 1 heaped tablespoon of the pea mixture and form it into a ball. Make all the balls the same way.

4 Heat the oil in a *kadhai* or deep fryer until it is very hot (375°F/ 190°C). Pick up a ball, flatten it into a croquette, and drop it into the hot oil. When the underside of the croquette has nicely browned (about 3 minutes), turn and fry the other side till it turns golden brown (about 2 minutes). Remove with a slotted spoon and drain on kitchen paper. Continue with the rest the same way. Serve hot or at room temperature.

Masala vada can be made several hours ahead and reheated, uncovered, in a 375°F/190°C/Gas 5 preheated oven for 8–10 minutes.

To maintain an interesting variation in flavour and a balance in nutrition, follow with a braised vegetable dish such as Hot and Sour Garlic-braised Aubergine (p. 185) or Malabar Coconut-and-Yogurt-braised Vegetables (p. 205).

SOFT BEAN DUMPLINGS

MEDU VADAI

◆

Medu vadai, literally translated, means 'soft silky dumplings', which is exactly what they are – a spongy, soft interior encased in a crisp skin. These bean dumplings, laced with chopped ginger, cracked peppercorn, and cumin, are a speciality of Karnataka, where they are served with the world-famous Mysore coffee. They are delicious served as a first course or with drinks. They are also used for making other delicacies listed in the following pages.

FOR 8–12 PERSONS

◆

6 oz/175 g white split gram beans (urad dal)
¼ pint/150 ml water
½ in/1 cm piece fresh ginger
¾ teaspoon cumin seeds
¾ teaspoon cracked whole black peppercorns
⅓ teaspoon ground asafetida (optional)
⅛ teaspoon bicarbonate of soda
1 teaspoon coarse salt, or to taste
Groundnut oil or corn oil (enough to fill a kadhai *or a deep fryer to a depth of 2 in/5 cm)*

1 Pick clean and wash beans.
2 Put the beans in a bowl and add enough water to cover by at least 2 in/5 cm. Soak for 4 hours, drain, and rinse the beans.
3 *To make the bean paste in a food processor*, add the beans to the container. With the metal blade attached, process for 1 minute. Add 4 tablespoons later, ginger, cumin, peppercorns, and asafetida, and continue processing, stopping the machine every 15 seconds to scrape down the sides, until the batter is light and fluffy, about 5 minutes. If necessary add 4 tablespoons more water.

To make the bean paste in a blender, place ¼ pint/150 ml water, ginger, cumin, peppercorns, and asafetida in container and blend for 20–30

seconds. Add drained beans gradually, and blend until you have a smooth paste. During blending, turn the machine on and off a few times and push the paste down the sides and away from the blade with a rubber spatula. (The whole process will take about 4–5 minutes.)

4 Transfer the bean paste to a clean bowl and beat with a whisk or fork until light and fluffy (about 10 minutes). Cover and let the paste rest at room temperature for 4 hours or until fermented and foamy.

5 Cut 6 squares of greaseproof paper 6 × 6 in/15 × 15 cm. Put 2 table-spoons oil in a small bowl, fill another small bowl with cold water, and keep these three items close to where you will fry the dumplings.

6 Stir bicarbonate of soda and salt into the bean paste. Make one dumpling at a time. Place one piece of greaseproof paper on the work board and brush it with some oil. Dip your fingers in cold water and scoop up enough bean paste to form a ball the size of a golf ball. Drop it onto the oiled wax greaseproof paper. Using your fingers, flatten the ball into a 2 in/5 cm round dumpling. With your fingertip, make a hole in the centre of the dumpling. Make 5 more dumplings on the remaining 5 pieces of greaseproof paper. When you have formed all 6 dumplings you are ready to fry the first batch. (You will make 4 batches altogether). A simpler method, followed by many Indian cooks, is to dip one's fingers in cold water, scoop up 2–3 tablespoons of bean paste, shape it into a ball, and fry it.

7 Heat the oil in a *kadhai* or deep fryer until moderately hot (325–350°F/ 165–180°C), lift one piece of greaseproof paper with the dumpling on it and hold it right over the oil. Using a knife or spatula dipped in water, slide the dumpling gently off the paper into the hot oil. Slide the remaining 5 dumplings into the oil in the same way. Fry one side for 3 minutes, then carefully flip them over with a slotted spoon and continue frying until the dumplings are light golden on the second side (another 3 minutes). Drain the dumplings on kitchen paper and continue with the remaining bean paste the same way.

VARIATION: The bean paste dumplings can be coated with chopped onions and green chilies before being fried. You will need about 12 oz/350 g chopped onion and 2 tablespoons chopped green chilies.

Serve immediately or set aside for several hours. To reheat, drop them in hot oil (375°F/190°C) for 30–45 seconds.

These delicately scented dumplings should be followed with a main dish containing plenty of spicy sauce such as Cauliflower,

Aubergine, and Potato in Herb Sauce (p. 180) or Sweet Peppers Stuffed with Cheese and Spring Onions in Sauce Afghan (p. 209).

BRAHMIN BEAN DUMPLINGS IN CHILI-LACED YOGURT SAUCE

DAHI VADAI

Dahi Vadai is a classic dish served at weddings and other religious festivals in the Brahmin households of southern and southwestern India. The dumplings are soaked in yogurt spiced with green and red chilies, coconut, and fresh ginger. It's a lovely yogurt salad that can be served as a side dish or by itself with a stuffed bread for a light meal.

FOR 8 PERSONS

◆

24 Soft Bean Dumplings (p. 152)
YOGHURT SAUCE:
1½ pints/800 ml plain yogurt
¼ pint/150 ml water
2 oz/60 g flaked coconut (fresh or frozen)
1 tablespoon shredded fresh ginger
4–6 hot green chilies, shredded
2 tablespoons light sesame oil or light vegetable oil
1½ teaspoons black mustard seeds
1–2 dry red chili pods, broken into bits, seeds discarded
1 teaspoon coarse salt, or to taste (optional)
Chopped fresh coriander for garnish

1 Put yogurt, water, coconut, ginger, and chilies into a shallow bowl. Mix well. Add the dumplings and with a rubber spatula gently turn them in the yogurt mixture to coat them well. Cover and let soak for 1 hour, or refrigerate for several hours.

2 Measure out the mustard seeds and chili bits and put them next to

the stove in separate piles. Heat the oil in a small frying pan. When it is very hot, add the mustard seeds. Keep a lid handy, as the seeds may spatter. As the spattering subsides, add the chili bits. Shake the pan for a few seconds until the chili bits turn a few shades darker. Lift the pan off the heat and pour the entire contents over the yogurt-dumplng mixture. Add salt to taste and gently turn the dumplings to coat them well with spices. Transfer to an attractive shallow serving dish and garnish with coriander.

This substantial first course needs only a simple pilaf and a few vegetables to complete a meal.

MADRAS SPLIT PEA CROQUETTES IN SPICY TOMATO SAUCE

RASA VADA

This is a simple and quick dish to put together provided you have the ingredients on hand. All you need to do is combine split pea croquettes and tomato-lentil broth. The croquettes soak up the juices and turn moist, plump and delicate. *Rasa vada*, a speciality of Madras, is loved by children and adults alike. It is served as tiffin or as a side dish with the main meal. I prefer to eat it as a first course. The gentle fragrance of the coriander-scented tomato-lentil broth mixed with the earthy flavour of peas produces an excellent sensation to one's palate before dinner.

FOR 8 PERSONS

24 Spicy Split Pea Croquettes (p. 150)
1½ pints/800 ml thick Curry-Laced Tomato-Lentil Broth (p. 172)
4 tablespoons chopped fresh coriander

1 Put the croquettes in a deep bowl. Add the curried broth and let soak for 1 hour and refrigerate, covered, for several hours.

2 To serve, warm the broth with croquettes gently until heated through. Place 3 croquettes in a soup bowl for each person. Pour some of the reserved broth over and garnish with chopped coriander.

These are good hot, warm or cold. For a contrast in flavour I like to serve a simple pilaf such as Coconut Pilaf with Toasted Sesame Seeds (p. 332).

TINY CRISP POORI BREADS

PAPDI

◆

MAKES ABOUT 8 DOZEN TINY CRISP POORIS

3 oz/90 g plain flour, plus additional for dusting
3 oz/90 g chapati *flour or wholemeal flour*
1 tablespoon semolina
¼ pint/150 ml warm water
Groundnut or corn oil enough to fill a kadhai *or a fryer to a depth of 3 in/8cm*

1 Put both flours and semolina in a bowl. Add the water and mix so that it adheres into a mass. Pick up the mass of dough and place it on a work board. Knead for 5 minutes. Brush hands and knuckles often with oil to prevent the dough from sticking to your hand as you knead. Cover the dough with a piece of cling film and let it rest for 10 minutes.

To make dough in a food processor, put both flours and semolina into the container with the steel blade attached. With the machine running pour the water through the feed tube in a steady stream. Process until the flour adheres together into a mass and forms a ball over the blade. Run the machine for 30 seconds, turning off the machine every 5–10 seconds, to knead the dough. Remove the dough to the work board. The dough is ready to be rolled (it needs no resting).

2 Divide the dough into 4 equal portions, shape each into a ball. Place one ball at a time on the work board (keep the remaining balls covered with cling film to prevent a crust from forming). Dust generously with flour and roll into a 9–10 in/23–25 cm circle. Cut out

round *pooris* with a plain 2 in/5 cm round biscuit cutter and prick with a fork to prevent them from puffing during frying. Roll and cut the 3 remaining portions of dough the same way. (These *pooris* may be rolled an hour ahead of time and kept covered with cling film.)

3 When ready to fry the *pooris*, heat the oil in the frying pan until very hot (375–400°F/190–200°C). Slip one round into the hot oil. When it rises to the surface, use the back of a slotted spoon to gently push the *poori* down into the oil for about 10 seconds or until it is puffed and the bottom is slightly browned. Turn it over and cook the other side for about 5 seconds. Baste the *poori* with oil, using a spoon, to make it crisp. With a slotted spoon transfer the *poori* to kitchen paper to drain. When the oil is hot again (375–400°F/190–200°C) repeat with the remaining rolled dough the same way.

Use *pooris* for making *Aloo Papdi Chat* (p. 158) and *Bhel-Poori* (p. 159).

CRISP POORIS AND POTATOES WRAPPED IN YOGURT AND TAMARIND SAUCE

ALOO PAPDI CHAT

The tiny crisp *pooris*, when they don't puff up completely, are not discarded. Instead they are combined with potatoes, herbs, and so on, and garnished with a contrasting sauce: sweetish-sour tamarind against cool yogurt and served as a *chat* called *aloo papdi*, another famous street vendor's snack from the northern province. *Aloo papdi* are excellent served with drinks; they are also a wonderful first course, but once assembled, they must be eaten right away.

FOR 8 PERSONS

¾ pint/450 ml plain yogurt, as tart as possible
1 tablespoon sugar
½ teaspoon coarse salt, or to taste
½ teaspoon roasted cumin, crushed once
48 crisp pooris (p. 156)
1 lb/500 g boiled potatoes, cut into ¼ in/5 mm cubes
¼ pint/150 ml Sweet and Spicy Tamarind Chutney (p. 293)
5–6 tablespoons chopped fresh coriander
Black pepper and hot red pepper powder
4–8 hot green chilies, chopped
5–6 tablespoons chopped spring onions

To serve, mix yogurt, sugar, salt, and cumin in a bowl. Arrange 6 tiny crisp *pooris* on one salad plate and distribute 4 tablespoons of potatoes over them evenly. Dribble 4 tablespoons of the yogurt mixture over the potatoes and *pooris*. Then dribble 1 tablespoon tamarind chutney evenly over the yogurt. Sprinkle each serving with 2 teaspoons coriander, a little black and red pepper, some chopped chilies, and 2 teaspoons of spring onion. Repeat on the seven remaining salad plates. Serve immediately.

BOMBAY SPICY AND CRUNCHY APPETIZER

BHEL-POORI

Mention *bhel-poori* to a native of Bombay, and immediately that person visualizes walking along the famous Marina Drive at Chowpati Beach nibbling this crunchy, sweetish-sour treat. *Bhel-poori* is the Bombay version of the northern Indian *chat*, except it is far more complex in flavour and texture. Indians do not bother making *bhel-poori* at home, partly because it is more fun to buy and eat them at the beach, and partly because it is too time-consuming. The following recipe is fairly simple, because it calls for ready-made *bhel* mix, now available in Indian grocers. This mix contains no preservatives and tastes good. With the addition of an appropriate sauce and a few other ingredients, this recipe reproduces the same delicious *bhel-poori* you might find at Chowpati Beach in Bombay.

FOR 8 PERSONS

48 crisp pooris *(p. 156)*
3 oz/90 g chopped onion
3 oz/90 g chopped, peeled, and seeded cucumbers
3 oz/90 g chopped tomato
3 oz/90 g chopped tart raw green mango or tart apple (optional)
6 oz/175 g bought bhel *mix*
6 oz/175 g Coriander Chutney *(p. 291)*
6 oz/175 g Sweet and Spicy Tamarind Chutney *(p. 293)*
1½ oz/45 g chopped fresh coriander
8–12 hot green chilies, chopped
½ teaspoon hot red pepper powder, ground
½ teaspoon black pepper
FOR GARNISH:
8 lettuce leaves
8 hot green chilies
8 lemon wedges

1 Coarsely crush the crisp *pooris* in a bowl. Set aside.
2 Mix onion, cucumber and tomato in another bowl. If you are using raw mango or apple, add that also. Set aside.
3 Put the *bhel* mix into a bowl. Set aside.
4 Put the chutneys in two separate bowls. Mix coriander and chopped chilies in another small bowl. Set aside.

All this can be done several hours ahead and kept (vegetables, chutneys, and herbs in the refrigerator) until you are ready to serve the *bhel-poori*.

At the time of serving, put all the ingredients in the order given in a large salad bowl or mixing bowl. Toss well. Serve spooned on salad plates lined with lettuce leaves. Garnish with chilies and lemon wedges.

Bhel-poori is a highly nutritive snack or first course. A simple dish such as Courgette Koftas in Creamed Tomato Sauce (p. 188) would be an appropriate main course.

FRITTERS

PAKODA

Indian fritters are distinctly different from all other kinds. They are spicy, crunchy, and aromatic because they are classically prepared with a chick-pea batter that is laced with fragrant herbs and spices. Every region has its own special formula for spicing the batter. For example, cumin and coriander are added in the north, while in the south asafetida is preferred. In the east, the Bengalis are fond of black onion seeds, while the Gujaratis put in carom, and so on. In addition to this, distinctly different cooking oils in which the fritters are fried provide yet another taste dimension. The same spinach fritters fried in sesame oil would taste quite different from ones fried in mustard oil. There is no choosing the best among them, as they are all absolutely delicious. Much depends upon the availability of fresh ingredients and one's mood and the composition of the meal itself.

Fritters are the most versatile appetizers in Indian cooking. You can follow them with any main dish as long as it is not another fried

preparation, such as *kafta*. They are also good at teatime and as snacks or for picnics, and now they are becoming a favourite with cocktails. Indians like them dipped in a spicy sauce such as Sweet and Spicy Tamarind Chutney, page 293, or Coriander Chutney, page 291.

SPICY VEGETABLE FRITTERS
WITH SPRING ONION

SABZI PAKODA

These simple fritters of aubergine, potatoes, and Indian cheese are the most popular fritter in northern India. This particular recipe is from Bangladesh (once part of India), where sweet aromatic onion seeds are used to flavour fritter batters. For variations you can make fritters with cauliflower, onions, or yam.

Since soybeans are becoming more and more popular in Indian vegetarian cooking, I have included beancurd as one of the main ingredients in a *pakoda*. Beancurd is healthy, and it is also delicious. You may, of course, substitute *paneer*.

FOR 6–8 PERSONS

6 oz/175 g chick-pea flour (besan)
2 tablespoons groundnut oil or corn oil
½ teaspoon turmeric
¾ teaspoon baking powder
2 tablespoons chopped fresh coriander
4 hot green chilies, finely chopped
½ pint/300 ml warm water (110°F/43°C)
½ teaspoon coarse salt, or as needed
1 teaspoon ground cumin
1 teaspoon garam masala (p. 77)
½ teaspoon hot red pepper powder
3 spring onion stalks with green parts, thinly shredded into 1 in/2.5 cm long pieces
½ teaspoon black onion seeds (kalaunji)

VEGETABLES:
1 small aubergine, unpeeled
1 medium baking potato, unpeeled
1 beancurd cake (or 4 oz/125 g sliced *Indian cheese cubes* (paneer) *or* *1 medium courgette, sliced ⅛ in/3 mm thick)*
Groundnut oil or corn oil (enough to fill *a* kadhai *or any fryer to a depth of 2½ in/6 cm)*

1 Put all the batter ingredients in a bowl and mix thoroughly until it is lump-free. The batter can be mixed in a blender or food processor, in which case mix all the ingredients except the spring onions and black onion seeds; fold them into the mixed batter separately. Let batter sit, covered, at room temperature for at least 30 minutes. The batter will keep in the refrigerator for 2 days.

2 Cut the aubergine into quarters. Cut each quarter into thin slices. Put the cut slices in a bowl of water to cover and set aside. Scrub the potato clean, leave the skin on, and cut it into ⅛ in/3 mm thick slices lengthwise. Add them to the bowl with the aubergine. Cut the beancurd cake in half. Cut each half into ½ in/1 cm slices. Put them or Indian cheese cubes (*paneer*) or courgette in another bowl.

3 Heat the oil in a *kadhai* or fryer until it is very hot (375°F/190°C). Drain the aubergine and potatoes and pat them dry on kitchen paper. Dip the vegetables and beancurd cake slices in the batter, one at a time, and gently dip them into the hot oil. Fry them, turning with a slotted spoon, until golden brown (3–4 minutes on each side). With a slotted spoon, transfer the fritters to a baking tray lined with kitchen paper to drain. Continue with all the vegetables the same way.

The fritters may be made several hours ahead. Just before serving, reheat them by frying them in hot oil (375°F/190°C) for a minute. If you want to make your fritters ahead of time, leave them slightly under-browned, that is, cook them for only 7–8 minutes, and then fry them for a minute or so just before you serve them. Serve immediately with Sweet and Spicy Tamarind Chutney (p. 293) or Herb-and-Spice-Laced Creamy Yogurt Salad (p. 275).

SAVOURIES

◆

BASIC TECHNIQUE OF MAKING
DRIED LACE POTATO CRISPS

SOOKHA JALIDAR ALOO

◆

If you happen to drop in at the home of a Punjabi from the north-western part of India, you are most likely to be welcomed with their usually gracious hospitality and served sweet milky tea with a few savouries, one of which will almost always be these spicy lace potatoes. The Punjabis' technique of preparing them is unique. First, the warm-water soaking releases a lot of starch from the potato slices, making them very crisp. Second, the potatoes are partially cooked before being dried. Finally, the Punjabis like their crisps spicy hot, so they coat them with red pepper powder.

MAKES 1½ PINTS/1 LITRE

BASIC TECHNIQUE:
4 large baking potatoes (about 2 lb/1 kg)
½ teaspoon hot red pepper powder (optional)

1 Peel the potatoes and make waffled potatoes using a mandoline or a similar vegetable cutting device. If you do not have such a device, simply slice the potatoes thinly, using a very sharp knife. (Make sure the slices are not too thin, as they will be boiled and handled prior to being fried. The approximate thickness of the slices should be ¹⁄₁₆ in/ 1.5 mm.)
2 Wash the slices thoroughly in several changes of warm water until the water runs clear and is no longer milky. Soak the slices in warm water for 2 hours. Drain, rinse, and drain again.
3 Bring a large quantity (6½ pints/4 litres) of water to a vigorous boil in a deep pot. Drop in the drained potato slices. Stir for 1 minute. Turn

off the heat, cover, and let the potato slices soak for 15 minutes. Drain the slices and spread them on kitchen paper. When they are thoroughly drained, put them in a bowl. Add hot red pepper powder if you are using it, and mix thoroughly to coat the slices.

4 Arrange the slices in a single layer on a baking tray and dry them for one full day, either in the sun or by using an electric food dryer (following manufacturer's directions), or in a very low oven.

Store the dried potatoes in airtight containers in a cool, dry place.

LACE POTATO CRISPS

JALIDAR ALOO

FOR 8 PERSONS

Dried lace potato crisps (p. 163)
Groundnut oil or corn oil (enough to fill a kadhai or a deep fryer to a depth of 3 in/8 cm)
Salt to taste, if desired

Heat the oil in a *kadhai* or deep fryer until very hot (375°F/190°C). Drop several potato slices into the hot oil (be careful not to add too many too fast, as the oil will foam and overflow). Fry until the froth subsides and the crisps are lightly coloured on the edge (about 3–4 minutes). Remove and drain on kitchen paper. While still warm, sprinkle with salt. Continue with the remaining slices the same way.

SPICY POTATO STICKS

ALOO KE LACHCHEE

Just as Westerners eat popcorn and sweets in cinemas, in India it is hot and spicy potato sticks. These potato sticks are irresistible, especially with cocktails.

Spicy potato sticks are available in Indian grocers, but they are also quite simple to make.

FOR 8 PERSONS

◆

4 large baking potatoes (about 2 lb/1 kg)
Groundnut oil or corn oil (enough to fill a large frying pan to a depth of 3/4 in/2 cm)
SPICES TO BE MIXED TOGETHER:
1/2 teaspoon ground cumin or garam masala (p. 77)
1/2 teaspoon salt, or to taste
1/2 teaspoon ground lemon crystals (p. 66), or 1 tablespoon mango powder
1 teaspoon caster sugar
1/4 teaspoon black pepper
1/4 teaspoon hot red pepper powder

1 Peel the potatoes and shred them, using a mandoline or any vegetable-cutting device, or cut them into thin (about 1/16–1/8 in/ 1.5–3 mm) slices. Stack several slices and cut into thin (about 1/16–1/8 in/1.5–3 mm thick) matchsticks.

2 Wash the potato sticks in several changes of warm water until the water no longer looks cloudy. Put the sticks in a bowl, add warm water to cover, and let them soak for at least 1/2 hour but preferably 2 hours. Drain and pat dry thoroughly on layers of kitchen paper.

3 Heat the oil in a frying pan until very hot (375°F/190°C). Add enough potato sticks to cover the oil without overcrowding. The oil temperature will automatically drop. Regulate the heat to between medium and medium-high. This slow frying will cook the potatoes to crackling crispness. When the potatoes are fried and brown, remove with a slotted spoon and drain briefly in a large colander. Transfer to a bowl. While the potatoes are still warm, sprinkle a little of the spice mixture on and toss to mix. Continue frying the remaining potato shreds the same way. Make sure to use all the spice mixture on the fried potatoes. They keep well for several days if stored in an airtight container in a cool, dry place.

SAVOURY CUMIN COUNTRY BISCUITS

NAMKEEN PARA

◆

These are similar to the Fragrant Wholemeal Biscuits (p. 167) except these are laced with cumin and cut into long diamond shapes. They are also less flaky and more cracklingly crunchy. A speciality of the Northern Province, *namkeen para* are regularly made in Indian homes as after-school snacks for children.

Namkeen para are traditionally prepared during Hindu festivals such as the Festival of the Lights (*Diwali*). They are also very good with drinks or a cup of tea.

FOR 8 PERSONS

◆

8 oz/250 g plain flour
1½ teaspoons cumin seeds
½ teaspoon cayenne pepper
1 teaspoon coarse salt, or to taste, if desired
4 oz/125 g melted clarified butter (usli ghee, p. 57) or vegetable shortening
6 tablespoons cold water, or more as needed
Additional plain flour for dusting
Groundnut oil or corn oil (enough to fill a kadhai or deep fryer to a depth of 3 in/8 cm)

1 Put the flour, cumin, cayenne, and salt in a large bowl. Add butter or shortening and mix with your fingers to blend thoroughly. Add 6 tablespoons water, mix, and form into a dough. It will be fairly soft dough. Divide the dough into two portions and roll roughly into a ball. Keep one ball covered with cling film to prevent a crust from forming, and place the other on the work board.

2 Dust the dough with flour and roll into a 9 in/23 cm circle or square, using a rolling pin. Using a sharp knife, cut into ½ in/1 cm wide strips. Cut each strip diagonally into 1 in/2.5 cm long pieces to make them diamond-shaped. Roll and cut the other ball of dough the same way.

3 Heat the oil in the deep fryer until very hot (375°F/190°C). Drop the pieces of dough in and deep-fry, stirring often, until pale golden

(5 minutes at the most). They should not overbrown and turn dark. Remove the fried *paras* with a slotted spoon and place on a baking tray lined with kitchen paper to drain. Continue with the remaining pieces of dough the same way. For best results, the fryer should not be crowded. Therefore, fry the *paras* in four batches.

Cool thoroughly and store in airtight containers. Stored in a cool, dry place, *paras* will keep for a couple of months.

FRAGRANT WHOLEMEAL BISCUITS

MATHIA

The classic snack of northern Indians, *mathia* can best be described as shortbread crackers. Generally enjoyed with a piece of tart pickle and a hot cup of tea, *mathia* is a traditional biscuit offered as part of the dowry gift by the bride's side to the bridegroom's family during the marriage ceremony.

The classic *mathia* is too rich and difficult to digest; therefore, I have developed a recipe using less fat. The flavour is as classical as ever and will most definitely be acceptable to the bridegroom's mother!

These crackers are great with drinks, ideal given as gifts, and also quite enjoyable with a bowl of soup.

FOR 8 PERSONS

6 oz/175 g chapati *flour (or a combination of whole and plain flours), plus additional flour for dusting*
5–6 tablespoons vegetable shortening
5–6 tablespoons milk
1 teaspoon salt
¾ teaspoon carom seeds or dried thyme
1½ teaspoons cracked whole black peppercorns
Groundnut oil or corn oil (enough to fill a kadhai *or deep fryer to a depth of 2 in/5 cm)*

1 Place the flour in a large bowl. Rub the shortening into it until the mixture resembles coarse cornmeal. Add milk, salt, carom, and black pepper and mix until you have a moist dough. Place the dough on a work surface and divide into three equal portions. Keep the dough covered with cling film so that a crust does not form.

2 Working with one piece of dough at a time, dust with flour and roll into an 8 in/20 cm round. Cut the round with a sharp knife into ¼ in/5mm wide strips. Cut each strip across into 3 in/8cm pieces. Roll and cut the remaining two pieces of dough in the same manner.

3 When you are ready to fry the biscuits, heat the oil in a *kadhai* or deep fryer until it is very hot (375°F/190°C). Drop several strips of dough into the hot oil. Be careful not to overcrowd the pan, as the oil will foam and overflow. Fry the dough, turning often, until the pieces look cooked and are barely coloured (about 3 minutes). Remove the biscuits with a slotted spoon and drain on kitchen paper. Continue with the rest of the biscuits the same way.

When cool, store in airtight containers in a cool, dry place.

FRIED MUNG BEANS

BHONA MOONG

◆

Gujarati Jains are known for their vegetarian cuisine – not just for its flavour or visual appeal but for its great nutritive value as well. Even their snacks are carefully thought out. Simple everyday mung beans are soaked, drained, and fried into a crisp, crunchy snack that is utterly delicious as well as protein-rich. These fried beans are marvellous with drinks, too.

MAKES ABOUT 8 OZ/250 G

◆

6 oz/175 g whole green mung beans (sabat moong*)*

Groundnut oil or corn oil (enough to fill a kadhai *or a deep fryer to a depth of 2½ in/6 cm)*

SPICES TO BE MIXED TOGETHER:
½ teaspoon ground lemon crystals (p. 66), or 1 teaspoon mango powder
½–1 teaspoon caster sugar
¼ teaspoon black pepper
Coarse salt to taste, if desired

1 Wash the beans in cold running water and put into a bowl. Add enough boiling water to cover the beans by 2 in/5 cm. Soak for 12–18 hours. Drain, wash the beans in cold water, and drain again.

2 Line a baking tray (such as sponge-roll tin) with layers of kitchen paper. Spread the beans on in a single layer and let dry for ½ hour.

3 While the beans are drying, start heating the oil. When the oil is very hot (375°F/190°C), add half the beans. Fry, stirring, until the froth of the oil subsides and the beans are clearly visible and sizzling (about 4–5 minutes). Remove immediately with a fine perforated spoon, drain on kitchen paper for 1 minute, and immediately transfer to a bowl. While the beans are still warm, sprinkle on half the spice mixture and toss well. Fry the remaining beans the same way, add to the bowl, and sprinkle on the remaining spice mixture. Mix and toss the beans. Cool completely. Store in airtight containers in a cool, dry place.

NOTE: The fryer should be deep enough to allow room above the level of the oil. When the beans are added, the oil foams dramatically, causing it to overflow. In addition, do not overfry beans as they become very hard to chew.

FRIED LENTIL WAFERS

PAPAD-TALA

Lentil wafers are the most popular food served with drinks all over India. The practice of making them at home has died out completely because the bought varieties are of excellent quality. Perhaps this is due to the fact that wafer-making is still a cottage industry in India, where millions of skilful women roll these paper-thin, perfectly round circles of lentil dough day after day. *Papad* can be found in all Indian shops, in many flavours: black pepper, hot red pepper, green chili, garlic, and so on. Choose according to your taste and the total flavour of the meal. Two recipes follow, one for fried *papad*, the other roasted.

FOR 4 PERSONS

◆

4–8 bought wafers
Groundnut oil or corn oil (enough to fill a kadhai *or a deep fryer to a depth of 1½ in/4 cm)*

Heat the oil in the *kadhai* or fryer. When it is hot (375°F/190°C), drop one wafer into the hot oil. Push the wafer down and swirl it around, using tongs, pressing it gently to keep it submerged at all times during cooking. The wafer will turn light and fluffy and expand enormously in size (about 10 seconds). Remove and drain on kitchen paper and continue with the remaining ones the same way. When slightly cool, the *papad* will turn crisp.

VARIATION: for Roasted Lentil Wafers (*Papad-Bhona*). These roasted lentil wafers are my father's favourite, since he never took much liking to fried foods. In this method the *papad* is held directly over the flame and roasted until fully cooked. Without oil, the *papad* tastes lighter, smoky, and spicier.

Serve these wafers just as you would serve fried wafers. Hold one wafer at a time with a pair of unserrated tongs and place directly over a burner with a high flame on. Roast, lifting and turning until fully cooked (1–1½ minutes). Be careful not to burn the wafer. The roasted wafer will have a few dark spots. Roast all the wafers the same way.

SOUPS

There are several dishes in Indian cooking that according to Western description will be categorized as soups. Since Indians do not have a tradition of serving a separate soup course, these soupy dishes are simply enjoyed along with the rest of the meal.

Many urban households in India in recent years have started serving these dishes and Indian adaptations of many classic French soups as a first course. I like spicy rich soups on cold wintery days and cool broths during the warm summer months.

For a light supper, serve these soups with a stuffed bread and a salad.

CURRY-LACED TOMATO-LENTIL BROTH

TOMATO RASAM

◆

This is the most famous soup of Madras, in southern India. A luscious tomato and lentil broth, it is gently perfumed with mustard seeds and curry. Because this soup is spicy and fragrant, it makes an excellent first course for a formal meal.

FOR 6–8 PERSONS

◆

1 lb/500 g ripe tomatoes, fresh or canned
6 oz/175 g cooked lentils (p. 254)
½ pint/300 ml water
1½ teaspoons ground cumin
2 teaspoons ground coriander
¼–½ teaspoon cayenne
1 table spoon minced onion
1 teaspoon minced garlic
2 teaspoons coarse salt, or to taste
1 tablespoon lemon juice
FOR SPICED BUTTER:
1 tablespoon usli ghee (p. 57)
1 teaspoon black mustard seeds
8 curry (kari) leaves (fresh or dry), or 2 tablespoons chopped fresh coriander

1 Blanch, peel, and cut the tomatoes in half. Scoop out the pulp and pips. Set aside the tomato shells, and mince the pulp and pips in a blender, a food processor, or with a sharp knife.

2 Put the lentils in a deep pot. Add ½ pint/300 ml water and whisk for a minute to crush some of the lentils. Add the puréed tomatoes, cumin, coriander, cayenne, onion, garlic, and salt, and bring to the boil. Lower the heat and cook at a gentle boil, partially covered, for 10 minutes. Add the lemon juice and tomato halves and continue cooking, uncovered, for 1 minute, until the tomatoes are heated and barely cooked. Turn off the heat. Keep the soup covered while you make the spiced butter.

3 Measure out the spices and put them next to the stove in separate piles. Heat the *ghee* in a small frying pan until very hot. Add the mustard seeds carefully. Keep a lid handy, as the seeds may fly all over. When the seeds stop spattering, add the curry leaves and turn off the heat. Pick up the pan and shake it for a few seconds. Pour the entire contents over the soup and mix well. If you are using coriander instead of curry leaves, add it now. This should be a rather thin soup. If it is too thick, add water. Serve piping hot in individual soup bowls.

This tasty soup goes well with just about any main dish. To maintain a southern flavour throughout the meal, you can serve Tanjore Broccoli and Mung Bean Stew with Coconut (p. 190) or, for contrast, Vegetables Braised in Yogurt and Spices, Patna-Style (p. 207), or Jain Coriander-Scented Millet and Mung Bean Pilaf (p. 226).

LEMON FLAVOURED MUNG BEAN BROTH

ELIMBICHIPAYAM RASAM

◆

In Tanjore, southern India, this soup is made with the essence of mung beans. The broth is then combined with spices, lemon juice, and freshly chopped coriander to produce a true delicacy. It is refreshingly light and has a faint lemony taste.

FOR 4 PERSONS

◆

3 oz/90 g cooked yellow split mung beans (p. 38)
2 hot green chilies, chopped
½ teaspoon ground cumin
¾ teaspoon black pepper
12 curry (kari) leaves (fresh or dry, optional)
1 pint/600 ml water
1 cucumber, peeled, cored, and sliced thin
Juice of ½ lemon
1 teaspoon coarse salt, or to taste
2 tablespoons usli ghee *(p. 57)*
½ teaspoon black mustard seeds
¼ teaspoon ground asafetida
2 tablespoons coarsely chopped fresh coriander leaves

1 Put the cooked beans, chilies, cumin, pepper, curry leaves, and water in a large pan and bring to the boil. Lower the heat and let it boil gently, covered, for 5 minutes. Add the cucumber and continue boiling for an additional 5 minutes. Turn off the heat. Stir in the lemon juice and salt. Keep the soup hot, covered, while you make the spicy butter.

2 Measure out the spices and put them next to the stove in separate piles. Heat the *ghee* in a small frying pan until it is very hot. Carefully add the mustard seeds. Keep a lid handy, as the seeds may splatter and fly all over. When the seeds stop splattering, add the asafetida and shake the pan for a few seconds. Pour the contents of the pan over the soup. Serve the soup piping hot, garnished with fresh coriander.

Follow the menu suggestions given for Curry-Laced Tomato-Lentil Broth (p. 172).

UDIPI CHILLED YOGURT SOUP

MOORU KOYAMBOO

◆

In Udipi, in southern India, from where most of the southern restaurant chefs come, a cool, refreshing yogurt soup is prepared, the likes of which I have neither seen nor tasted elsewhere. I suspect the magic lies in the local milk from which the buttermilk is made. No wonder Lord Krishna, the cowherd who always craved buttermilk and cream, is associated with Udipi. I love this soup and serve it on warm summer days.

FOR 6 PERSONS

◆

1¼ pints/700 ml plain yogurt
¾ pint/450 ml buttermilk
1½ teaspoons coarse salt, or to taste
2 teaspoons shredded or grated fresh ginger
2–4 hot green chilis, minced
3 oz/90 g julienned sweet green pepper
3 oz/90 g julienned sweet red pepper
3 oz/90 g julienned tomatoes
4 tablespoons light sesame oil or light vegetable oil
2 teaspoons black mustard seeds
12 curry (kari) leaves (fresh or dry)
¼ teaspoon ground asafetida

1 Put the yogurt and buttermilk in a bowl and beat with a whisk or a wooden spoon until the mixture is well blended. Stir in the salt, ginger, and chilies. Cover and chill thoroughly.

2 Mix the peppers and tomatoes in another bowl. Sprinkle on a little salt, toss gently, cover, and chill.

3 When you are ready to serve, pour the yogurt mixture into a soup tureen. Place the vegetables carefully on it. If you are pouring the soup into individual soup bowls, distribute the yogurt mixture evenly and then place the julienned vegetables on each. (Do not worry if some of the vegetables sink into the yogurt.)

4 Measure out the spices and place them next to the stove in separate piles. Heat the oil in a small frying pan over high heat. When it is very hot, add the mustard seeds. Keep a lid handy, as the seeds may splatter and fly all over. When the seeds stop splattering, turn off the heat and add the curry leaves and asafetida, and shake the pan for a few seconds – just long enough to brown the leaves and bring out the aroma of the asafetida. Pour the entire contents of the pan over the soup.

5 To serve, mix the spices and vegetables gently into the yogurt.

This simple, delicate soup may be followed by any main dish. For a southern flavour, serve Madras Fiery Aubergine, Lentil, and Chili Stew (p. 194).

COLD MALABAR AVOCADO COCONUT SOUP

AVCADOO KOYAMBOO

The Malabar Muslims in Kerala do wonderful things with avocado. Here is one of the delicious soups they have created just to bring out the flavour of avocado and bind it in harmony with the sweetness of coconut and spices. This soup is an excellent first course in a formal meal.

FOR 6 PERSONS

1 large ripe avocado
4 oz/125 g flaked coconut (fresh or unsweetened, tinned)
½ pint/300 ml plain yogurt, as tart as possible
2 hot green chilies

| ½ teaspoon ground cumin |
| 2 tablespoons lemon juice |
| 1 teaspoon coarse salt, or to taste |
| 1 large clove garlic |
| 1¼ pints/700 ml water |
| 2 tablespoons finely chopped fresh coriander |

1 Peel the avocado and remove the stone. Cut off 6 thin slices, wrap in cling film, and save for the garnish. Put the remaining avocado along with the coconut, yogurt, garlic, chilies, cumin, lemon juice, salt, and ½ pint/300 ml water into the container of a food processor or blender and process until it is throughly liquefied. Add another ¼ pint/150 ml water and blend.

2 Transfer the soup to a bowl and stir in the remaining ½ pint/ 300 ml of water. Mix well and chill the soup thoroughly.

Serve in cream soup bowls garnished with slices of avocado and some freshly chopped coriander.

This beautiful, pale jade-coloured soup with a hint of coconut should ideally be followed by an equally subtle main dish. A good choice would be Cauliflower, Aubergine, and Potato in Herb Sauce (p. 180).

CREAM OF CURRIED VEGETABLE AND SPLIT PEA SOUP

SABZI SHORVA

◆

This is one of the most popular vegetarian soups in Indian restaurants. The flavour in the broth comes from the gently fried spices and the intermingling of the vegetables and peas. The soup keeps well in the refrigerator and improves in flavour with time.

FOR 6 PERSONS

◆

4–5 *tablespoons* usli ghee *(p. 57)*
1 *tablespoon Curry Powder Master Recipe (p. 73) or bought*
3 *oz/90 g finely chopped onion*
3 *oz/90 g finely chopped carrots*
3 *oz/90 g finely chopped celery*
½ *pint/300 ml water*
6 *oz/175 g finely puréed fresh tomatoes (or 4 fl oz/125 ml tinned tomato purée)*
6 *oz/175 g cooked split peas (p. 254)*
¼ *teaspoon black pepper*
2 *teaspoons coarse salt, or to taste*
¼ *pint/150 ml single cream or milk*
Chopped coriander for garnish

1 Heat the *ghee* in a deep pot over medium-high heat. When it is very hot, add the curry powder and immediately add the onion, carrots and celery. Sauté the vegetables, stirring often to ensure that they brown evenly, for 5 minutes. Add ½ pint/300 ml water, the tomatoes, peas, pepper, and salt. Cover and cook over low heat until the vegetables are tender (10 minutes). Add enough cream or milk to mellow the soup as well as thin it.

2 Heat the soup thoroughly and serve garnished with chopped fresh coriander.

I often serve this soup for a light but complete meal in itself, accompanied only by a piece of bread and a salad. For an elaborate affair try following it with Bean Curd Dumplings with Tomatoes in a Fenugreek-Laced Yogurt Sauce (p. 213).

ONE-DISH MAIN COURSES/ ONE-DISH MEALS

There are many dishes in Indian cooking that are meals in themselves or at least are so hearty that all one needs is a loaf of bread and some salad to complete the meal. These dishes often contain several ingredients and take some extra care to prepare. For that reason Indians often reserve them for special occasions, such as for entertaining, for wedding feasts, and other celebrations.

There are also certain preparations that are associated with specific occasions. For example, at Sunday lunch in northern India one almost always expects *kadhi*, the dumplings in yogurt sauce, or *channa*, chickpeas in spicy sauce. Stuffed breads with pickles and rice casseroles are specialities of the northwestern and northeastern regions of India. Certain foods are prepared on specific religious festivals, such as Rice and Mung Bean Casserole (p. 219) during the Festival of *Kanu*. These dishes are usually very well balanced nutritionally.

For your convenience I have organised the recipes according to their major ingredients, such as vegetables combined with dairy products, vegetables combined with pulses, and so on. For entertaining these dishes make excellent main courses. You may serve them alone or with side dishes, depending upon how elaborate a menu you are planning.

VEGETABLES

◆

CAULIFLOWER, AUBERGINE, AND POTATO IN HERB SAUCE

SABZI KORMA

◆

Korma is the classic Moghul technique of braising vegetables in a thick, nut-rich sauce. In this process the vegetables retain their flavour and shape during cooking. Thus *korma* dishes are considered one of the most elegant preparations in vegetarian cooking and often occupy the centre place at the banquet table. Here the vegetables (the cauliflower, aubergine, and potato) are cooked in a fennel-and-coriander-scented and almond-tomato sauce. The toasted sesame garnish adds an interesting texture as well as a nutty flavour to the dish.

FOR 4–6 PERSONS

◆

6 tablespoons light vegetable oil
8 oz/250 g onions, finely chopped
2 teaspoons garlic, finely chopped
2 tablespoons grated or crushed fresh ginger
4 tablespoons minced fresh coriander
1 oz/30 g ground blanched almonds
1 tablespoon ground coriander
½ teaspoon ground fennel
½ teaspoon cayenne pepper
¼ teaspoon turmeric
4 oz/125 g tinned tomato purée (or 2 medium-size tomatoes puréed with skin and 2 teaspoons tomato concentrate)
1 teaspoon paprika
½ pint/300 ml water
1 medium cauliflower, core and stalk removed, and cut into 1½ in/4 cm florets
1 small aubergine, unpeeled, cut into 1½ in/4 cm cubes
2 medium potatoes, peeled and cut into 1½ in/4 cm cubes
1½ teaspoons ground roasted cumin seeds or garam masala (p. 77)
2 teaspoons coarse salt, or to taste
1 tablespoon toasted sesame seeds

1 Measure out the spices and place them next to the stove in separate piles. Heat the oil in a large heavy frying pan over medium-high heat. Add the minced onion and fry, stirring, until browned (about 10 minutes). Stir in the garlic and ginger and continue cooking for another 2 minutes. Add the minced coriander and almonds, and cook for 2 more minutes.

2 Stir in the ground coriander, fennel, cayenne, and turmeric, and let the spices sizzle for a few seconds. Add the puréed tomatoes and paprika, reduce the heat to low, and cook for 2 minutes. Stir constantly to prevent sticking and burning.

3 Add ½ pint/300 ml water, cauliflower, aubergine, and potatoes; raise the heat to high and bring to the boil. Lower the heat and simmer, covered, for 30 minutes or until the cauliflower is cooked but still crisp. Turn off the heat and stir in the cumin or *garam masala* and salt. Let stand, covered, for 30 minutes, allowing the flavours to blend, before you serve.

Serve sprinkled with sesame seeds.

For a complete meal serve any bread that is light and flavourful, such as Dill and Garlic Barley Bread with Shredded Green Chilies (p. 318). For a more elaborate meal include a few side dishes such as Spicy Mushrooms with Ginger and Chilies (p. 244) and Bengal Red Lentils with Spices (p. 258).

STUFFED CAULIFLOWER WITH TART TOMATO-CORIANDER SAUCE

GOBHI MASALLAM

◆

Gobhi masallam is the vegetarian counterpart of the famous Moghul dish from the city of Lucknow called *murgh massallam*, in which the whole chicken, wrapped in spices, is pot roasted. In the vegetarian version a whole head of cauliflower is used instead. This dish has also become a classic in India. The whole cauliflower, served beneath a crust of onion, almonds, and chilies, looks stunning, particularly when it is sliced into wedges and served with this brilliant red tomato sauce.

FOR 4–6 PERSONS

◆

1½–1¾ lb/750–875 g *cauliflower, core, stalk, and leaves removed*

FOR THE STUFFING MIXTURE:

6 tablespoons light vegetable oil
8 oz/250 g finely chopped onion
1 tablespoon finely chopped garlic
1½ tablespoons finely chopped fresh ginger
6 hot green chilies, minced
¼ teaspoon cayenne pepper
¼ teaspoon black pepper
1½ tablespoons ground coriander
½ teaspoon ground fennel
2 tablespoons ground blanched almonds
1 teaspoon coarse salt, or to taste
1 tablespoon plain flour
2 tablespoons sliced blanched almonds
4–6 coriander sprigs, for garnish
¾ pint/450 ml Tomato-Coriander Sauce (see following recipe)

1 Preheat oven to 400°F/200°C/Gas 6.

2 Steam the whole cauliflower for 8 minutes. Remove the cauliflower and let it cool completely. Set aside.

3 Measure out the spices and place them next to the stove in separate piles. Heat 4 tablespoons of the oil in a frying pan over medium-high heat for 2 minutes. Add the onion and fry, stirring constantly, for 10 minutes or until lightly browned. Add the garlic and ginger and fry for 2 more minutes. Add the chilies and continue frying for an additional minute.

4 Add all the other ingredients from cayenne to flour; mix well and continue frying for 2 minutes. Add about 4 tablespoons water, stir well, and continue cooking until the mixture turns into thick paste. Turn off the heat and let the stuffing mixture cool.

5 Stuff half the spice mixture into the spaces between the florets of the cauliflower. This takes a little effort, but try to put in as much as possible. Spread the remaining half over the top of the cauliflower and pat it down (the spreading will be patchy). Place the stuffed cauliflower in a shallow baking dish or tray. Sprinkle almonds over it and dribble the remaining 2 tablespoons of oil all over it.

6 Bake the cauliflower in the middle level of the oven for 25–30 minutes, or until the spice coating looks nicely browned, glazed, and crisp.

To serve, place the cauliflower on a heated serving platter and arrange the coriander sprigs around it. Scrape off any brown bits and spices clinging to the baking dish and stir into the tomato sauce. Transfer the sauce to a small bowl or sauce boat. Serve the cauliflower cut into 4–8 wedges. Pour a little sauce over each and garnish with a coriander sprig.

TOMATO-CORIANDER SAUCE

◆

MAKES ¾ PINT/450 ML

◆

3 tablespoons light vegetable oil
3 oz/90 g chopped onion
2 teaspoons ground cumin
1 lb/500 g fresh ripe or tinned, drained tomatoes, puréed
½ pint/300 ml water
Coarse salt, to taste
2 tablespoons chopped fresh coriander

Heat the oil in a small pan over medium-high heat. When it is very hot, add the onion and fry, stirring constantly, for 6–8 minutes or until light brown. Add the cumin and continue frying for 1 more minute. Add the tomato purée, ½ pint/300 ml water, and salt; mix well and bring to the boil. Simmer gently over low heat, uncovered, for 15 minutes, stirring often. Turn off the heat and stir in chopped coriander.

This makes a lovely late-supper dish accompanied by Basic Baked Wholemeal Bread (p. 306) and a North Indian Vegetable Salad (p. 268) and a yogurt salad (pp. 275–279). For an elaborate meal serve a few side dishes such as Bengal Green Beans and Potatoes Smothered in Mustard Oil (p. 232) and Sweet and Sour Bombay Lentils (p. 264).

HOT AND SOUR GARLIC-BRAISED AUBERGINE

KHATTI BHAJI

◆

Every region in India has one great aubergine preparation it can boast about. In Punjab it is *khatti bhaji*, meaning sour aubergines, because in this dish the aubergines are braised in a large amount of tomatoes. Usually sliced onion, potatoes, and green chilies are added to enhance the flavour as well as increase the quantity of the dish. The characteristic flavour of *khatti bhaji* comes from the sliced garlic and mustard oil used in cooking the vegetables.

FOR 6 PERSONS

◆

1 large aubergine, unpeeled
8 oz/250 g baking potatoes
½ pint/300 ml mustard oil (or light vegetable oil or a combination)
5 tablespoons sliced garlic
12 oz/375 g thinly sliced onions
4–8 hot green chilies, thickly shredded
½ teaspoon turmeric
½–1 teaspoon cayenne pepper
1 lb/500 g thinly sliced tomatoes
1½ teaspoons coarse salt, or to taste

1 Cut the aubergine with its skin in half lengthwise. Cut each half across into halves. Cut each quarter into long slices about ⅜ in/1 cm thick. Scrub the potatoes clean under cold running water and pat them dry. Cut the potatoes into half lengthwise. Cut each half into long thin slices about ⅜ in/1 cm thick. Put the aubergine and potato slices in a large bowl of water and set aside.

2 Measure out the spices and place them next to the stove in separate piles. Heat the mustard oil in a very large *kadhai* or a large heavy frying pan until very hot and smoking. Turn off the heat and let the oil

cool for a few minutes (if you are using vegetable oil or a combination of mustard and vegetable oils, skip this step). Heat the oil again over high heat. When it is very hot, add the garlic and cook, stirring and turning, for 2 minutes or until it begins to colour.

3 Add the onion and continue cooking for 5 minutes. Add the chilies and cook for 2 minutes more. Add the turmeric and cayenne and let it sizzle for 30 seconds.

4 Add the aubergine, mix the ingredients, and cook, turning the vegetables to distribute the spices and adjusting the heat as necessary, for 8 minutes or until the aubergine softens slightly and begins to fry. Add the potatoes and continue cooking, turning them, for 3 minutes. Add the tomatoes along with the salt and reduce the heat to medium-high. Cook the vegetables, turning them constantly, for 10 minutes. Finally reduce the heat to medium-low and let the vegetables fry, undisturbed, until they are soft.

This garlicky dish needs only a bowl of plain cooked rice and a simple lentil purée side dish (*dal*) to complete a meal. For an elaborate meal include a simple vegetable such as Dry-Fried Pointed Gourd with Coriander (p. 248) and Sweet and Fragrant Pineapple Chutney (p. 298).

BOTTLE GOURD STUFFED WITH SPICY POTATOES IN TOMATO-HERB SAUCE

ALOO BHARA LAUKI

◆

Lucknow, the Moghul city of the *nawabs* (Moslem princes) in the Northern Province of India, is known for turning out elaborate vegetarian dishes. Even a simple vegetable in the hands of these northerners takes on a suave appeal. In this dish a whole gourd is hollowed out and stuffed with a mustard-scented spicy potato mixture. It is then baked in a coriander-ginger sauce and presented whole at the table. The stuffed gourd is usually prepared for banquets, formal entertainments, and special buffet-style dinners.

FOR 6 PERSONS

◆

1 lb/500 g bottle gourd (about 2 small ones), or use 2 large cucumbers
FOR THE SPICY POTATO STUFFING:
2 tablespoons mustard oil or light vegetable oil
½ teaspoon ground cumin
¼ teaspoon ginger powder
½ teaspoon mango powder or 2 teaspoons lemon juice
2 medium-size potatoes, boiled till soft, peeled, and coarsely mashed
2–4 hot green chilies, chopped
1 tablespoon molasses
FOR THE SAUCE:
1 tablespoon light vegetable oil
2 tablespoons minced onion
1 teaspoon minced garlic
2 teaspoons grated or crushed fresh ginger
¼ teaspoon cayenne pepper
4 oz/125 g tinned tomato purée
Coarse salt, to taste
½ pint/300 ml water
3 tablespoons chopped fresh coriander
Coriander sprig for garnish

1 Preheat oven to 400°F/200°C/Gas 6.

2 Peel the gourd or cucumber. Using an apple corer, scoop out the centres, leaving a shell ½ in/1 cm thick. Finely mince the scooped-out flesh of the gourd.

3 Measure out the spices and place them next to the stove in separate piles. Heat the mustard oil in a pan until it is very hot and smoking. Turn off the heat and let the oil cool briefly (skip this step if you are using light vegetable oil). Heat the oil again and add the minced gourd. Stir-fry the gourd over medium heat for 1 minute. Add the cumin, ginger powder, and mango powder and continue frying for 30 seconds or more. Add the potatoes and chilies, mix to coat them well with the spices, and fry for 5 minutes. Turn off the heat and stir in the molasses.

4 Stuff the gourd with the filling. Place the stuffed gourd in a shallow baking dish that will hold them snugly.

5 To make the sauce, heat the oil in the same pan over high heat. When it is hot, add the onion, garlic, and ginger. Cook, stirring constantly, for 1 minute. Add the cayenne, tomato purée, salt, and water and bring to the boil. Stir in the chopped coriander.

6 Pour the tomato-herb sauce over the stuffed gourd. Cover tightly with foil and bake in the middle of the oven for 30 minutes (45 minutes if you want softer gourd). Remove the pan from the oven and let the dish rest undisturbed for 5 minutes before serving.

Transfer the stuffed gourd to a heated serving platter. Spoon the sauce over it and garnish with coriander. Serve sliced ½–1 in/1–2.5 cm thick, preferably diagonally, with the sauce.

Follow the menu suggestions given for Cauliflower, Aubergine, and Potatoes in Herb Sauce (p. 180).

COURGETTE KOFTAS IN CREAMED TOMATO SAUCE

MALAI KOFTA

◆

In the holy city of Banaras this *kofta* is made with bottle gourd. Courgettes also work extremely well. In keeping with the tradition of the classic Brahmin cooking of northern India, no garlic is used in this dish.

FOR 6 PERSONS

FOR KOFTA BALLS:
1 recipe Spicy Courgette Koftas (p. 142)
FOR THE SAUCE:
4 medium tomatoes, quartered

6 hot green chilies
1½ in/4 cm piece fresh ginger, peeled
5 tablespoons groundnut oil
2 teaspoons ground cumin
¾ teaspoon turmeric
2 tablespoons ground almonds or peanuts
2 teaspoons paprika
2 teaspoons garam masala *(p. 77)*

1 To make the sauce, put the tomatoes, chilies, and ginger into the container of a blender or food processor and process until finely puréed. Heat the oil in a heavy pan over medium-high heat. When it is hot, add all the ingredients from the cumin to the *garam masala*, and immediately add the puréed tomato mixture and bring to the boil. Lower the heat and boil the sauce gently for 20 minutes. Turn off the heat. Measure the sauce. You should have 1½ pints/800 ml; if not, add enough water to bring it to that amount. Set aside for several hours, covered, or refrigerate overnight.

2 When you are ready to serve, heat the sauce until it is boiling gently. Add the *kofta* and simmer until thoroughly heated through.

Follow the menu suggestions given for Cauliflower, Aubergine, and Potato in Herb Sauce (p. 180).

VEGETABLE-PULSE COMBINATIONS

◆

TANJORE BROCCOLI AND MUNG BEAN STEW WITH COCONUT

TANDOO KOOTOO

◆

As the name suggests, this is a southern Brahmin dish from the holy city of Tanjore, the home of the Meenakshi Temple. In India this stew is made with a special variety of spinach that has thick, meaty stems. Broccoli stalks, surprisingly, make a good substitute.

FOR 4–6 PERSONS

◆

1½ lb/750 g broccoli
5 oz/150 g split yellow mung beans (moong dal)
⅛ teaspoon turmeric
¾ pint/450 ml water or more
⅓ teaspoon ground asafetida
1½ teaspoons coarse salt, or to taste
1½ teaspoons sambaar *powder (p. 75) or Curry Powder Master Recipe (p. 73)*
¾ pint/450 ml water
1 teaspoon cumin seeds
4 oz/125 g fresh flaked coconut
4 hot green chilies
4 tablespoons water
4 tablespoons usli ghee *(p. 57) or a combination of unsalted butter and light vegetable oil*
1 teaspoon black mustard seeds
8 curry (kari) leaves (fresh or dry, optional)
2 tablespoons chopped fresh coriander

1 Cut the broccoli stalks from the florets and peel stalks. Slice them into ¼ in/5 mm pieces. Cut the florets into 1 in/2.5 cm pieces. Set aside.

2 Pick clean the beans and put them along with the turmeric and ¾ pint/450 ml water in a heavy pan and bring to the boil. Cook the beans, partially covered, over medium-high heat for 15 minutes or until the beans are barely cooked. If the water evaporates too quickly, add more as needed.

3 Add the broccoli stalks and tops, asafetida, salt, and *sambaar* along with ¾ pint/450 ml water. Mix well and continue cooking, partially covered, for 8 more minutes or until the vegetables are barely cooked.

4 While the vegetables are cooking, put the cumin, coconut, chilies, and 4 tablespoons water into the container of a blender or food processor and process until finely puréed.

5 Add the coconut purée to the broccoli-mung bean mixture and cook for 2 more minutes or just long enough to remove the raw flavour from the cumin and coconut. Turn off the heat.

6 Heat the *ghee* in a small frying pan over high heat. When it is very hot, add the mustard seeds. Keep a lid handy, as the seeds may fly all over. When the spattering begins to subside, take the pan off the heat, add the curry leaves, and let sizzle for 15–20 seconds. Immediately pour the entire contents of the pan over the stew, mix well, and serve sprinkled with chopped coriander.

To relish fully the delicate flavours of this dish, serve only plain boiled rice and a simple vegetable such as Spicy Curried Potatoes (p. 249). For an elaborate meal start with one of the *rasams* from the soup section. Serve Southern Carrot Salad with Peanuts and Mustard Seeds (p. 269) and Courgette and Yogurt Salad (p. 276) as side dishes. A good choice of pickle would be Madras Hot Star Fruit Chutney (p. 299).

HEARTY BLUE MOUNTAIN CABBAGE AND TOMATO STEW

MUTTAKOS SAMBAAR

◆

A speciality of my grandmother's from the Blue Mountains, commonly known as the Nilgiri Hills, this incredibly simple yet delicious stew is made with lentils, cabbage, tomatoes, and onions, and flavoured with curry. The hot spices are kept to a minimum to heighten the flavours of the vegetables. I often serve the stew as a light lunch, in large bowls accompanied by a piece of bread or a little rice.

FOR 6–8 PERSONS

◆

6 oz/175 g yellow lentils (toovar dal) or red lentils (masar dal)
1¼ pints/700 ml water
¼ teaspoon turmeric
12 oz/375 g ripe tomatoes, quartered
8–12 curry (kari) leaves
4 tablespoons light vegetable oil
1½ teaspoons black mustard seeds
⅓ teaspoon fenugreek seeds (optional)
1 tablespoon sambaar powder (p. 75) or Curry Powder Master Recipe (p. 73)
1 medium-size onion, peeled and cut into 1 in/2.5 cm pieces
1½ lb/750 g cabbage (stem and tough leaves removed), chopped into 1 in/2.5 cm pieces
2 teaspoons coarse salt, or to taste
3–4 tablespoons chopped fresh coriander
3 tablespoons usli ghee (p. 57) or unsalted butter (optional)

1 Pick clean the lentils, then put them in a bowl and wash thoroughly in several changes of water. Put the lentils in a large pan, add the

1¼ pints/700 ml water and the turmeric, and bring to the boil. Lower the heat to medium and cook, partially covered, for 30 minutes or until the lentils are fully cooked.

2 Add the tomatoes and curry leaves, mix well, and turn off heat. Take out about half the tomato-lentil mixture and process in a food processor or blender until finely puréed. Return it to the pan.

3 Measure out the spices and place them right next to the stove in separate piles. Heat the oil in a large pan over high heat. When the oil is very hot, add the mustard seeds. Keep a lid handy, as the seeds may fly all over. As the seeds are spattering, add the fenugreek. When the fenugreek turns dark brown add the *sambaar* or curry powder, let sizzle for a second or two and immediately add the onion and cabbage. Stir well and quickly for 2 seconds. Cook the vegetables, uncovered, for 4–5 minutes. Turn down the heat a little if they begin to brown too much or too rapidly.

4 Add the lentil mixture, mix thoroughly, and bring to the boil. Cook the stew over a medium heat, covered, for 20 minutes, or until the vegetables are done but still crisp. Stir in the salt to taste and a little chopped coriander.

Serve in a soup tureen or individual bowls, garnished with chopped coriander. If desired, pour a teaspoon or two of *usli ghee* on top.

Follow the menu suggestions for Tanjore Broccoli and Mung Bean Stew with Coconut (p. 190).

MADRAS FIERY AUBERGINE, LENTIL, AND CHILI STEW

PITLAI

Laced with chilies and then more chilies, *pitlai* is one of the hottest preparations in all of southern cooking. The characteristic taste of *pitlai* comes from the flavour of a fried spiced paste consisting of coconut, chilies, coriander, and various pulses that are infused in the sauce. For a milder taste decrease the quantity of chilies.

FOR 4–6 PERSONS

FOR THE SPICE PASTE:
3 tablespoons light sesame or light vegetable oil
2 tablespoons yellow split peas (channa dal)
1 tablespoon split white gram beans (urad dal)
5 tablespoons coriander seeds
1 teaspoon black peppercorns
12 dry red chili pods
3 tablespoons desiccated coconut (khopra)
¼ pint/150 ml water, or more
2 lb/1 kg aubergine, unpeeled, cut into 1 in/2.5 cm cubes
1½ teaspoons coarse salt, or to taste
1 teaspoon turmeric
1¼ pints/700 ml water
6 oz/175 g cooked yellow or red lentils (p. 254)
FOR THE SPICE-PERFUMED BUTTER:
2 tablespoons usli ghee (p. 57) or light vegetable oil
2 teaspoons black mustard seeds
½ teaspoon ground asafetida
8–10 curry (kari) leaves, fresh or dry (optional)

1 Heat the oil in a small frying pan over medium-low heat for

3 minutes. Pick clean the peas and the beans and add them to the oil and fry, stirring, for 1 minute or until they just begin to fry. Add the coriander and peppercorns and continue frying for 1 more minute. Add the chili pods and fry all the ingredients until the pulses turn light golden and the spices smell fried. Add the coconut, mix the ingredients for 15 seconds, and turn off the heat. Put the spice mixture into the container of an electric blender along with ¼ pint/150 ml water. Process until it reduces to a fine sauce. If necessary, add more water. Set aside.

2 Put the aubergine, turmeric, and water in a large heavy saucepan and bring to the boil. Cook the aubergine cubes over medium-high heat, covered, for 5 minutes. Add the cooked lentils, mix well, and continue cooking for 1 more minute.

3 Add the ground spice paste and salt to taste. Stir well, but carefully, to distribute the spices evenly into the aubergine. Turn off heat.

4 Measure out the spices and place them right next to the stove in separate piles. Heat the *ghee* or oil in a small frying pan over high heat. When it is very hot, add the mustard seeds. Keep a lid handy, as the seeds may fly all over. When the spattering subsides, take the pan off the heat, and add the asafetida and curry leaves. Let the spices and herbs sizzle in the *ghee* for 10–15 seconds, then pour the entire contents of the pan over the aubergine. Gently stir to fold in the spices. Heat throughly before serving.

Follow menu suggestions given for Tanjore Broccoli and Mung Bean Stew with Coconut (p. 190).

JAMMU BLACK BEANS AND AUBERGINE WITH MUSTARD OIL

PAHADI MAA DAL

◆

This robust preparation of beans, tomatoes, yogurt, and fresh ginger, bursting with the fragrances of mustard oil and spices, is a speciality all along the lower slopes of the Himalayas, including Jammu and Simla. In this recipe, aubergine is used not as a vegetable but a thickener, to give body to the sauce. This *dal* preparation is very mild. For a hotter flavour, increase the quantity of cayenne pepper and, if desired, garnish with shredded green chilies.

FOR 6 PERSONS

6 oz/175 g whole black gram beans (sabat urad)
3 tablespoons finely chopped fresh ginger
8 oz/250 g chopped onion
1 sweet green pepper, seeded and chopped
1–4 hot green chilies, minced
½ teaspoon cayenne pepper
2 teaspoons paprika
1 tablespoon ground coriander
½ pint/300 ml plain yogurt
1 pint/600 ml water
8 oz/250 g aubergine, unpeeled, cut into ¾ in/2 cm cubes
8 oz/250 g ripe tomatoes, chopped
1½ teaspoons coarse salt, or to taste
FOR THE MUSTARD OIL
4–5 tablespoons mustard oil, or light vegetable oil and 1 teaspoon dry mustard powder
1 tablespoon cumin seeds, crushed
8 oz/250 g finely chopped onion
6 tablespoons chopped fresh coriander

1 Pick clean the beans and wash thoroughly in several changes of water and put them in a bowl. Add enough water to cover the beans by at least 1½ in/4 cm. Let soak for 8 hours or overnight. Drain and rinse the beans, then drain again.

2 Put the beans in a heavy pot along with the ginger, onion, green pepper, chilies, cayenne, paprika, coriander, yogurt, and ½ pint/ 300 ml of the water, and bring to the boil. Lower heat and cook, covered, for 1 hour. Add the remaining ½ pint/300 ml water and continue cooking, covered, for 30 minutes or until the beans are cooked.

3 Add the aubergine and tomatoes, mix well, and cook for 30 minutes longer or until the vegetables are cooked and very tender – the contents of the pan will now look like a thick stew. Keep the *dal* on a low simmer while you make the spice-perfumed butter. Add salt to taste.

4 Measure out the spices and place them next to the stove in separate piles. Heat the mustard oil in a small frying pan over high heat until it is smoking. Turn off the heat and let cool for a couple of minutes. (If you are using vegetable oil, skip this step. Also do not add mustard powder yet.) Heat the oil again over a high heat. When it is very hot, add the cumin. When the cumin turns dark brown (about 10 seconds), add the onions and fry, stirring constantly, until they turn caramel brown (15 minutes). If you are using mustard powder, add it now. Add 4 tablespoons chopped coriander; let it sizzle in oil for a few seconds, then immediately pour the entire contents of the pan over the *dal*. Mix thoroughly and serve sprinkled with the remaining chopped coriander.

This creamy bean dish is best enjoyed with plain cooked rice or Yogurt Bread (p. 314). Mustard-Flecked Hot Tomato Chutney (p. 295) and Courgette and Yogurt Salad (p. 276) would make a good accompaniment. For an elaborate meal serve a side-dish vegetable such as Bitter Gourd with Fragrant Potato Stuffing (p. 239).

COORG-STYLE HOT AND GARLICKY BLACK BEANS WITH LOTUS ROOT

COORG URAD DAL

Coorgis have one distinctive feature about their cooking. It is fiery hot – all the way. This black bean dish is no exception. Coorgi food, influenced by Maharashtrian and Mysorian cuisine, is spiced with asafetida, cumin, and coriander. Chilies in all varieties and in large quantities are added for flavour and pungency. This unique version of Coorgi black beans with lotus root was given to me by my sister Chitra. The lotus root gives the beans an earthy aroma and a crunchy texture.

FOR 6 PERSONS

6 oz/175 g whole black gram beans (sabat urad dal)
1¼ pints/700 ml water
1 lb/500 g lotus root (or water chestnuts or potatoes)
2 teaspoons coarse salt, or to taste
FOR THE SPICE-PERFUMED BUTTER:
4 tablespoons light sesame oil or groundnut oil
½ teaspoon ground asafetida
2 teaspoons minced garlic
1½ tablespoons grated or crushed fresh ginger
4 hot green chilies, chopped
1 tablespoon ground cumin
1 teaspoon cayenne pepper
1 teaspoon turmeric
4 tablespoons minced fresh coriander
Lemon juice
6 hot green chilies for garnish

1 Pick clean beans and rinse in several changes of water and put them in a bowl. Add enough water to cover by at least 1½ in/4 cm. Soak for

8 hours or overnight. Drain and rinse thoroughly, then drain again.

2 Put the beans in a pot along with 1¼ pints/700 ml water and bring to the boil. Lower heat and cook, covered, for 45 minutes.

3 While the beans are cooking, prepare the lotus root. Peel the lotus root or water chestnuts and cut into ⅛ in/3 mm thick slices. Wash them thoroughly and drain. (If you are using potatoes, peel and cut them into ½ in/1 cm cubes.)

4 Add the lotus root and salt to the beans and continue cooking, covered, for 15 more minutes. Keep the *dal* on a low simmer while you make the spice-perfumed butter.

5 Measure out the spices and place them right next to the stove in separate piles. Heat the oil in a small frying pan over medium heat. When it is hot, add the asafetida and let sizzle for 15 seconds. Add the garlic, ginger, and chilies and fry, stirring and shaking the pan, for 30 seconds. Add the cumin, cayenne, and turmeric and let sizzle for 30 seconds. Add the coriander, shake the pan for a few seconds, and pour the entire contents of the pan over the simmering beans. Add the lemon juice – about 2 tablespoons or to taste. Mix thoroughly. Serve garnished with green chilies.

Follow the serving suggestions given for Madras Fiery Aubergine, Lentil, and Chili Stew (p. 194).

MANALI UNRIPE PEACH AND CHICK-PEAS WITH FENNEL

MANALI AADOO DAL

◆

Along the slopes of the Himalayan Mountains lies Manali, where fruit orchards dot the countryside. Here, as a special treat, fruits are picked unripe and cooked with chick-peas in a delicate fennel-and-ginger-scented sauce. Naturally, mustard oil plays an important role in imparting the distinct characteristic flavour of this dish.

FOR 4 PERSONS

◆

5–6 tablespoons mustard oil or light vegetable oil
1½ teaspoons cumin seeds
¾ teaspoon fennel seeds
3 tablespoons shredded fresh ginger
8 oz/250 g minced onion
5 hot green chilies, chopped
1½ tablespoons ground coriander
2 tablespoons ground almonds
1 lb/500 g unripe hard peaches (or nectarines) peeled, stoned, and sliced thickly
8 oz/250 g drained cooked chick-peas
1 teaspoon mango powder (or 1 tablespoon lemon juice)
½ teaspoon garam masala *(p. 77)*
Coarse salt to taste

1 Measure out the spices and place them right next to the stove in separate piles. Heat the oil in a heavy pan until very hot and smoking. Turn off this heat and let the oil cool briefly. (If you are using vegetable oil, omit this step.)
2 Heat the oil again over medium-high heat. When it is hot, add the cumin and fennel. When they turn dark brown (about 10 seconds), add the ginger and let sizzle for 10–15 seconds. Add the onion and fry,

stirring constantly, until light golden (about 8 minutes). Add the chilies, coriander, and almonds; continue cooking for 2 more minutes.
3 Add the peaches and toss well to coat with spices. Stir in the chick-peas and mango powder. If mixture looks very thick, add a few tablespoons of water. Cover and cook over low heat for 20 minutes or until all the flavours have blended and the peaches are cooked. Stir in *garam masala* and salt and serve.

Follow the menu suggestions given for Jammu Black Beans and Aubergine with Mustard Oil (p. 196).

PUMPKIN AND SPLIT PEAS WITH CAMPHOR BASIL

LAU DAL

◆

Cooking pumpkin with yellow split peas is extremely popular all through the eastern regions. In Assam, near the Burma border, the tribeswomen who live in the hills add a local herb, camphor basil, to lend the dish a sweet distinctive aroma. I love the hypnotic flavour of camphor basil. Since it is not sold here, I use a mixture of sweet basil and star anise. The result is unbelievably good.

FOR 4–6 PERSONS

◆

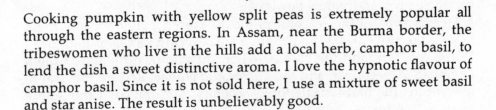

5–6 tablespoons fresh camphor basil leaves (kapoor tulsi) or 5–6 tablespoons sweet basil leaves and 4 star anise sections
6 oz/175 g yellow split peas
Pinch turmeric
3 bay leaves
1 small onion, peeled and chopped
¾ pint/450 ml water
2 lb/1 Kg pumpkin, peeled and cut into 1½ in/4 cm cubes
1 teaspoon sugar
1½ teaspoons coarse salt, or to taste
½ pint/300 ml water

FOR THE SPICED BUTTER:

5 tablespoons usli ghee (p. 57) or a combination of unsalted butter and light vegetable oil
1½ teaspoons cumin seeds
2 tablespoons shredded fresh ginger
2–4 hot green chilies, shredded

1 Cut the basil leaves into ¼ in/5mm wide shreds; set aside.

2 Put the peas, turmeric, bay leaves, onion, and star anise (if you are using sweet basil) in a deep pot with ¾ pint/450 ml water and bring to the boil. Cook over medium heat, partially covered, for 20 minutes.

3 Add the pumpkin pieces along with ½ pint/300 ml water, sugar, and salt and bring to the boil again. Lower the heat and continue cooking, covered, for 20 more minutes. Turn off the heat. Transfer to a serving dish or individual bowls.

4 Measure out all the seasonings for the spiced butter and put them next to the stove. Heat the *ghee* in a small frying pan over high heat. When it is hot, add the cumin. When the cumin turns dark brown (about 15–20 seconds), add the ginger and chilies. Reduce the heat to low and let the herbs sizzle for 30 seconds. Add the basil and let the mixture fry for 30 seconds. Pour all of it over the pumpkin-pea mixture. Mix with a fork just once or twice to streak it with the spiced butter. Serve immediately.

This mellow stew is best enjoyed with bread and a bowl of Smoked Aubergine and Yogurt Salad (p. 277). Quick Onion, Tomato, and Cucumber Relish (p. 290) adds a nice cool spicy touch.

Sun-Dried Bean Dumplings in Spicy Tomato Sauce

VADEE

In the valley of Kashmir, the northernmost state of India, not much grows in the winter. Therefore, on cold winter days while the chilling winds circle through the winding canals, the *Chinar* trees, and the snowcapped Himalayan Mountains, the Kashmiri women are busy turning sun-dried bean dumplings and vegetables into mouth-watering delicacies in their homes. This recipe for *vadee* (meaning 'dried dumpling' or a dish made with it), a speciality of the *Kashmiri pandits*, is flavoured with aromatic fenugreek leaves and sweet mustard oil. The addition of potatoes makes it quite substantial.

You do not have to transplant yourself to Kashmir to enjoy this dish. Commercially prepared dried dumplings called *vadee* are available in Indian grocers.

FOR 8 PERSONS

1 recipe spicy sun-dried bean dumplings (badian), homemade (recipe follows) or bought
8 tablespoons mustard oil or light vegetable oil
12 oz/375 g thin-sliced onion
3 tablespoons shredded ginger
1½ teaspoons ground cumin
1½ teaspoons ground coriander
1 teaspoon turmeric
½ teaspoon cayenne pepper
1½ oz/45 g chopped fresh fenugreek leaves (or 2 teaspoons dry fenugreek leaves, kasoori methi, or 5 oz/150 g chopped fresh spinach)
4 medium tomatoes, chopped
3 medium-size potatoes, peeled and cut into ¼ in/5mm thick slices
2½ pints/1.5 litres water
4 tablespoons chopped fresh coriander
1 teaspoon coarse salt, or to taste
8–12 curry (kari) leaves (fresh or dry, optional)

1 If you are using shop-bought *vadee*, break them up into small pieces.
2 Heat the mustard oil in a very large shallow pan until it is very hot and smoking. Turn off the heat and let the oil cool briefly. (Omit this step if you are using vegetable oil.) Heat the oil again and add *vadee*.

Fry them over medium-high heat, turning them often, until they are nicely browned (about 2 minutes). Remove with a slotted spoon to a reserved plate and set aside.

3 To the same oil add the onion and ginger. Fry, stirring constantly, until the onion turns golden brown (about 15 minutes). Add the cumin, coriander, turmeric, and cayenne. Stir for 1 minute, and immediately add the fenugreek and tomatoes. Mix well and cook, stirring, until the sauce looks thick and pulpy (about 10 minutes).

4 Add the fried *vadee*, potatoes, and 2 pints/1 litre water and bring to the boil. Lower the heat and cook, covered, for 30 minutes. Check once or twice to make sure the sauce is not evaporating too quickly. Stir in the remaining ½ pint/300 ml water and half the chopped coriander. Turn off the heat and let the dish rest, covered and undisturbed, for 15 minutes. Stir in the salt and curry leaves.

To serve, garnish with the remaining chopped coriander. This dish should be served with either plain cooked rice or a simple bread such as Nirvana Special Balloon Bread (p. 310) or Fennel-Scented Sweet Flaky Bread (p. 309), accompanied with a yogurt drink. For a more elaborate meal follow the menu suggestions given for Jammu Black Beans and Aubergine with Mustard Oil (p. 96).

SUN-DRIED BEAN DUMPLINGS

BADIAN

◆

MAKES ABOUT 100 BADIES

6 oz/175 g split yellow mung beans (moong dal) or split white gram beans (urad dal)
4 hot green chilies
¼ in/5 mm thick slice fresh ginger, peeled
¼ teaspoon cumin seeds
¼ teaspoon ground asafetida
1 teaspoon coarse salt
½ teaspoon coarsely crushed black pepper

1 Pick over and clean the beans, then rinse them thoroughly in water. Put the beans in a bowl and add enough water to cover by 1 in/2.5 cm. Soak for 8 hours. Drain and once again rinse the beans. Drain well.

2 Put the beans along with the chilies, ginger, cumin, and asafetida into the container of a food processor or blender and process until coarsely ground (about 1½–2 minutes), turning off the machine every half minute to push mixture down. Add the salt and pepper and process for an additional 15 seconds. Transfer the mixture to a bowl.

3 Line a sponge-roll tin with double layers of muslin. Scoop the mixture by teaspoonfuls and drop onto the muslin.

4 Air-dry the bean mixture outdoors (keep in the shade, however) for 3–4 days or until they are fully dry. Or place the tin in a warm oven with the oven door slightly open for 1 hour. Turn off the oven and leave the tin with the dumplings in the oven for 1–2 days or until fully dry.

Store dumplings in airtight containers. They will keep fresh up to 3 months.

VEGETABLE-DAIRY COMBINATIONS

◆

MALABAR COCONUT-AND-YOGURT-BRAISED VEGETABLES

AVIAL

◆

Avial is the masterpiece of Malabar. It carefully and ingeniously combines the products of the region to produce the most complex and flavourful dish imaginable. *Avial* is made by cooking several varieties of root and green vegetables in a cumin-scented yogurt-coconut sauce. Star fruit or unripe mango is added to lend the necessary tart flavour, since tamarind is in short supply in Malabar. Besides, the brown colour of tamarind would ruin a perfect, pearly white sauce. Lentils, too, are scarce in Malabar; therefore, the flavouring and rich consistency of the sauce are achieved by a mixture of thick coconut pulp and yogurt. Finally, the touch that sets Malabar food apart from all others is the addition of freshly pressed coconut oil, perfumed with *kari* leaves and asafetida, to the dish just before serving.

NOTE: The coconut oil must be absolutely fresh and not oily tasting. If you are not sure, then simply use any other oil suggested.

FOR 6–8 PERSONS

◆

6–8 small red wax potatoes (about 1 lb/500 g)
12 oz/375 g green beans
¾ pint/450 ml water
2 medium sweet green peppers
⅓ teaspoon turmeric
6 oz/175 g shelled green peas (fresh or frozen)
4 oz/125 g packed fresh flaked coconut
1½ teaspoons cumin seeds
4 hot green chilies
¼ pint/150 ml water
¼ pint/150 ml plain yogurt
1 teaspoon coarse salt, or to taste
FOR SPICED BUTTER:
2 tablespoons coconut oil (or light sesame oil, or groundnut oil)
12 curry (kari) leaves (fresh or dry)
¼ teaspoon ground asafetida

1 Scrub and clean the potatoes under cold running water and pat dry on towels. Cut them, unpeeled, into halves (cut large ones into quarters). Clean and snap off the ends of the beans and cut them into 1 in/2.5 cm long pieces. Wash and cut the green peppers into halves, core and seed, and cut them into 1 in/2.5 cm pieces.
2 Put the potatoes and beans in a heavy non-metallic pot along with the turmeric and ¾ pint/450 ml water and bring to the boil. Cook the

vegetables over medium heat, partially covered, for 7 minutes.

3 Add the peas and cook for 3 more minutes. Drain the vegetables in a colander.

4 Put the coconut, cumin, and chilies along with ¼ pint/150 ml water into the container of an electric blender or a food processor. Process until the contents are reduced to a fine purée.

5 Put the cooked vegetables back into the same pot along with the puréed coconut mixture and bring to the boil. Simmer over low heat, covered, for 8 minutes. Beat the yogurt with a whisk or fork until well blended and add to the simmering vegetables along with salt to taste. Continue cooking for another 2 minutes. Keep the stew at a low simmer while you make the spiced butter.

6 Heat the oil in a small frying pan over high heat. When the oil is hot, take the pan off the heat and add the curry leaves and asafetida. Let the spices sizzle for 5 seconds. Immediately pour the entire contents of the pan over the stew. Mix well and serve.

Avial is delicious and satisfying as a luncheon entrée, served with plain boiled rice and some lentil wafers. A fine beverage to serve would be Lemonade with Ginger (p. 360).

VEGETABLES BRAISED IN YOGURT AND SPICES, PATNA-STYLE

PATNA KORMA

◆

Patna, the capital of Bihar, has a very old and rich history. Once the centre of the ancient kingdom of Magadha, this is the land where Buddha wandered restlessly until he found enlightenment just one hundred miles south, in Gaya. The food of the region reflects the rich heritage acquired over several thousand years; it is simple yet intriguingly flavoured, and the spicing is complex yet subtle. This braised vegetable dish scented with cumin and coriander is wrapped in a delicate sauce of yogurt, almonds, and tomatoes. You may substitute carrots in place of potatoes.

FOR 6 PERSONS

8 tablespoons light vegetable oil
6 oz/175 g onion, finely chopped
2 tablespoons ground cumin
2 tablespoons ground coriander
½ teaspoon turmeric
¼–½ teaspoon cayenne pepper (optional)
¼–½ teaspoon black pepper
½ teaspoon minced garlic
3 tablespoons grated or crushed fresh ginger
½ pint/300 ml plain yogurt
4 tablespoons tomato purée (fresh or tinned)
2 tablespoons ground almonds
2 medium potatoes, peeled and quartered
1 small aubergine, unpeeled, cut into 1½ in/4 cm cubes
2 medium courgettes, cut into 1½ in/4 cm thick slices
8 oz/250 g yard long beans or green beans, cut into 2 in/5 cm pieces
¼ pint/150 ml water
1½ teaspoons coarse salt, or to taste
¾ teaspoon garam masala *(p. 77)*
Chopped fresh coriander for garnish

1 Measure out the spices and place them next to the stove in separate piles. Heat the oil in a heavy-bottomed pan over medium-high heat. When hot, add the onions and fry, stirring, until light-brown (about 8 minutes). Add the cumin, coriander, turmeric, cayenne, and black pepper. Mix well, and let sizzle for 5 seconds. Add the garlic and ginger and cook for 2 more minutes. Add the yogurt 2 tablespoons at a time, and cook, stirring the mixture, until it looks thick and pulpy.

2 Add the tomato purée and ground almonds and continue cooking for 2 more minutes, stirring to prevent sticking and burning. Add the potatoes and mix well. Reduce the heat and cook, covered, until potatoes are barely done (8 minutes). Add the aubergine, courgettes, and beans, along with ¼ pint/150 ml water and salt. Stir well and continue cooking, covered, for 20 more minutes. Sprinkle on the *garam masala* and serve garnished with chopped coriander.

To serve as a simple luncheon dish accompany with a bread such as Dill and Garlic Barley Bread with Shredded Green Chilies (p. 318) or Tomato Pilaf (p. 326). For an elaborate meal follow the serving suggestions given for Cauliflower, Aubergine, and Potato in Herb Sauce (p. 180).

SWEET PEPPERS STUFFED WITH CHEESE AND SPRING ONIONS IN SAUCE AFGHAN

PESHAVARI BHARA MIRCH

◆

In Peshawar, the northwest frontier region of Pakistan (once a part of India), tiny sweet green pepper halves are stuffed with fresh moist cheese (*paneer*) and potatoes and then pan-roasted. The potatoes develop a crackling crust and a wonderfully smoky flavour. The pepper halves are served robed in a fennel-and-cumin-scented tomato sauce. For a variation you can use onions in place of peppers. This visually appealing dish is ideal for company.

FOR 4 PERSONS

4 medium sweet green or red peppers
Indian cheese (paneer) made with 3 pints/2 litres milk (p. 52), or 4 bean curd cakes (about 4 oz/125 g)
3 oz/90 g finely chopped spring onions, white and green parts
4 hot green chilies, minced
5 tablespoons finely chopped fresh coriander
2 tablespoons plain flour
7 tablespoons light vegetable oil
½ teaspoon cumin seeds
2 tablespoons grated or crushed ginger
4 medium potatoes, boiled, peeled, and coarsely mashed
1 tablespoon lemon juice
¾ teaspoon coarse salt, or to taste
½ pint/300 ml Sauce Afghan (see following recipe)
Coriander sprig for garnish (optional)

1 Wash and wipe dry the peppers. Cut each neatly into halves. Remove membrane from inside the peppers to make room for the stuffing.

2 Put the cheese, spring onions, chilies, coriander, and flour in a small bowl. Mix thoroughly and set aside.

3 Heat 3 tablespoons of the oil in a frying pan over medium-high heat. When it is hot, add the cumin. When the cumin turns dark brown (15 seconds), add the ginger and let sizzle for 10 seconds. Add the potatoes and fry, stirring, until they are well coated with the oil and the spices and begin to brown. Turn off the heat. Stir in the lemon juice and salt. Let the potatoes cool a little.

4 Divide the cheese mixture and the potato mixture equally into 8 portions. Stuff the pepper halves first with the cheese mixture, packing it down lightly. Top the cheese mixture with the potato mixture and, using a spatula, smooth the top. (Each pepper half now is stuffed with 2 fillings, cheese at the bottom and potatoes on the top.)

5 Heat the pan over medium-high heat. When it is hot, add 3 tablespoons oil and immediately lay the stuffed peppers, cut side down, in a single layer and cook the peppers, uncovered, until the potatoes develop a nice brown crust. Check to ensure peppers are not sticking.

6 Gently turn the peppers upside down. Dribble the remaining 1 tablespoon oil around the peppers. Reduce the heat to medium and continue cooking, shaking the pan often, until the peppers are cooked but still crunchy (10–12 minutes).

Serve the peppers crusty potato side up, arranged in Sauce Afghan in a shallow serving dish. Garnish, if desired, with a coriander sprig.

SAUCE AFGHAN

PESHAVARI SHORVA

◆

MAKES ½ PINT/300 ML

◆

6 tablespoons light vegetable oil
3 oz/90 g minced onion
3 hot green chilies
1 large clove garlic, minced
2 medium tomatoes, finely chopped
½ teaspoon ground cumin
½ teaspoon ground fennel
5 tablespoons plain yogurt, lightly mixed with a fork
⅓ teaspoon coarse salt, or to taste

Heat the oil in a small pan until very hot. Add onion and cook over medium heat until beginning to turn brown (about 10 minutes). Add all the other ingredients and continue cooking until the oil separates from the gravy and the sauce looks fried. This will take about 30 minutes. During cooking, add about 3 tablespoons water and stir often to prevent sticking and burning. Turn off the heat, measure the sauce, and add enough water to make a little over ½ pint/300 ml. Return the sauce to the pan and heat thoroughly before serving.

Peshavari bhara mirch makes an excellent luncheon dish. You may serve a refreshing drink such as Iced Yogurt Drink with Mint (p. 365). For an elaborate meal add Aubergine and Potatoes Laced with Fenugreek (p. 240).

BEAN CURD DUMPLINGS WITH TOMATOES IN A FENUGREEK-LACED YOGURT SAUCE

HYDERABAD TAMATAR KADHI

◆

Kadhi are one of the most popular preparations of Indian vegetarian cuisine. Created in the Northern Province of India, this classic recipe consists of fried chick-pea-batter dumplings, simmered in a seasoned yogurt sauce. In northern India they are traditional at Sunday brunch, served over a bed of rice. Today their popularity has spread to many other regions. Inevitably many interesting and delicious variations have sprung up: in Sindh *kokum* fruit forms the sauce instead of yogurt; in Rajasthan fenugreek and spinach replace some of the dumplings. In Bengal *kadhi* are flavoured with five-spice blend (p. 82), while in Punjab they use fennel and cumin seeds. In this recipe from Hyderabad the *kadhi* are made with tomatoes and flavoured with fenugreek seeds. And I make the dumplings with bean curd, as I think it lends a lovely flavour to the dish in addition to being highly nutritive.

FOR 6–8 PERSONS

◆

8 oz/250 g chick-pea flour (besan)
2 teaspoons ground coriander
¼ teaspoon cayenne pepper
4 tablespoons plain yogurt
¼ pint/150 ml warm water, or more as needed
Pinch bicarbonate of soda
½ teaspoon coarse salt, or to taste
1 onion, peeled and sliced thin
1 potato, peeled and sliced thin
2 bean curd cakes, cut into ½ × ½ × 1 in/ 1 × 1 × 2.5 cm pieces
Groundnut or corn oil (enough to fill a deep fryer to a depth of 3 in/7.5 cm)

FOR THE SAUCE:

1 pint/600 ml plain yogurt
3 oz/90 g chick-pea flour (besan)
2½ pints/1.5 litres cold water
½ teaspoon turmeric
2 teaspoons ground coriander
1½ teaspoons coarse salt, or to taste
4 tablespoons light sesame oil or light vegetable oil
½ teaspoon fenugreek seeds
1 teaspoon cumin seeds
4 hot green chilies, minced
4 medium tomatoes, cut in half
2 medium onions, sliced thin

1 To make the batter for the dumplings, mix the chick-pea flour, coriander, cayenne, yogurt, water, bicarbonate of soda, and salt to a smooth, thick paste. Beat the batter until it is light and foamy (this will take 15 minutes by hand or 5 minutes in a food processor). Let the batter rest for 2 hours in a warm place (omit this step if you are making the batter in the food processor).

2 To make the dumplings, heat the oil in a utensil for deep frying to 325°F/165°C. Dip the onions, potatoes, and bean curd in the batter and deep-fry until they are light golden (5–8 minutes). If you have any batter left, drop it by spoonfuls into the hot oil and deep-fry them the same way.

3 Fill a large bowl with cold water. Drop in the dumplings and let them soak for 1 minute. Drain on kitchen paper and transfer them to a bowl.

4 To make the sauce, mix yogurt, chick-pea flour, water, turmeric, coriander, and salt in a bowl and keep it ready next to the stove.

5 Measure out the spices and place them next to the stove in separate piles. Heat the oil in a large deep pot over medium-high heat. When it is hot, add fenugreek. After 5 seconds, add the cumin. When both turn dark brown (15–20 seconds), add chilies and immediately add the yogurt mixture, stirring vigorously with a whisk to prevent lumping. Bring the sauce to the boil and add the dumplings. Lower the heat and cook, uncovered, for 45 minutes, stirring often to prevent sticking. Add the tomatoes during the last 3 minutes of cooking.

6 While the sauce is cooking, pat the onions dry. Heat the same oil in deep fryer until very hot (375–400°F/190–200°C). Add sliced onion in batches and fry until it turns caramel brown. Remove and drain on kitchen paper. Set aside until needed.

7 When ready to serve, ladle into soup bowls and garnish with fried sliced onion.

Serve the dumplings with either plain cooked rice or Nirvana Special Balloon Bread (p. 310), accompanied by a yogurt drink or a fruit punch.

KASHMIR BRAHMIN VEGETARIAN KEEMA

MATAR SHUFTA

◆

Matar shufta is the famous vegetarian counterpart of *keema-matar* (in Hindi, *keema* means 'minced meat', and *matar* 'peas'). A classic dish of the Kashmiri Brahmins, known as *Kashmiri pandits*, *matar shufta* is made with a milk fudge that is spiced and fried to look like minced meat. Surprisingly, the dish bears a striking resemblance to *keema matar*. It is a rich and heavy preparation; therefore, serve it in moderate portions. If you have any Vegetarian Keema left use it to stuff vegetables as in Baked Courgettes Stuffed with Vegetarian Keema and Bulgur (p. 228).

FOR 4 PERSONS

◆

8 oz/250 g milk fudge (khoya, p. 53), or ½ pint/300 ml cottage cheese mixed with 4 tablespoons dry milk powder
3 tablespoons usli ghee (p. 57), walnut oil, or a light vegetable oil (4 tablespoons if using cottage cheese and milk powder)
2 teaspoons cumin seeds
¼ teaspoon ground asafetida
1½ tablespoons ground coriander
½ teaspoon ground cardamom
¼ teaspoon ginger powder
½ teaspoon cayenne pepper
6 tablespoons plain yogurt
6 oz/175 g cooked green peas (fresh or frozen)
¼ pint/150 ml water
2 teaspoons paprika
1 tablespoon shredded fresh ginger
2–3 hot green chilies, chopped
2–3 tablespoons fresh chopped coriander
½ teaspoon garam masala (p.77)

1 Put the milk fudge in a bowl and crumble it with your fingers.

2 Heat a heavy-bottomed pan over medium-high heat. When it is hot, add 1 tablespoon *ghee* and the milk fudge and fry, stirring constantly, until it is fried and well browned (about 3–4 minutes, 6–8 minutes for cottage cheese). If the fudge browns too fast, decrease the heat to medium or medium-low. Transfer the fried fudge grains to a bowl.

3 Measure out the spices and place them right next to the stove in separate piles. Add the remaining 2 tablespoons *ghee* to the same pan. When it is hot, add the cumin. When the cumin turns dark (about 10 seconds), add the asafetida, coriander, cardamom, ginger, and cayenne, and shake the pan for a couple of seconds. Immediately add the yogurt. Cook, stirring, until the fat begins to separate and the sauce looks thick and fried (3–5 minutes).

4 Add the browned fudge and stir to distribute the pieces evenly into the fudge. Immediately add the peas, water, paprika, ginger, and chilies, and mix again. Cook over low heat, uncovered, for 2 minutes. Turn off the heat and fold in half the chopped coriander and half the *garam masala*.

Serve sprinkled with the remaining chopped coriander and *garam masala*. For a luncheon or light supper, serve this gorgeous dish with Fennel-Scented Sweet Flaky Bread (p. 309) and a cool yogurt drink. For something more elaborate choose several side dishes to compose a meal, as just about anything goes with *matar shufta*.

VEGETABLE-PULSE-DAIRY-GRAIN COMBINATIONS

◆

FRAGRANT RICE AND MUNG BEAN WITH POTATOES AND SWEET PEPPERS

KHICHDEE

Khichdee is a creamy porridge of rice and yellow mung beans laced with turmeric and cumin butter. It is the first solid food given to an infant in India because it is mild flavoured and easy to digest. It is also the basic diet of a person at home with a cold or the flu. I love the creamy consistency and subtle flavour of this dish. If I have it at lunch, I like to add a little sautéed sweet peppers and potatoes to make it more interesting.

FOR 6–8 PERSONS

3 oz/90 g long-grain rice
6 oz/175 g yellow mung beans (moong dal)
⅛ teaspoon turmeric
2½ pints/1.5 litres water
1½ teaspoons coarse salt, or to taste
6 tablespoons usli ghee (p. 57) *or light vegetable oil*
2 medium potatoes, peeled and cut into ¼ in/5 mm pieces
2 green peppers, cored and chopped into ¼ in/5 mm pieces
1 tablespoon cumin seeds
¼ teaspoon hot red pepper powder
Paprika
Black pepper

1 Pick over the rice and beans and put in a bowl. Wash them thoroughly in several changes of water. Add them to a large pan along with ¹⁄₁₆ teaspoon turmeric and 1½ pints/800 ml of the water and bring to the boil. Reduce the heat and cook, partially covered, for 30 minutes. Stir often to make sure the mixture doesn't stick or burn. Add the remaining pint/600 ml water and continue cooking for an additional 20 minutes. Add salt to taste and turn off the heat. Cover to keep the porridge warm while you make the vegetables and the spiced butter.

2 Place a medium-size frying pan over high heat until it is very hot. Add 2 tablespoons of the *ghee* along with the potatoes and remaining turmeric. Reduce the heat to medium and turn-fry the potatoes for 3 minutes. Add the green peppers and continue frying for 3 more minutes. Lower the heat and cook, covered, for 5 minutes, or until the potatoes are soft. Turn off the heat. Transfer to a warm serving dish.

3 When you are ready to serve, transfer the porridge to a serving bowl. Wipe the frying pan clean, add the remaining *ghee*, and heat over high heat. When it is very hot, add the cumin. When the cumin turns several shades darker (about 10–15 seconds), add the red pepper and pour the entire contents all at once over the porridge. Sprinkle a little paprika and black pepper on top and serve immediately, accompanied with the potatoes and peppers.

To serve individually, put about ½ pint/300 ml *khichdee* in individual soup bowls, sprinkle a few tablespoons of fried vegetables on it, and serve. For a richer taste, spoon on a teaspoon of *usli ghee*.

RICE AND MUNG BEAN CASSEROLE
WITH CUMIN AND BLACK PEPPER

VEN PONGAL

◆

Ven pongal is the southern version of *khichdee* (opposite), except it is more like a moist pudding that is studded with fried cashew nuts, cracked black peppercorns, cumin, and ginger. The *usli ghee* folded into the *pongal* before it is served tempers the spices and imparts a very delicate aroma.

Ven pongal, although cooked in many homes nowadays, is basically a *prasadam*, meaning 'divine food' usually prepared in temples and accepted as a blessed offering from the deity. Since the Mysore Brahmins, called *Iyangar*, are the best-known chefs of this rice casserole, it only follows that the best *ven pongal* is made in the *Iyangar* temples of Lord Vishnu. My mother often made this *pongal* on Sundays for brunch, which we enjoyed with spicy-tart sauces.

Pongal means 'boiled', referring to the boiled rice. It is based upon the several-thousand-year-old tradition of celebrating the new harvest year in March or April by cooking the freshly harvested rice and chanting *'pongal-pongal'* when the rice comes to the boil.

FOR 4 PERSONS

6 *tablespoons* usli ghee (*p. 57*) or 6 *tablespoons unsalted melted butter* *mixed with a little oil*
3 oz/90 g yellow mung beans (moong dal), *picked clean*
6 oz/175 g long-grain rice
1¼ pints/700 ml water
1½ teaspoons coarse salt, or to taste
1½ teaspoons cumin seeds
1½ teaspoons cracked black peppercorns
1 tablespoon chopped fresh ginger
8 tablespoons chopped roasted cashew nuts

1 Heat 2 tablespoons of the *ghee* over medium-high heat in a large pan until it is hot (about 2 minutes). Add the mung beans and cook, stirring, for 2 minutes. Add the rice and continue cooking for 30 seconds more. Add 1¼ pints/700 ml of the water and the salt, and bring to the boil, stirring well so the rice and beans will not lump.

2 Reduce the heat to medium and cook, partially covered, for 10 minutes. Stir a couple of times just to make sure the mixture is cooking evenly. Cover the pan tightly, reduce the heat to the lowest point, and continue cooking for an additional 10 minutes. Turn off the heat.

3 Heat the remaining 4 tablespoons of *ghee* in a small frying pan.

When it is very hot, add the cumin, peppercorns, and ginger. Let the spices sizzle for 5 seconds, then immediately pour the fragrant *ghee* with all the spices over the rice-and-bean mixture. Mix carefully but thoroughly. Let the rice rest for 5 minutes before using.

Serve garnished with roasted cashew nuts and accompanied with Tomato-Onion Sauce (p. 287), or Hot and Spicy Tamarind Sauce with Peanuts (p. 286).

INDIAN CHEESE AND SWEET PEPPER PILAF

PANEER-MIRCH PULLAO

Here is a simple yet very elegant and tasty pilaf of basmati rice made with Indian cheese (*paneer*) and sweet peppers. This pilaf, fragrant with Moghul spices, is also very beautiful because of the contrast of the bright peppers against the cheese.

FOR 6 PERSONS

12 oz/375 g basmati rice
1½ pints/800 ml water
8 tablespoons light vegetable oil
Indian cheese (paneer) *made with 1½ pints/800 ml milk (p. 52)* *and cut into ½ × ½ × 1 in/1 × 1 × 2.5 cm pieces*
1½ teaspoons black (or white) cumin seeds
½ teaspoon fennel seeds
7 oz/200 g minced onion
1 teaspoon minced garlic
2 teaspoons grated or crushed fresh ginger
½ teaspoon garam masala *(p. 77)*
2 teaspoons coarse salt, or to taste
2 sweet green peppers, seeded *and cut into ½ in/1 cm thick slices*
1 sweet red pepper, seeded *and cut into ½ in/1 cm thick slices*
1 teaspoon lemon juice

1 Wash the rice in several changes of water and place it in a large bowl. Add 1½ pints/800 ml water, and let soak for 30 minutes. Drain the rice, reserving the water, and set aside.

2 While the rice is soaking, heat 5 tablespoons of the oil in a large, non-stick frying pan over medium heat. When it is hot, add the pieces of *paneer*. Keep a pot lid handy, as the moisture from the cheese may release explosively, causing tiny particles of cheese to fly all over. Fry the cheese, turning carefully, until the pieces are lightly browned (3–5 minutes). Transfer to a plate and set aside. Set aside the frying pan with the oil to sauté peppers in later.

3 Heat the remaining 3 tablespoons of the oil in a heavy-bottomed pan over medium-high heat. When it is hot, add the cumin and fennel seeds. When the spices start turning brown, add the onion and cook, stirring, until onion begins to brown (about 5 minutes). Add the garlic and ginger and fry for an additional 2 minutes.

4 Add the drained rice, the reserved water, *garam masala*, and salt; stir well and bring to the boil. Lower the heat and cook, partially covered, for 15 minutes or until most of the water is absorbed into the rice.

5 While the rice is cooking, place the frying pan with the oil in it over high heat. When the oil is hot, add the slices of green and red pepper and fry, turning them, until they look slightly cooked but are still very crisp (4–5 minutes). If the peppers start smoking, reduce the heat to medium-high or medium. Sprinkle with lemon juice. Lower the heat and keep the peppers warm while the rice is cooking.

6 Uncover the rice, add the peppers and the pieces of *paneer* along with the collected juices and oil, and fold them into the rice gently. Place the cover on tight, reduce the heat to the lowest possible level, and let the rice steam for 10 minutes, placing the pan over a wok ring or a pair of tongs. Turn off the heat and let the rice rest undisturbed and covered, for 5 minutes. Carefully transfer the pilaf to a serving platter, fluffing it as you do so.

For a simple meal serve the pilaf with a yogurt salad and relish. A good salad choice is Courgette and Yogurt Salad (p. 276). For an elaborate meal choose a side dish or vegetable that does not contain peppers and a spicy fragrant *dal* such as Banaras Yellow Lentils with Peppered Mango Slices (p. 257).

MYSORE CINNAMON-SCENTED LENTIL AND RICE CASSEROLE WITH VEGETABLES AND CASHEW NUTS

BESE BELE OLIANNA

◆

Bese bele olianna is the famous vegetarian speciality from Bangalore. The dish contains innumerable ingredients – vegetables, nuts, seasoning, lentils, beans – all of which are cooked with even more spices, herbs, and flavourings. During the cooking *bese bele* acquires an intriguing flavour that is hard to analyse or describe. Its characteristic taste is special *masala*, which has a pronounced cinnamon and clove aroma.

FOR 6–8 PERSONS

◆

1½ in/4 cm round ball tamarind pulp
½ pint/300 ml boiling water
4 medium onions
3 medium potatoes
8 oz/250 g aubergine
6 fl oz/175 ml usli ghee (p. 57) or unsalted butter
3 oz/90 g raw cashew nuts, broken into bits
3 oz/90 g cut green beans
3 oz/90 g green peas, fresh or frozen
¼ pint/150 ml water
6 oz/175 g cooked yellow lentils (p. 254)
2 teaspoons coarse salt, or to taste
12 oz/375 g long-grain rice, cooked
5 tablespoons bese bele *Powder* (p. 76)
2 teaspoons black mustard seeds
1 tablespoon yellow split peas (channa dal)
1 tablespoon white split gram beans (urad dal)
3 in/8 cm stick cinnamon
2 dry red chilies, broken into pieces

2 hot green chilies, slit and seeded
12 curry (kari) leaves (fresh or dry, optional)
Usli ghee for garnish, if needed
Lemon wedges for garnish

1 Put the tamarind pulp in a small bowl, add ½ pint/300 ml boiling water, and let it soak for 15 minutes. Mash the pulp, using a spoon or your fingers. Strain the liquid into another small bowl, squeezing the pulp as much as possible, and set aside. Discard the fibrous residue.

2 Peel and slice the onions. Cut the potatoes, with their skins on, into halves lengthways. Cut the aubergine, with its skin, into ½ in/1 cm thick 1 in by 2 in/2.5 by 5 cm slices. Put the potatoes and the aubergine in a bowl of water. Set aside.

3 Measure out the spices and place them next to the stove in separate piles. Heat 2 tablespoons of the *ghee* in a pan until hot. Add the cashew nuts and sauté over medium heat until they are barely coloured (3–4 minutes). Transfer with a slotted spoon to a bowl and set aside to be used later as a garnish.

4 Add 4 more tablespoons of the *ghee* to the pan. Add the onions, the thoroughly drained potatoes and aubergine, and the green beans and peas. Over medium-high heat lightly brown the vegetables, turning them constantly (about 6–8 minutes). Add ¼ pint/150 ml water. Lower the heat and cook the vegetables, covered, until barely done (5 minutes). Uncover, add the tamarind liquid and the cooked lentils, mix well, and continue cooking, partially covered, for 10 minutes. If necessary, add a little water if the lentils become too thick and stick to the bottom of the pan. Stir in a little salt to taste.

5 Add the rice and the *bese bele* powder. Gently fold to distribute the spice powder and rice evenly in the lentil-vegetable mixture. Reduce the heat to the lowest point and keep the dish steaming while you make the spiced butter.

6 Heat 3 tablespoons of the *ghee* in a small frying pan over medium heat. When it is hot, add the mustard seeds. Keep a lid handy, as the seeds when added may fly all over. When the splattering subsides a little, add the split peas. When the peas begin to change colour, add the gram beans and cinnamon. When both peas and beans look light brown (about 3 minutes), add the red chilies and let sizzle for 15–30 seconds. Add the green chilies and curry leaves, take the pan off the fire, and let them sizzle for 15–20 seconds; then pour the entire contents of the pan over the rice mixture. Add the remaining *usli ghee* and as much additional salt as you find necessary, and gently fold the mixture in, as you would fold in egg whites.

7 Cover tightly with a lid (for a better airtight seal, place a sheet of foil over the pan before the lid). Reduce the heat to the lowest point and raise the pan off the burners slightly (this can be done either by using a wok ring or a pair of metal tongs). Let the *bese bele* steam for 10 minutes, and then turn off the heat. Let it rest for 5 minutes, undisturbed. If the rice has become too thick and dry, fold in a little water. The *bese bele* should have a creamy consistency.

Serve *bese bele* garnished with fried cashew nuts and lemon wedges. If desired, you can pour a little more *usli ghee* over it.

JAIN CORIANDER-SCENTED MILLET AND MUNG BEAN PILAF

AHMADABAD JAIN PULLAO

◆

The Jains in Ahmadabad cook with several other grains besides rice and wheat. This millet pilaf is one example. It is made with sweet spices and vegetables, very much the way an authentic rice pilaf is prepared. Millet pilaf is heat-producing, therefore you won't want to eat much of it during the summer. It is a meal in itself and needs no accompaniment. You may, however, serve a vegetable or yogurt salad with it.

FOR 6 PERSONS

◆

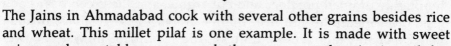

3 oz/90 g whole mung beans (sabat moong)
6 oz/175 g millet
2 bay leaves
6 tablespoons usli ghee (p. 57), or light vegetable oil
1½ teaspoons mustard seeds
1½ teaspoons cumin seeds

2 medium-size onions, chopped
4 hot green chilies, chopped
1 tablespoon finely chopped fresh ginger
1 teaspoon ground cumin
2 teaspoons ground coriander
¼ teaspoon turmeric
Juice of 1 lemon
1½ teaspoons coarse salt, or to taste
½ pint/300 ml water
1½ teaspoons Gujarati garam masala (p. 79) or garam masala (p. 77)
4 tablespoons chopped fresh coriander
1 medium cucumber, peeled and sliced
1 large tomato, sliced

1 Pick clean the mung beans and put in a bowl, add enough water to cover by at least 2 in/5 cm, and soak for 8 hours or overnight. Drain, rinse the beans thoroughly, drain again, and set aside.

2 Measure out the spices and place them right next to the stove in separate piles. Place the millet, bay leaves, and 2 tablespoons of the *ghee* in a large pan over high heat for 2 minutes. Reduce the heat to medium and fry the millet, stirring, for 5 minutes or until it is light golden. Put the cooked millet in a bowl and set aside.

3 Add the remaining 4 tablespoons of *ghee* to the pan and increase the heat to medium-high. When the *ghee* is very hot, add the mustard and cumin seeds. Keep the lid handy, as the seeds may spatter. When the spattering subsides, add the onions, chilies, and ginger and cook, stirring, for 6 minutes or until the onions are lightly browned. Add the ground cumin, coriander, and turmeric. Mix well and continue frying for another minute.

4 Add the reserved millet, the drained beans, the lemon juice, and the salt, and mix thoroughly. Add ½ pint/300 ml water, and bring to the boil. Lower the heat and cook, covered, for 30 minutes or until the beans and millet are cooked but still firm to the bite.

5 Transfer the mixture to a heated serving platter, sprinkle with Gujarati *garam masala* or *garam masala* and with chopped coriander. Serve garnished with slices of cucumber and tomato.

BAKED COURGETTES STUFFED WITH VEGETARIAN KEEMA AND BULGUR

BHARA HARA KADDOO

◆

This is another meat-lookalike created with Kashmiri vegetarian *keema*. The mock meat is combined with cracked wheat and stuffed into courgette halves and then baked. The cracked wheat, in addition to providing important nutrients and a marvellous texture, acts as a sponge to absorb the excess moisture in the courgettes.

FOR 4 PERSONS

◆

4 medium tender young courgettes, each about 5–6 in/12.5–15 cm long
1 tablespoon light vegetable oil
3 oz/90 g onion, finely chopped
4 oz/125 g fine-grain bulgur
1 recipe Kashmir Brahmin Vegetarian Keema (p. 216)
1 recipe Tomato-Coriander Sauce (p. 184)

1 Preheat the oven to 350° F/180° C/Gas 4.
2 Wash the courgettes thoroughly and cut neatly into halves length-wise. Using a spoon, scrape out the centres, leaving shells ¼ in/5 mm thick. Chop the scraped courgette flesh finely.
3 Mix the oil, onion, bulgur, vegetarian *keema*, and the chopped courgettes. Stuff the courgette shells with the mixture. Place the stuffed courgette halves in a baking dish that will hold them in one layer snugly. Cover tightly with foil.
4 Bake in the middle of the preheated oven for 40–45 minutes. Remove and serve accompanied with sauce.

This lovely dish is substantial enough to be served as a luncheon or light supper accompanied with any bread or a simple rice pilaf.

SIDE
DISHES

An Indian meal always includes several side dishes consisting of cooked vegetables, pulses, raw vegetables, and a yogurt preparation. The logic of this composition is to provide one's body with the perfect balance of protein, carbohydrates, minerals, and vitamins all at the same time, so that they can combine, interact, and be absorbed by the body in the most nutritional way possible.

Side dishes of vegetables are usually simple preparations. For a light meal one or more of these side-dish vegetables can be served in place of a main-dish preparation. The seasonings and cooking techniques used to make them vary from region to region. The most common technique is called turn-frying (or stir-frying), or *bhonao* in Hindi, in which the vegetable pieces are constantly turned in the pan with a slotted spoon until they are cooked and fried.

Spicily perfumed pulse purées called *dal* always accompany an Indian vegetarian meal to provide protein, calories, and, most important, the necessary moisture and sauce needed in the meal.

Vegetable salads are another important feature of an Indian vegetarian meal. They are called by different names in different parts of India. In Maharashtra, for example, they are called *kosumbara* and are always eaten as a first course before the rest of the meal.

Indian yogurt salads are in a class by themselves. There is no equivalent of these wonderful preparations in any part of the world. They are made by combining yogurt with fruits, nuts, or vegetables (raw, boiled, roasted, or smoked) and then seasoning them with spices and herbs. In the northern regions of India yogurt salad is known as *raita* and is usually laced with roasted spices, while in the southern regions it is called *pachadi* and flavoured with a spicy oil dressing. Many of these yogurt salads are so delicious I often make a light meal of them accompanied by a bowl of rice or a loaf of bread.

VEGETABLES

♦

CURRIED AVOCADO WITH GINGER AND GREEN CHILIES

AVCADOO MASIAL

♦

The Moslems in Malabar are called *moplas,* meaning 'sons-in-law' or 'the honoured ones.' This is because they are the descendants of the Arab settlers who came to India four hundred years ago, married the local girls, and stayed. The *moplas* love avocado, particularly in this spicy salad. It is generally enjoyed in its own right or with their famous rice flour bread. *Avcadoo masial* should be served with a southern meal as a side dish.

FOR 4 PERSONS

♦

1 large ripe avocado
Juice of 1 lime or 1 small lemon
4 tablespoons finely chopped fresh coriander
8 curry (kari) leaves (fresh or dry, optional)
Coarse salt, to taste
FOR THE SPICED BUTTER:
1 tablespoon coconut oil, light sesame oil, or light vegetable oil
1 teaspoon black mustard seeds
1 teaspoon minced garlic
3 oz/90 g chopped onion
½ teaspoon Curry Powder Master Recipe (p. 73)
2–4 hot green chilies, minced

1 Cut the avocado in half. Remove the stone and scoop out the pulp with a spoon. Chop the pulp roughly. Blend in the lime juice, coriander, curry leaves, and salt. Set aside.

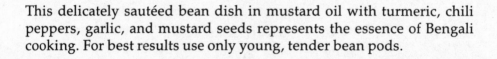

2 Heat the oil in a small frying pan over medium-high heat. When it is hot, add the mustard seeds. Keep a lid handy, as the seeds may spatter and fly all over. When the spattering stops, add the garlic and let sizzle for 5 seconds. Add the onion and cook, stirring, until limp (about 3 minutes). Add the curry powder and chilies, mix, and continue cooking for 1 more minute. Add the avocado mixture and turn off the heat. Stir to mix all the ingredients. Serve at room temperature.

BENGALI GREEN BEANS AND POTATOES SMOTHERED IN MUSTARD OIL

BANGLA ALOO SEM

◆

This delicately sautéed bean dish in mustard oil with turmeric, chili peppers, garlic, and mustard seeds represents the essence of Bengali cooking. For best results use only young, tender bean pods.

FOR 4 PERSONS

◆

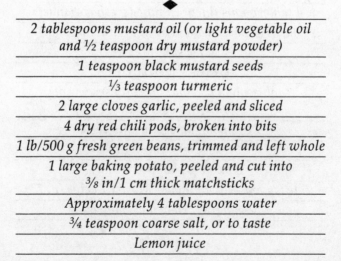

2 tablespoons mustard oil (or light vegetable oil and ½ teaspoon dry mustard powder)
1 teaspoon black mustard seeds
⅓ teaspoon turmeric
2 large cloves garlic, peeled and sliced
4 dry red chili pods, broken into bits
1 lb/500 g fresh green beans, trimmed and left whole
1 large baking potato, peeled and cut into ⅜ in/1 cm thick matchsticks
Approximately 4 tablespoons water
¾ teaspoon coarse salt, or to taste
Lemon juice

1 Put the mustard oil in a heavy frying pan and heat to smoking. Turn off the heat and let the oil cool briefly. (Omit this step if you are using light vegetable oil. Do not add mustard powder yet.)

2 Measure out the spices and place them next to the stove in separate piles. Heat the oil again over medium-high heat. When it is hot, add the mustard seeds. Keep a lid handy, as the seeds may spatter and fly all over. When the spattering subsides, add the turmeric, garlic, and chili bits and fry, shaking the pan, until the garlic turns light golden (about 20–30 seconds).

3 Add the beans and potatoes. Let the vegetables sizzle undisturbed for 1 minute (if necessary reduce the heat to medium). Fry the vegetables, turning them, for 5 minutes. Add about 4 tablespoons water along with the salt. If you are using light vegetable oil, add the mustard powder now and mix well. Reduce the heat to low or medium-low and cook, covered, until the vegetables are thoroughly cooked (about 25 minutes). There will be a little liquid left in the pan. Uncover and continue cooking, turning and tossing the vegetables until they look dry and glazed (3–4 minutes). If necessary increase the heat a little. Turn off the heat. Sprinkle on a little lemon juice (about 1–2 teaspoons) to taste.

NOTE: For a milder dish, discard the seeds of the chili pods.

These beans are delicious, even cold as a salad. Although cooked in the authentic Bengali style, the beans go well with any northern or western Indian menu. To maintain the Bengali flavour serve Bengal Red Lentils with Spices (p. 258) accompanied by plain cooked rice, or Nirvana Special Balloon Bread (p. 310).

SPICY YARD BEANS WITH CHICK-PEA MORSELS

BESAN KI BHAJI

◆

This is yet another technique of cooking with *dal*. Here chick-pea flour is moistened and treated like a vegetable. In Kanauj in the north of India, the tender green pods of black-eyed beans, called yard long beans, are cooked with a highly spiced chick-pea flour to produce this unusual speciality. The contrast of sweet and crunchy beans against the spicy, dumpling like chick-pea morsels is sensational.

FOR 6 PERSONS

◆

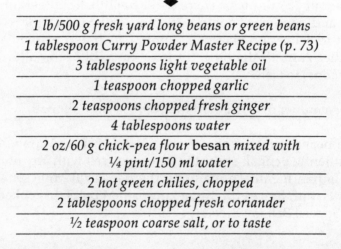

1 lb/500 g fresh yard long beans or green beans
1 tablespoon Curry Powder Master Recipe (p. 73)
3 tablespoons light vegetable oil
1 teaspoon chopped garlic
2 teaspoons chopped fresh ginger
4 tablespoons water
2 oz/60 g chick-pea flour besan mixed with ¼ pint/150 ml water
2 hot green chilies, chopped
2 tablespoons chopped fresh coriander
½ teaspoon coarse salt, or to taste

1 Trim the beans and cut into ¼ in/5 mm pieces. Sprinkle over them the curry powder and toss to coat the beans well. Set aside.

2 Measure out the spices and place them right next to the stove in separate piles. Heat the oil in a pan over medium-high heat for 2 minutes. Add the garlic and ginger and let sizzle for 30 seconds or until they begin to brown and flavour the oil. Add the beans and fry, turning and tossing, for 5 minutes. Add 4 tablespoons water, lower the heat and cook, covered, for 15 minutes or until the beans are cooked.

3 Uncover, stir the beans, and pour onto them the chick-pea flour solution along with the chilies and coriander. Do not stir; let the batter cook (about 1 minute), until it resembles a thick custard.

4 Continue to fry, gently turning the mixture, for 5 minutes. The chick-pea mixture will become little morsels of dough and scatter among the beans. Serve hot or warm with southern stews such as Tanjore Broccoli and Mung Bean Stew with Coconut (p. 190).

BEETROOT SMOTHERED WITH BEET GREENS

CHUKANDAR SAAG SABZI

Indians hate to throw away any ingredient that can be put to good use. It is therefore not unusual for an Indian cook to chop an entire bunch of beetroot complete with their greens and cook them together. In this recipe sweet tender beetroot slices are cooked in the moisture of their succulent greens. The dish is flavoured in the Central Province style, with aromatic groundnut oil, mustard, and cumin seeds.

FOR 4 PERSONS

1 large bunch beetroot with their greens
5 tablespoons groundnut oil
1 teaspoon black mustard seeds
1 tablespoon ground coriander
¼ teaspoon ground fenugreek
¼ teaspoon turmeric
½ teaspoon cayenne pepper
8 oz/250 g minced onion
1 tablespoon grated or crushed fresh ginger
1 teaspoon coarse salt, or to taste
1 teaspoon roasted cumin seeds, crushed

1 Cut off the stalks and leaves from the beetroot bunch. Chop the leaves and discard the stalks. Peel the beetroot and cut into ⅛ in/3 mm thick slices.

2 Measure out the spices and place them next to the stove in separate piles. Heat the oil in a large pan over high heat. When the oil is hot, add the mustard seeds. Keep a lid handy, as the seeds may fly all over. When the seeds stop spattering, add the coriander, fenugreek, turmeric, and cayenne and follow at once with the onion. Fry until the onion begins to turn light brown (about 6 minutes), stirring constantly.

3 Add the beetroot along with the greens and continue to cook, turning the vegetables until the greens are wilted. Stir in the ginger gently and cook, covered, over low heat for 20 minutes. Uncover, add salt to taste, and continue cooking until most of the liquid in the pan has evaporated and the beetroot looks glazed. Stir in the cumin gently.

Serve warm, at room temperature, or cold.

Variation: For Cauliflower Smothered with Cauliflower Greens (*Gobhi Sabzi*), substitute 1 small cauliflower (with all the greens attached) for the beetroot and greens. Also, before serving, sprinkle with chopped fresh coriander.

TURN-FRIED BITTER GOURD AND MIXED VEGETABLES IN MUSTARD SAUCE

SHOKHTO

An authentically traditional Bengal meal always begins with *shokhto*, a mixed vegetable preparation containing bitter gourd. The Bengalis consider bitter gourd essential for the health of mind and soul, because of its great medicinal value and its bitter taste. It is also definitely good on the palate.

FOR 4 PERSONS

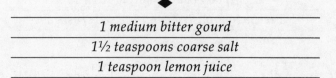

1 medium bitter gourd
1½ teaspoons coarse salt
1 teaspoon lemon juice

¼ teaspoon turmeric
1 lb/500 g raw vegetables (see Note) peeled and cut into small cubes or thin slices
3 tablespoons mustard oil (or 3 tablespoons light vegetable oil and ½ teaspoon dry mustard powder)
1 teaspoon panch phoron (p. 82)
2 bay leaves
2 dry red chili pods
1 tablespoon chopped fresh ginger
⅓ teaspoon turmeric
4 tablespoons water
1 teaspoon sugar
¾ teaspoon coarse salt, or to taste
1½ teaspoons dry mustard mixed with 2 tablespoons water

NOTE: A combination of green banana, green beans, potatoes, broccoli, carrot, aubergine, turnip, radish, and green peas works well.

1 Cut the bitter gourd in half and scrape out the pips and fibrous centre. Cut into slices ½ in/1 cm thick. Mix the salt, lemon juice, and turmeric in a bowl. Add the bitter gourd slices and toss well. Let them soak in the lemon-turmeric mixture for a minimum of 1 hour; 4 hours are ideal. Then squeeze the gourd pieces to extract as much juice as possible. Be careful not to squeeze too hard or you may crush the bitter gourd. Rinse thoroughly and drain. Set aside. This step is essential: It rids the gourd of its bitterness.

2 Put the prepared vegetables and bitter gourd in a bowl. Measure out the spices and place them next to the stove. Heat the oil in a large heavy pan until it smokes. Turn off the heat and let the oil cool a little. (Omit this step if you are not using mustard oil. Do not add mustard powder yet.)

3 Heat the oil again over medium-high heat until it is very hot. Turn off the heat and add the *panch phoron* spices. When the spices turn several shades darker and release their aroma (about 15 seconds), add the bay leaves and chili pods and turn the heat to medium-high. When the bay leaves look a little brown (about 15 seconds), add the ginger, turmeric, and vegetables. Turn-fry the vegetables for 5 minutes. Add 4 tablespoons water along with the sugar, salt, and ½ teaspoon dry mustard (if you are using light vegetable oil) and blend well. Lower the heat and cook, covered, for 20 minutes or until the vegetables are cooked but still hold their shape. Uncover, raise the heat, and continue cooking, turning the vegetables until they look fried and glazed.

4 Pour in the mustard paste mixture and cook for 2 more minutes.

Follow the menu suggestions given for Bengal Green Beans and Potato Smothered in Mustard Oil (p. 232).

BITTER GOURD WITH SPICY ONION STUFFING

BHARA KARELA

◆

Bitter gourd filled with a fennel-and-fenugreek-scented spicy onion stuffing exemplifies the classic garlic-free cooking of the northern Brahmins. The bitter gourds are first tempered by soaking in a turmeric, lemon juice, and salt mixture, then cooked and squeezed to extract their bitter juice.

FOR 4 PERSONS

◆

1 lb/500 g tender young bitter gourds (about 4)
4½ teaspoons coarse salt
1 tablespoon lemon juice
¾ teaspoon turmeric
SPICE MIXTURE FOR FILLING:
1 tablespoon fennel seeds
1 tablespoon coriander seeds
1½ teaspoons cumin seeds
¾ teaspoon fenugreek seeds
½ teaspoon mango powder
½ teaspoon coarse salt

| ½ teaspoon cayenne pepper (optional) |
| 4 tablespoons light vegetable oil |
| 8 oz/250 g onion, finely chopped |

1 Peel the outer rough skin of the bitter gourds. Make a slit all the way along the length of each. Mix the salt, lemon juice, and turmeric in a small bowl and rub this mixture inside the cavities of the gourds. Let them soak for 8 hours or overnight. Drain well, squeezing very lightly. Put the gourds in a large saucepan, add enough water to cover, and bring to the boil. Cook, uncovered, for 6 minutes or until they are tender. Drain and squeeze again. Set aside.

2 Measure out the spices and place them next to the stove in separate piles. Heat a frying pan about 9–12 in/20–30 cm in diameter over high heat until very hot. Add the fennel, coriander, cumin, and fenugreek and dry-roast, shaking the pan, until they release their aroma and look a few shades darker (about 3 minutes). Transfer to a plate and cool thoroughly. Using a spice or coffee grinder, grind them to a powder. Blend in the mango powder, salt, and cayenne.

3 Heat 3 tablespoons of the oil in the same frying pan and add the onion. Over high heat fry the onion, stirring constantly, for 7 minutes or until lightly coloured. Turn off the heat and blend in the spice mixture. Transfer the mixture to a bowl.

4 Stuff the bitter gourds with the spicy onion mixture, distributing it evenly. Secure the stuffed gourds by wrapping each one with kitchen string (this will ensure that the filling will not fall out during the next step).

5 Heat the remaining tablespoon of oil in the same frying pan over high heat for 1–2 minutes. Add the stuffed bitter gourds and fry, turning them often, for 4 minutes or until they are heated through and begin to brown. Reduce the heat to medium and continue frying, turning, until nicely browned all over (about 8 minutes). Remove the string and discard. If desired, slice into neat rounds before serving.

Variation: For Bitter Gourd with Fragrant Potato Stuffing (*Bhara Karela Aloo*), use potatoes in place of onions. This dish is popular because many Hindu Brahmins, particularly in the holy cities of Banaras, Allahabad, and Haradwar, are forbidden to include onions in their diet. Follow the recipe as given, except substitute 2 medium potatoes (about 8 oz/250 g), boiled, peeled, and coarsely mashed, for the onion, and omit the fennel seeds.

AUBERGINE AND POTATOES LACED WITH FENUGREEK

ALOO BAIGAN

◆

Aubergine and potatoes are a popular combination throughout northern India. They can be spiced Moghul-style (as is done in Indian restaurants) or with regional flavourings. My favourite is a version from the eastern extremities of the Northern Province near Nepal, in which the vegetables are first fried to develop a roasted flavour and then steamed in their own moisture. Cayenne pepper, fenugreek, and tart mango powder bring out the essence of that region's cooking.

FOR 4 PERSONS

◆

1 lb/500 g aubergines
1 lb/500 g potatoes
¾ teaspoon turmeric
1½ tablespoons ground coriander
½–1 teaspoon cayenne pepper
1½ teaspoons coarse salt
4 tablespoons light vegetable oil
¾ teaspoon fenugreek seeds
1 teaspoon mango powder

1 Cut the aubergines, unpeeled, into 1 in/2.5 cm pieces or cubes. Peel the potatoes and cut them into 1 in/2.5 cm cubes. Put the vegetables in a bowl. Sprinkle on the turmeric, coriander, cayenne, and salt, and mix well to coat evenly with the spices.

2 Heat the oil in a large pan over high heat for 3 minutes. Add the fenugreek and fry until it turns dark brown (10–15 seconds). Add the vegetables, shake the pan a few times, and let the vegetables sizzle undisturbed for 1–2 minutes. Fry the vegetables, turning them, for 5 minutes or until the spices start clinging to the vegetables and the aubergine looks limp and begins to steam. Lower the heat and cook, covered, for 20 minutes, turning the vegetables often to ensure that they are cooking evenly. Be careful not to break the fragile pieces of vegetables. Sprinkle on the mango powder and fry uncovered, turning them regularly, for 5 minutes or until they look glazed. Serve warm or at room temperature.

Aloo baigan can be served with any meal as long as it doesn't contain potatoes or aubergine. I love it by itself with Nirvana Special Balloon Bread (p. 310) and Punjab Five-Jewel Creamed Lentils (p. 266).

SPICY AUBERGINE IN GINGER-TAMARIND SAUCE

MASALA VANGI

◆

The classic speciality of the Maharashtrians from Bombay is made by braising aubergines that have been coated with cinnamon, cloves, and coconut in a sweetish-sour tamarind sauce. The recipe calls for the long thin aubergines available in Asian greengrocers. In India these aubergines are picked when very tender and young, hardly 4–5 in/10–13 cm long, and ½–¾ in/1–2 cm in diameter. They are sweet, flavourful, and seedless. Small baby aubergines (1½ in/4 cm–2 in/5 cm long) make excellent substitutes. They are practically seedless and needn't be secured with string since they are so tiny.

FOR 4–6 PERSONS

◆

½ in/1 cm round ball tamarind
4 tablespoons boiling water
1 lb/500 g thin, long aubergines or 9–10 baby aubergines
3 tablespoons light vegetable oil
1½ teaspoons minced garlic
2 teaspoons ground coriander
¼ teaspoon ground cinnamon
⅛ teaspoon ground cloves
2 oz/60 g coconut (fresh or tinned, unsweetened)
1–2 teaspoons cayenne pepper
½ teaspoon coarse salt, or to taste
2 tablespoons molasses or brown sugar
½ teaspoon black mustard seeds
Ginger-Tamarind Sauce (recipe follows)

1 Put the tamarind in a nonmetallic bowl. Add 4 tablespoons boiling water and let it soak for 30 minutes. Mash the pulp using a spoon or your fingers. Strain the liquid into another small bowl, squeezing the pulp as much as possible. Save the fibrous residue for making the sauce.

2 Slit the aubergines lengthways to within ¾ in/2 cm of the stem end so that each aubergine remains in one piece.

3 Measure out the spices and place them next to the stove in separate piles. Heat 2 tablespoons of the oil in a large frying pan over medium-high heat for 1 minute. Add the garlic and fry for 30 seconds. Add the coriander, cinnamon, and cloves; fry for 15 more seconds. Stir in the coconut and cayenne, continue frying, stirring, until lightly toasted (about 20 minutes). Turn off the heat and stir in the salt, tamarind liquid, and molasses, and mix well.

4 Stuff the aubergines with the spicy coconut mixture. Secure them by tying with string.

5 Heat the remaining 1 tablespoon oil in the same pan over medium-high heat. When it is hot, add mustard seeds. Keep a lid handy, as the seeds may spatter and fly all over. When the seeds stop spattering, add the aubergines in one layer. Fry the aubergines, turning them often, for 3–4 minutes. Reduce heat to medium or medium-low and cook them, covered, for 10–12 minutes or until they are soft and cooked through. Turn off heat. Transfer them to a serving platter, pour Ginger-Tamarind Sauce over them, and serve immediately.

GINGER-TAMARIND SAUCE

◆

Tamarind residue from recipe
¼ pint/150 ml boiling water
½ teaspoon cornflour
1 tablespoon shredded fresh ginger

1 Put tamarind residue in a nometallic bowl, add ¼ pint/150 ml boiling water, and let soak for 30 minutes. Mash the residue using a spoon or your fingers. Strain the liquid into another small bowl, squeezing the pulp as much as possible. Discard the fibrous residue.

2 Put tamarind water in a nonmetallic pan along with cornflour; mix well and bring to the boil. Cook for 2 minutes. Turn off heat and stir in ginger shreds.

NOTE: For a hotter flavour, stir 4 chopped hot green chilies into sauce.

SPICY MUSHROOMS WITH GINGER AND CHILIES

KHOMBI TARKARI

Northern Indians, particularly those along the lower slopes of the Himalayan Mountains, adore mushrooms. They sauté them with spices, stew them in tomato sauces, or add them to pilaf. In this recipe the mushrooms are sautéed in a spicy onion-garlic-ginger paste. Roasted cumin and fresh coriander are added to impart a refreshing flavour. I love this dish cold as an appetizer with drinks, or wrapped in a bread as a snack, or folded into a simple Tomato Pilaf (p. 326) for a light supper. Of course, the mushrooms are also good by themselves as a side dish.

Fresh morels or chanterelles can be cooked the same way.

FOR 4 PERSONS

3 tablespoons groundnut oil
6 oz/175 g chopped onion
1 tablespoon chopped fresh ginger
2 teaspoons finely chopped garlic
2 hot green chilies, minced
¼ teaspoon turmeric
1½ lb/750 g mushrooms, cleaned and cut into 1 in/2.5 cm pieces
½ teaspoon coarse salt, or to taste
1 teaspoon roasted cumin seeds, crushed
1 teaspoon lemon juice
2 tablespoons chopped fresh coriander, for garnish

1 Measure out the spices and place them right next to the stove in separate piles. Heat the oil in a *kadhai*, wok, or large frying pan over medium-high heat for 3 minutes. Add the onion and cook, stirring, for 3 minutes. Add the ginger, garlic, and chilies, and cook for 2 more minutes.

2 Add the turmeric, mushrooms, and salt. Cook, turning them, until all the moisture released by the mushrooms evaporates and the mushrooms begin to fry (about 15 minutes). Lower the heat, sprinkle on the cumin and the lemon juice, mix well, and continue cooking until the mushrooms absorb the lemon juice and look fried (about 5 minutes). Turn off the heat and serve warm, at room temperature, or cold, sprinkled with chopped fresh coriander.

FRAGRANT BUTTER-LACED PURÉED MUSTARD GREENS

SARSOON KA SAAG

◆

Every community in the world has a basic food that it refers to as its soul food. For the Punjabi Sikhs of Amritsar, the home of the Golden Temple, it is mustard greens cooked to a velvety purée and laced with ginger shreds, garlic slivers, and unsalted butter. The classic recipe for this dish calls for a mixture of mustard greens and a green called *bathua*, which acts as a binder for the sauce in addition to lending a marvellous flavour. *Bathua* is hard to find; therefore you may substitute spinach in its place.

FOR 6 PERSONS

◆

1¼–1½ lb/625–750 g fresh mustard greens
1 lb/500 g fresh spinach greens or one 10 oz/300 g packet frozen leaf spinach
4 oz/125 g fresh fenugreek leaves, or 3 tablespoons dry fenugreek leaves (kasoori methi)
4 tablespoons cornmeal (preferably yellow)
2 hot green chilies, chopped
½ teaspoon asafetida, or 2 oz/60 g minced onion
1 pint/600 ml water
1 medium sweet green pepper, seeded, and chopped
2 teaspoons cornflour dissolved in 2 tablespoons water
1¼ teaspoons coarse salt, or to taste
4–6 tablespoons usli ghee (p. 57) or unsalted butter
4 tablespoons shredded or sliced fresh ginger
2–4 tablespoons thickly sliced garlic

1 Snip the stems off the tender leaves of both the mustard and spinach greens. For more mature spinach leaves, fold the leaf vertically along the stalk and with one hand pull away the stalk, including the portion attached to the leaf's underside.

2 Rinse the mustard greens, spinach, and fenugreek in several changes of water until all the sand has been washed away. Chop the greens coarsely.

3 Put the cornmeal, chilies, asafetida, and 1 pint/600 ml water in a deep pot and bring to the boil. Add the chopped greens, or, if you are using frozen and dried greens, add them now. Add the green pepper and cook, stirring, until the greens have wilted and the liquid comes to the boil. Lower the heat and cook at a low simmer, covered, for 1 hour, or until the greens are thoroughly cooked. When the greens are slightly cool, purée them in batches, using a blender or food processor, until smooth and creamy.

4 Return the purée to the same pot, add the cornflour mixture, and cook over low heat until thickened and smooth (6–10 minutes). Add salt to taste, and keep the purée on a low simmer while you make the spice-perfumed butter.

5 Heat the *ghee* or butter in a small frying pan until hot. Reduce the heat to medium-low and add the ginger and garlic and let cook, sizzling, for 3 minutes or until the seasonings begin to brown. Turn off the heat.

Transfer the purée to a large shallow serving dish and gently pour the butter with the ginger and garlic over it. Stir just a few times to lace the purée with butter in streaks.

DRY-FRIED POINTED GOURD
WITH CORIANDER

KONDROO SABZI

Pointed gourd, called *kondroo* or *tindola*, a delicacy in northern India, is wonderful stir-fried or stewed in a spicy sauce, both of which I enjoyed as a child. This recipe demonstrates the way it is prepared in my mother's home in New Delhi. If you cannot get fresh pointed gourd, the tinned variety is a decent substitute. Serve with a simple flaky bread (p. 309) or Rice and Mung Bean Casserole with Cumin and Black Pepper (p. 219).

FOR 3–4 PERSONS

◆

1½ lb/750 g fresh kondroo (tindola) *or* two 14 oz/425 g tins
2–3 tablespoons light vegetable oil
¼ teaspoon turmeric
¼ teaspoon cayenne pepper
2 teaspoons ground coriander
Coarse salt to taste, if desired

1 Cut fresh *kondroo* into quarters, lengthwise. If you are using tinned, drain the *kondroo* halves (there should be 8–12 pieces in a tin) and rinse thoroughly in several changes of water. Drain, squeezing lightly to remove excess water, and cut in half lengthwise.

2 Heat the oil in a large frying pan for 2 minutes over high heat. Reduce the heat to medium and add all the spices. Immediately add the sliced *kondroo*, toss well to coat them with spices, and fry for 3 minutes or until lightly browned.

3 Reduce the heat to medium-low and cook the vegetables covered for 10–12 minutes, turning them often. Uncover and fry *kondroo* until most of the moisture evaporates and the vegetables look fried and slightly shrivelled (5–8 minutes). The flavour of the *kondroo* will come out only when it is well fried. Add salt if desired.

SPICY CURRIED POTATOES

OORLA-KAYANGA KARI

◆

From south India, here is the simplest of recipes for preparing curry *(kari)* of potatoes. All you need is boiled potatoes and a generous amount of good curry powder. For authentic flavour use Indian sesame or coconut oil.

FOR 6 PERSONS

◆

2 lb/1 kg boiling potatoes
2 tablespoons Curry Powder Master Recipe (homemade, p. 73, or bought)
3–4 teaspoons light sesame oil, coconut oil, or light vegetable oil
Coarse salt, to taste

1 Boil the potatoes in their jackets in water to cover until tender but firm. Drain and peel them. Cut the potatoes into slices 1½ in/4 cm thick and put them in a bowl. Sprinkle the curry powder over the potatoes while they are still warm. Sprinkle 3–4 tablespoons water over them and toss carefully to coat potato pieces evenly with the spice mixture. Set aside for 15 minutes to allow the potatoes to cool.

2 Heat the oil in a *kadhai* or large frying pan over high heat for 2 minutes. Add the potatoes and sprinkle on salt to taste. Reduce heat to medium to medium-high and fry the potatoes, turning them until nicely browned (12–15 minutes). The potatoes will develop a crisp crust when brown. Serve warm, at room temperature, or cold.

TINY NEW POTATOES SMOTHERED IN FENUGREEK LEAVES

METHI ALOO

◆

A classic dish from New Delhi and popular throughout the north, *methi aloo* is made with potatoes as tiny as cranberries. The potatoes are cooked in the vapour of the fenugreek greens, which are wilted in black-pepper-laced unsalted butter. These beautifully flavoured potatoes are best enjoyed with a simple bread or Rice and Mung Bean Casserole with Cumin and Black Pepper (p. 219).

FOR 4 PERSONS

1 lb/500 g tiny new potatoes or small red wax potatoes, cut into halves, unpeeled
¼–½ lb/125–250 g fresh fenugreek leaves, or 2 tablespoons dry fenugreek leaves (**kasoori methi***)*
4–6 tablespoons unsalted butter
½ teaspoon black pepper
½ teaspoon garam masala *(p. 77)*
½ teaspoon mango powder or 1½ teaspoons lemon juice
Coarse salt, to taste

1 Scrub the potatoes clean under cold running water. Drain. Wash the fresh fenugreek leaves in several changes of water, drain, and finely chop them.

2 Heat 2 tablespoons of the butter in a pan until melted. Add the potatoes and gently fry them over medium-high heat for 5–6 minutes or until they look lightly fried and their skins begin to shrivel. Add the chopped fenugreek and continue cooking for 3 more minutes or until the greens look wilted and limp. Sprinkle on the black pepper, add the remaining butter, and mix well.

3 Lower the heat and cook, covered, until the potatoes are done (about 20 minutes). Check often and stir to ensure that they are not burning. (There is usually no water added to this dish. The potatoes cook in the butter vapour. If, however, you find the potatoes looking dry due to quick and excessive evaporation, add a few tablespoons water during the cooking. After the potatoes are done, uncover, and increase the heat and continue cooking until all excess moisture evaporates.)

4 Sprinkle on the *garam masala*, mango powder, and salt; mix well and fry the potatoes, turning them, until they are well coated with the spices and glazed (about 5 minutes). Serve warm, at room temperature, or cold.

TURN-FRIED CURRIED TARO ROOT

ARBI (GHUIAN) KI SABZI

◆

The Rajasthanis of western India use *ajwain* or carom seeds to flavour vegetables. In this recipe taro root, a popular root vegetable with a potato-like texture, is stir-fried with cayenne, turmeric, and carom seeds. The spicing is subtle to allow the sweet flavour of taro to be enjoyed to its fullest. Serve *arbi sabzi* with a simple bread such as Nirvana Special Balloon Bread (p. 310).

FOR 4 PERSONS

◆

1½ lb/750 g taro root (arbi)
¾ teaspoon turmeric
¾ teaspoon cayenne pepper
Coarse salt, to taste
4 tablespoons peanut oil
½ teaspoon carom seeds (ajwain)

1 Put the taro roots in a pot along with water to cover and bring to the boil. Cook, covered, for 12–15 minutes or until the taro roots are tender and can be peeled easily. Drain and cool briefly. Peel the taro roots and cut the flesh into ½ in/1 cm thick slices.

2 Put the taro root slices in a mixing bowl. Sprinkle on the turmeric, cayenne, and salt; toss well.

3 Heat the oil in a large frying pan over medium-high heat. When it is hot, add the carom seeds and let sizzle for 10 seconds. Add the spice-coated taro root slices and fry, turning and tossing, until they are well browned and fried (about 15 minutes). If necessary reduce the heat to medium.

Serve warm or at room temperature.

COURGETTES IN MILK SAUCE WITH CHILI FLAKES

PAAL KOOTOO

◆

This is one of the most unusually flavoured dishes from Tanjore, India. The courgette is first cooked in sweetened milk sauce as though it were a dessert, but then it is flavoured with light sesame oil laced with chili pepper, mustard seeds, and spicy gram beans. Traditionally the dish is made with green pumpkin, but courgettes make a good substitute. This dish usually accompanies a spicy southern stew such as Madras Fiery Aubergine, Lentil, and Chili Stew (p. 194) and a bowl of plain boiled rice.

FOR 4 PERSONS

◆

1 lb/500 g very tender young courgettes
½ pint/300 ml milk
3 tablespoons jaggery or brown sugar
½ teaspoon coarse salt
2 teaspoons cornflour dissolved in 2 tablespoons milk or water
1–2 tablespoons light sesame oil or light vegetable oil
½ teaspoon black mustard seeds
¾ teaspoon split white gram beans (urad dal)

4 dry red chili pods, broken into bits
(discard seeds for a milder flavour)

1 Scrub the courgettes clean under cold running water and wipe dry. Cut them into ¼ in/15 mm thick slices. Steam courgettes and set aside.

2 Mix the milk, brown sugar, and salt in a pan and bring to the boil over medium-high heat. Add the cornflour mixture and cook, stirring constantly, until the sauce thickens (about a minute). Add the steamed courgettes and continue cooking until the vegetables are heated through. Turn off the heat.

3 Heat the oil in a small frying pan over high heat until very hot. Add the mustard seeds. Keep a lid handy, as the seeds may spatter and fly all over. When the seeds begin to spatter, add the beans. When the beans turn light brown and the seeds stop spattering, add the chili bits. Shake the pan a few times to make sure all the chili bits are coated with hot oil, then immediately pour the contents of the pan over the vegetable sauce mixture. Stir to mix the ingredients and serve.

PULSES

DAL

COOKED LENTILS, PEAS, AND BEANS, MASTER RECIPE

GALA HUA DAL

This is the basic recipe for cooking lentils or beans. Many southern and southwestern regional recipes call for cooked lentils or beans to be stirred gently into a dish near the end of cooking. Therefore, it may be a good idea to make them a day ahead and have them ready when you begin the actual cooking.

MAKES 2 PINTS/1 LITRE THICK LENTIL OR BEAN PURÉE

8 oz/250 g yellow lentils (arhar dal), *or red lentils* (masar dal), *yellow split peas or yellow mung beans* (moong dal)
¼ teaspoon turmeric

1 Pick lentils, peas, or beans clean and wash thoroughly in several changes of water.

2 Put the lentils, peas, or beans in a deep pot along with the turmeric and 2 pints/1 litre water; bring to the boil. Stir often to make sure they do not lump together. Cook over medium heat, partially covered, for 40 minutes (25 minutes for red lentils and mung beans). Cover, reduce heat, and continue cooking for an additional 20–25 minutes (10 minutes for red lentils and mung beans) or until soft.

3 Turn off heat and measure the purée. There should be 2 pints/1 litre purée; if not, add enough water to bring to that quantity. For a more ground purée, beat lentils, peas, or beans with a whisk for 3–5 minutes. Cooked *dal* can be kept for 3 days, refrigerated. Cooked lentils and beans thicken considerably and become gelatinous with keeping. They also reduce in volume considerably. Therefore remember to make allowance for such evaporation.

SPROUTED MUNG BEANS WITH COCONUT AND WHOLE SPICES, MAHARASHTRIAN-STYLE

USAL

Lightly sprouted mung beans (p. 87) are very popular with Gujaratis and Maharashtrians. In this recipe sprouted beans are steamed in the vapour of mustard-, cumin-, and asafetida-laced butter and then dressed with fresh coconut and coriander before being served. This preparation, called *usal*, has one special addition – the sweetish-sour fruit *kokum* – which gives the dish its characteristic flavour. You may, of course, use lemon juice and a little sugar instead. *Usal* is served with a Maharashtrian meal in all the southwestern regions of India accompanied by a bowl of plain cooked rice and a vegetable such as Spicy Aubergine in Ginger-Tamarind Sauce (p. 242).

FOR 4–6 PERSONS

6 oz/175 g whole mung beans, sprouted (p. 87)
2 tablespoons usli ghee *(p. 57) or light sesame or vegetable oil*
1 teaspoon mustard seeds
1 teaspoon cumin seeds
¼ teaspoon ground asafetida
¼ teaspoon turmeric
½ teaspoon cayenne pepper
1 tablespoon powdered jaggery or brown sugar
1 teaspoon Marathi *garam masala (p. 80) or garam masala (p. 77)*
¾ teaspoon coarse salt, or to taste
4–6 mangosteen fruit pieces (kokum) (or 1 tablespoon lemon juice and 1 teaspoon sugar)
5–6 tablespoons water
3 tablespoons chopped fresh coriander
3 tablespoons flaked coconut (fresh or tinned, unsweetened)

1 Rinse sprouted beans thoroughly in cold water. Drain and set aside.
2 Measure out the spices and place them right next to the stove in separate piles. Heat the *usli ghee* in a large frying pan over medium-high heat. When it is hot, add the mustard seeds. Keep a lid handy, as the seeds may spatter and fly all over. When the seeds are spattering, add the cumin. When the cumin turns brown (about 15 seconds), add the asafetida, turmeric, and cayenne. Stir for 5 seconds, add the sprouted beans, and mix well. Sprinkle on the jaggery, Marathi *garam masala*, and salt, and continue frying, turning and tossing, for 2–3 minutes, until all the ingredients are well blended.
3 Bury the *kokum* fruit in the beans and pour about 5–6 tablespoons water over it.
4 Lower the heat and cook, covered, for 25 minutes, or until the beans are cooked but still quite crunchy. Uncover, fluff the beans, and turn off the heat. Gently stir in more salt if necessary, some of the coriander, and the coconut.

Cool completely and serve at room temperature, sprinkled with the remaining coriander and coconut.

BANARAS YELLOW LENTILS WITH PEPPERED MANGO SLICES

BANARASI ARHAR DAL

◆

Banaras arhar dal, a dish reminiscent of the north Indian countryside – mango groves, coriander patches, and fields of lentils stretching to the horizon – is in fact a simple, humble dish and quite easy to make. The lentils are first cooked to a smooth, creamy consistency. Then the mango slices, spiced with cayenne, cumin, and *garam masala*, are folded into the *dal*. Finally fresh coriander is added to perfume and mix the flavours.

In my mother's home, as a child, I ate this *dal* with a simple baked bread or a bowl of fluffy plain rice and a vegetable side dish, the most memorable being Bitter Gourd with Spicy Onion Stuffing and with Fragrant Potato Stuffing (pp. 238 and 239).

FOR 6–8 PERSONS

◆

8 oz/250 g yellow lentils (toor dal) *or red lentils* (masar dal)
½ teaspoon turmeric
1 small green mango, peeled, pitted, and sliced *(or 8 slices dry mangoes or 2 tablespoons* *mango powder)*
1½ teaspoons coarse salt, or to taste
FOR THE SPICED BUTTER:
4–5 tablespoons usli ghee *(p. 57)* *or light vegetable oil*
1½ teaspoons cumin seeds
½ teaspoon cayenne pepper
teaspoon garam masala *(p. 77)*
4 tablespoons finely chopped fresh coriander

1 Pick clean, wash, and cook the lentils and turmeric following the instructions on page 254, except add dried mango slices or mango powder (if you are using one of them) a half-hour before the end of cooking. Stir in the salt. Keep the *dal* over a low simmer while you make the spiced butter.

2 Measure out the spices and place them right next to the stove in separate piles. Heat the *usli ghee* in a small frying pan over medium-high heat. When it is hot, add the cumin. When the cumin turns dark brown (about 12 seconds), add the mango slices (if you are using them). Fry the mangoes, turning and tossing them, until they look slightly soft and cooked (about 8 minutes). Reduce the heat, if necessary.

3 Sprinkle on the cayenne and the *garam masala*, and continue cooking, turning the mangoes, for 2 more minutes. Turn off the heat and pour the entire contents of the pan over the *dal*. Add half the chopped coriander and mix well. Serve sprinkled with the remaining coriander.

BENGAL RED LENTILS
WITH SPICES

BENGALI MASAR DAL

◆

Of all the pulses available in India, the Bengalis favour red lentils the most, and they inevitably prepare them in one classic way. In this technique the lentils are first cooked with turmeric and green chilies until they become a purée. This smooth purée is infused with two flavourings. The first, consisting of fixed seasonings, is added near the end, while the lentils are cooking. The second, the spiced butter with chili pods, garlic, and whole spices, is gently folded into the *dal* just before it is served. The resulting *dal* is spicy, utterly delicious, and my very favourite. I love it with plain rice and a simple vegetable preparation on the side.

FOR 6–8 PERSONS

◆

FOR COOKING THE *DAL*:
8 oz/250 g red lentils (masar dal)
6 hot green chilies

½ teaspoon turmeric
2 pints/1 litre water
1½ teaspoons coarse salt, or to taste
FOR FLAVOURING THE *DAL*:
4 tablespoons usli ghee *(p. 57) or light vegetable oil*
6 oz/175 g minced onion
1 tablespoon grated or crushed fresh ginger
6 oz/175 g finely chopped tomatoes
FOR THE SPICED BUTTER:
2 tablespoons usli ghee, *or light vegetable oil*
1 tablespoon panch phoron *mix, (p. 82)*
4 bay leaves
4 dry red chili pods
2 teaspoons minced garlic (optional)

1 Pick clean, wash, and cook the *dal* using the lentils, chilies, turmeric, salt, and 2 pints/1 litre of water, following the instructions on page 254, to step 2.

2 While the lentils are cooking, heat the *usli ghee* in a large frying pan over medium-high heat. When it is hot, add the onion and fry, stirring constantly, until golden brown (about 10 minutes). Add the ginger and tomatoes and continue frying until the tomatoes are cooked and the contents reduce to a thick pulp (about 8 minutes). Stir constantly to prevent sticking and burning.

3 Blend the fried onion-tomato paste and salt to taste into the *dal*; continue cooking for an additional 10–15 minutes or until the flavours have blended in. Keep the *dal* on a low simmer while you make the spiced butter.

4 Measure out the spices and place them next to the stove in separate piles. Heat the *usli ghee* in a small frying pan over medium-high heat. When it is hot, add the *panch phoron*. When the mustard seeds are spattering and the cumin turns a little darker (about 15 seconds), add the bay leaves and chili pods. Continue frying until the chili turns dark (15–20 seconds), turning and tossing them. Turn off the heat, add the garlic, and let mixture fry, sizzling for 25 seconds or until it looks light golden. Pour the entire contents of the pan over the *dal*, mix well, and serve.

YELLOW MUNG BEANS LACED WITH HERBS

MOONG DAL

◆

This golden yellow purée of mung beans with a hint of ginger, chilies, and cumin is one of my favourite *dals*. Its delicate mellow flavour blends with just about any dish. The *dal* is flavoured with the spiced butter in the popular Bihari style of eastern India. *Moong dal* can be served with rice as well as bread. Just remember always to garnish the *dal* with loads and loads of fresh fragrant coriander.

FOR 4–6 PERSONS

◆

6 oz/175 g split yellow mung beans (moong dal)
¼ teaspoon turmeric
1½ pints/800 ml water
¾ teaspoon coarse salt, or to taste
FOR THE SPICED BUTTER:
3–4 tablespoons light vegetable oil
1½ teaspoons cumin seeds
1 tablespoon chopped fresh ginger
2–4 hot green chilies, chopped
1 tablespoon lemon juice
4 tablespoons chopped fresh coriander
Cayenne pepper or paprika (optional)

1 Pick clean and wash mung beans thoroughly in several changes of water.

2 Put the beans along with turmeric and 1½ pints/800 ml water in a deep saucepan and bring to the boil. Cook the beans, partially covered, over low heat for 35–40 minutes or until the beans are fully cooked and soft when pressed between the fingers. Check the beans and stir a few times during cooking. Turn off the heat and beat the *dal* with a whisk or wooden spoon for 1 minute or until the *dal* turns into thick purée.

Stir in salt to taste. Turn on the heat and keep the *dal* at a low simmer while you make the spice-perfumed butter.

3 Heat the oil in a small frying pan over medium-high heat. When it is hot, add the cumin. When the cumin turns dark brown (about 12 seconds), add the ginger and chilies and continue frying for 30 seconds or until the oil is laced with the scent of the seasonings. Turn off the heat and pour the entire contents of the pan over the *dal*. Add the lemon juice and half the chopped coriander and stir a few times – just enough to mix some of the perfumed oil into the *dal*. Serve sprinkled with the remaining coriander and, if desired, a little cayenne or paprika.

WHOLE MUNG BEANS AND SPINACH IN A SPICY TOMATO BUTTER

PALAK MOONG

◆

Cooking beans or lentils with fragrant greens is a common technique throughout India. In this version from New Delhi, the beans and spinach are first cooked with turmeric and then laced with a highly fragrant and spicy mixture of chilies, tomatoes, fresh coriander, and *garam masala*. This *dal* is absolutely outstanding and can easily be served as a complete meal in itself. Traditionally bread is served with it, but I think rice goes just as well.

FOR 4–6 PERSONS

◆

6 oz/175 g whole mung beans (sabat moong)
¼ teaspoon turmeric
2½ pints/1.5 litres water
12 oz/375 g fresh spinach (or a 10 oz/300 g pack frozen leaf spinach)
1 teaspoon coarse salt, or to taste
FOR THE SPICY TOMATO BUTTER:
4–5 tablespoons usli ghee *(p. 57) or light vegetable oil*
1½ tablespoons cumin seeds
6 oz/175 g finely chopped onion
1 tablespoon chopped fresh ginger
1½ teaspoons minced garlic
3 tablespoons chopped fresh coriander
3 hot green chilies, minced
2 medium red ripe tomatoes, chopped
½ teaspoon garam masala *(p.77)*

1 Pick clean and wash the beans in several changes of water. Put the beans in a deep saucepan along with the turmeric. Add 2½ pints/1.5

litres water and bring to the boil. Lower the heat and cook, partially covered, for 1½ hours. The beans should cook slowly to develop a creamy softness as well as to remain whole and plump.

2 While the beans are cooking, snip the stalks off the spinach leaves. Rinse in several changes of water until all the sand is washed away and chop fine (if you are using frozen spinach, defrost thoroughly).

3 Add the spinach to the beans, mix thoroughly until the greens wilt, and continue cooking, covered, for an additional 15–20 minutes. Stir in salt to taste. Keep the *dal* on a low simmer while you make the spicy tomato butter.

4 Heat the *usli ghee* or oil in a small frying pan over medium-high heat. When it is hot, add the cumin. When the cumin turns dark brown (about 12 seconds), add the onion. Fry the onion, stirring constantly, until golden brown (10–12 minutes). Add the ginger, garlic, coriander, and chilies, and fry for an additional 2 minutes. (If the seasonings seem to be browning too fast, reduce the heat to medium.)

5 Add the tomatoes and continue frying until the tomatoes are cooked and the contents of the pan look thick and pulpy. The fat will separate from the pulp. Pour the entire mixture over the *dal*, add the *garam masala*, and blend well. Let the *dal* simmer, covered, for 5 minutes before you serve it.

SWEET AND SOUR BOMBAY LENTILS

AMTI

No traditional Maharashtrian meal can be considered complete without a bowl of *amti* served on the side. *Amti* is made by cooking lentils with jaggery and the sweetish-sour fruit *kokum* and lacing it with a spice-perfumed butter. *Amti* has a sweet and sour taste and a brothy consistency. It is traditionally eaten poured over plain rice, although it's good all by itself, as a soup.

FOR 6–8 PERSONS

4 *mangosteen fruits* (kokum) *or* one ¾ *in/2 cm round tamarind pulp*
8 *oz/250 g yellow lentils* (arhar dal), *red lentils* (masar dal), *or yellow split peas*
½ *teaspoon turmeric*
2 *tablespoons light vegetable oil*
2 *pints/1 litre water*
1 *tablespoon powdered jaggery or brown sugar*
1½ *teaspoons coarse salt, or to taste*
FOR THE SPICE-PERFUMED BUTTER:
3–4 *tablespoons* usli ghee, (p. 57), *or light vegetable oil*
1 *teaspoon cumin seeds*
1 *teaspoon black mustard seeds*
¼ *teaspoon fenugreek seeds*
½ *teaspoon turmeric*
½ *teaspoon cayenne pepper*
2 *teaspoons* Marathi garam masala *(p. 80) or* garam masala *(p. 77)*
3 *tablespoons chopped fresh coriander*
3 *tablespoons flaked coconut* (fresh or tinned, unsweetened)

1 If you are using tamarind, soak it in ¼ pint/150 ml boiling water in a nonmetallic bowl for a half-hour. Strain the liquid, squeezing out of the pulp as much juice as possible. Discard the fibrous residue.

2 Pick clean, wash, and cook the lentils using turmeric, oil and 2 pints/1 litre water and following all the instructions on page 254 to step 2. Add *kokum* or tamarind juice and jaggery, and cook for an additional 10 minutes. Stir in salt to taste. Turn off the heat and beat the *dal*, using a whisk or a wooden spoon, for a minute to smooth and thicken the purée. Keep the *dal* on a low simmer while you make the spice-perfumed butter.

3 Measure out the spices and place them right next to the stove in separate piles. Heat the *usli ghee* in a small frying pan over medium-high heat. When it is hot add the cumin, mustard seeds, and fenugreek. When the spices turn dark brown and the spattering of the mustard seeds subsides, add the turmeric, cayenne, and Marathi *garam masala* or the *garam masala*. Let the spices sizzle for a second or two and immediately pour the entire contents of the pan over the *dal* and mix well. Let the *dal* cook for an additional 5 minutes. Serve it sprinkled with coriander and coconut.

Punjab Five-Jewel Creamed Lentils

PANCH RATAN DAL

◆

Panch ratan means 'five jewels.' The classic recipe calls for five varieties of lentils and beans to be combined and flavoured with cayenne pepper, cumin, and turmeric. The five seasonings and herbs that always flavour this *dal* are onion, garlic, ginger, chilies, and coriander. I have omitted the green chilies in this recipe as, together with cayenne, the *dal* tends to get quite hot. If you like a very hot taste, add 4 chopped green chilies to the recipe.

Panch ratan dal is delicious and filling. It goes beautifully with bread and rice alike.

FOR 8 PERSONS

FOR COOKING THE LENTILS:
6 oz/175 g yellow split peas
3 oz/90 g split white gram beans (urad dal)
1½ oz/45 g split yellow mung beans (moong dal)
1½ oz/45 g red lentils (masar dal)
½ teaspoon turmeric
2 teaspoons coarse salt, or to taste
6–8 tablespoons light vegetable oil
2 medium-size onions, peeled and sliced thin
2 teaspoons minced garlic
2 teaspoons grated or crushed fresh ginger
3 medium-size tomatoes, sliced into *¾ in/2 cm thick wedges*
FOR THE SPICED BUTTER:
1½ teaspoons cumin seeds
½ teaspoon cayenne pepper
1 teaspoon paprika, more for sprinkling
3–4 tablespoons chopped fresh coriander

1 Pick clean, wash, and cook the *dal*, using all the ingredients for cooking lentils except salt and following all the instructions on page 254 to step 2. Stir in the salt to taste. Keep the lentils on a low simmer while you make the fried seasonings.

2 Heat 4–6 tablespoons of the oil in a large frying pan over medium-high heat. Add the onions and cook, stirring constantly, until they turn light brown (15–18 minutes). Add the garlic and ginger, and continue cooking for 2 more minutes. Increase the heat to high, add the tomatoes, and fry, turning them carefully and shaking the pan, until they look slightly browned and cooked (about 5 minutes). Pour the entire contents of the pan over the *dal* and gently stir to mix. Continue simmering the *dal* while you make the spiced butter.

3 Wipe clean the frying pan and place it on medium-high heat. Add the remaining 2 tablespoons of the oil. When it is hot, add the cumin. When the cumin turns dark brown (about 12 seconds), add the cayenne and paprika. Immediately pour the entire contents of the pan over the *dal*, scraping the mixture out with a rubber spatula. Stir a few times, just to streak the *dal* with the spiced butter. Serve sprinkled with coriander and more paprika.

VEGETABLE SALADS

◆

NORTH INDIAN VEGETABLE SALAD

SALAAT

◆

This is a simple salad of sliced cucumbers, tomatoes, daikon radish (*mooli*), and potatoes that usually accompanies a formal banquet as well as a north Indian meal. The dressing can be as simple as lemon juice, or highly intricate, with a mustard-, garlic-, and cumin-laced creamy, tangy base. This salad has a familiar yet a very unusual taste. If you want, you can include sliced mushrooms, celery, carrots, green peppers, and Indian cheese (*paneer*).

FOR 6 PERSONS

◆

2 medium cucumbers
6 in/15 cm piece daikon radish (mooli)
4 medium ripe tomatoes
12 oz/375 g (6 small) waxy potatoes, unpeeled, boiled
Lettuce leaves
2–3 tablespoons roughly chopped fresh coriander leaves
1–2 hot green chilies, shredded (optional)
1 recipe North Indian Salad Dressing (recipe follows)

1 Peel the cucumbers and radish and cut them neatly into thin slices. Wash the tomatoes, wipe them dry, and cut them into similar slices. Cut the potatoes also into thin slices.
2 Arrange the sliced vegetables attractively on a platter over lettuce leaves. Sprinkle on the coriander and chilies, if you are using them. Dribble on 4–5 tablespoons of salad dressing and serve.

NORTH INDIAN SALAD DRESSING

SALAAT SAO

MAKES ABOUT ½ PINT/300 ML

◆

¼ pint/150 ml light sesame or vegetable oil
¼ pint/150 ml double cream
4 tablespoons lemon juice
¾ teaspoon minced garlic
1 teaspoon crushed or grated fresh ginger
½ teaspoon ground cumin
1 tablespoon sugar
Coarse salt, to taste

Blend all the ingredients in a bowl, using a whisk, a wooden spoon, or a blender or food processor. Cover and refrigerate for half an hour before using.

The dressing keeps well in the refrigerator, covered, for up to two days.

SOUTHERN CARROT SALAD
WITH PEANUTS AND MUSTARD SEEDS

KOOSMALI

In the southern and southwestern regions of India, vegetable salads are made with chopped or minced vegetables. There are many varieties (as you will note in the next few recipes), but they all contain lemon juice and green chilies and are usually laced with a mustard seed-oil dressing.

This salad of grated carrots with peanuts and cream or yogurt, called *koosmali*, is popular with Anglo-Indians in Bangalore. The addition of cream makes the salad richer and milder.

FOR 6 PERSONS

1 lb/500 g carrots
1 tablespoon **usli ghee** *(p. 57), or light vegetable oil*
1 teaspoon black mustard seeds
2 hot green chilies, shredded, seeds discarded
¼ teaspoon ground asafetida
1 tablespoon sugar
8 curry (kari) leaves, fresh or dried
Coarse salt, to taste
1 teaspoon lime (or lemon) juice
4 tablespoons sour cream or plain yogurt (or a combination of the two)
2 tablespoons chopped roasted peanuts or cashew nuts

1 Peel carrots and shred them, using an Indian vegetable shredder (*kaddoo kas*, p. 97), a mandoline, or similar vegetable cutting device. If you do not have one, simply use the coarse blade of a vegetable grater or a food processor.

2 Heat the *usli ghee* in a *kadhai* or large frying pan over high heat. When it is hot, add the mustard seeds. Keep a lid handy, as the seeds when added may spatter and fly all over. As the spattering begins to subside, add the chilies and let sizzle and fry for 15 seconds. Add the asafetida, sugar, and curry leaves; shake the pan for 10–15 seconds, or until the sugar heats and begins to melt. Add the carrots and quickly toss to coat them well with spices and sugar. Continue until the carrots lose their raw smell (2–3 minutes). Put in a bowl. When cool, add salt, lime juice, and cream, and mix well. Serve at room temperature or chilled, sprinkled with peanuts or cashew nuts.

Keeps well in the refrigerator, covered, for up to two days. Add peanuts or cashew nuts just before serving.

SPROUTED MUNG BEAN SALAD, ANDHRA-STYLE

KOSUMBARA

In Hyderabad the Andhra Moslems, who are of southern heritage, boast of a rich culinary history acquired from their cross-cultural ties with the northern Moghuls and the southern Madras Brahmins. This simple, easy-to-prepare salad is one example. Notice the absence of mustard-seed dressing and the addition of tomatoes and black pepper. This salad keeps well for several hours, covered, at room temperature.

FOR 6 PERSONS

6 oz/175 g whole mung beans, sprouted (p 87)
3 medium-size cucumbers, peeled and grated
4 tablespoons flaked coconut (fresh or tinned, unsweetened)
1 medium tomato, peeled, seeded, and shredded
4 tablespoons chopped fresh coriander
4 hot green chilies, finely chopped
Coarse salt, to taste
4 tablespoons lemon juice
½ teaspoon black pepper

Put all the ingredients in a bowl. Toss well and marinate for 2 hours. Serve at room temperature or cold.

TANJORE THREE-BEAN SALAD WITH SPICES

SHONDAL

◆

Shondal is the bean salad from Tanjore, in the south of India. It is prepared as a divine food and offered to Sarasvati (goddess of knowledge and wisdom) during the Festival of *Dashahra* (September–October) and then eaten. The classic vegetarian recipe is made with just chick-peas and contains, naturally, no garlic. I like to make this salad with a mixture of tender young broad beans, black-eyed beans, and chick-peas, and season it intensely.

You may serve this with any southern meal. It is delicious as a snack, too. The salad keeps well at room temperature, covered, for a day.

FOR 8 PERSONS

12 oz/375 g fresh black-eyed beans, cooked
12 oz/375 g fresh broad beans (or one 10 oz/300 g packet frozen beans), cooked
1¼ lb/625 g cooked chick-peas (or tinned chick-peas, drained and rinsed)
Juice of 2 small lemons
Coarse salt, to taste
2 tablespoons light sesame or light vegetable oil
2 teaspoons black mustard seeds
8 dry red chili pods, broken into bits
1 tablespoon sliced garlic (optional)
⅓ teaspoon ground asafetida (optional)
4 oz/125 g flaked coconut (fresh or tinned, unsweetened)
2 tablespoons finely chopped fresh coriander

1 Put first three ingredients in a bowl along with the lemon juice and salt. Toss well to mix.

2 Heat the oil in a small frying pan over high heat. When it is hot add the mustard seeds. Keep a lid handy, as the seeds may spatter and fly all over. When the spattering subsides add chili bits and garlic and let sizzle for a few seconds, until garlic turns light pink. Add asafetida and immediately pour the entire contents of the pan over the bean mixture. Toss well to distribute the spices. Stir in coconut and coriander.

Serve at room temperature or cold.

CUCUMBER AND PEANUT SALAD, MAHARASHTRIAN-STYLE

KHAMANG KAKDI

Khamang kakdi is one of the most popular salads of Maharashtra. Made with grated cucumber, peanuts, mint, and coriander, it is laced with cumin, mustard, and turmeric. The addition of sugar in the presence of lemon juice is a typical Maharashtrian trademark designed to lend a sweet-sour flavour to food.

The Brahmins add a pinch of asafetida to perk up their onion- and garlic-free cooking. For best flavour the salad should be served soon after it is made.

FOR 6 PERSONS

◆

3 large cucumbers
5–6 tablespoons roasted peanuts (salted or unsalted), ground to a fine powder
3 tablespoons chopped fresh coriander
1½ tablespoons chopped fresh mint leaves (optional)
2 teaspoons sugar
Juice of 1 small lemon

FOR THE SPICED BUTTER:
2 tablespoons usli ghee (p. 57), or light vegetable oil
¾ teaspoon black mustard seeds
¾ teaspoon cumin seeds
¼ teaspoon ground asafetida
⅛ teaspoon turmeric
8 hot green chilies, shredded
Coarse salt to taste

1 Peel the cucumbers and cut them in half lengthwise. Using a spoon, scrape out the seeds. Grate the cucumbers, using the coarse blade of a grater or food processor. Put the cucumber in a colander and squeeze hard to extract any excess moisture, and put it in a bowl. Add the next five ingredients and toss well.

2 Heat the *usli ghee* in a small frying pan over high heat. When it is very hot, add the mustard seeds. Keep a lid handy, as the seeds may spatter and fly all over. As the seeds are spattering, add the cumin and continue cooking until mixture turns several shades darker (15–20 seconds). Add the asafetida, turmeric, and chilies, shake the pan for a few seconds, and pour the entire contents of the pan over the cucumber. Add salt, and toss well to coat the vegetables with spices.

Serve immediately. If you do not plan to serve immediately, do not add peanuts, sugar, or salt until serving time.

YOGURT SALADS

HERB-AND- SPICE-LACED
CREAMY YOGURT SALAD

MASALA DAHI

This is the yogurt salad that is served in most Indian restaurants under the name *raita*, used as a sauce for fried food, fritters, dumplings, and bread, or to put out the fire in your mouth caused by scorchingly hot food. The salad keeps well in the refrigerator, covered, for up to two days.

FOR 4 PERSONS

½ pint/300 ml plain yogurt
¼ pint/150 ml soured cream
½ tablespoon minced fresh mint leaves (or ½ teaspoon dried mint leaves, powdered, optional)
1 tablespoon minced fresh coriander
¾ teaspoon ground roasted cumin seeds
¼ teaspoon cayenne pepper (optional)
¼ teaspoon black pepper
2 teaspoons sugar
½ teaspoon coarse salt, or to taste
3 oz/90 g minced cucumber, tomato, or a combination (optional)
Paprika for garnish

Blend all the ingredients in a bowl, cover, and chill thoroughly until needed. Serve sprinkled with paprika.

COURGETTE AND YOGURT SALAD

PACHADI VALLERIKA

◆

Flavoured in the classic southern manner – mustard seeds, chili pods, and asafetida in sesame oil dressing – this salad generally accompanies a southern meal. I think it's wonderful served with any meal with spicy brown sauces and delicate pilafs.

FOR 6 PERSONS

◆

1½ lb/750 g tender young courgettes
½ pint/300 ml plain yogurt
2 tablespoons minced fresh coriander
Coarse salt, to taste
2 tablespoons light sesame or light vegetable oil
1½ teaspoons black mustard seeds
4–8 dry red chili pods
¼ teaspoon ground asafetida (optional)

1 Scrub the courgettes under cold running water. Pat dry on towels. Shred the courgettes, using an Indian vegetable shredder *(kaddoo kas)*, a mandoline, or a similar vegetable cutting device. If you do not have one, simply use the coarse blade of a vegetable grater or a food processor.

2 Bring about 5 pints/3 litres of water to the boil. Add the shredded courgettes, stir once, and immediately remove from heat. Drain and rinse in cold water. Drain again, squeezing and pressing to extract any excess moisture from the courgettes, and transfer to a serving bowl. Add yogurt, coriander, and salt, and mix well.

3 Heat the oil in a small frying pan over high heat. When it is hot, add the mustard seeds. Keep a lid handy, as the seeds may spatter and fly all over. As the spattering subsides, add the chili pods and continue cooking until the chili pods turn several shades darker (about 15 seconds). If the chilies brown too fast, take the pan off the heat. Add the asafetida (if you are using it) and immediately pour the entire contents of the pan over the courgette-yogurt mixture. Mix well and serve, or refrigate until needed.

Keeps well, covered, in the refrigerator for a day.

SMOKED AUBERGINE AND YOGURT SALAD

BAIGAN KA RAITA

This yogurt salad is my absolute favourite. The smoky pulp of sweet aubergine against smooth, creamy yogurt with a fiery interlude of spices is sensational. Serve this salad with pilafs, breads, and especially with a north Indian meal. For a variation you can substitute roasted green, yellow, and red peppers; roasted onions; or roasted shallots – all finely shredded – for the aubergine.

FOR 6 PERSONS

1 large aubergine or 2 small ones
1 large tomato, blanched, peeled, seeded, and chopped
5–6 tablespoons finely chopped spring onions, white and green parts
½ pint/300 ml plain yogurt
4 tablespoons sour cream
Coarse salt, to taste
3 tablespoons light vegetable oil
1 tablespoon shredded fresh ginger
½ teaspoon or less cayenne pepper
5–6 tablespoons finely chopped fresh coriander
1½ teaspoons roasted cumin seeds, crushed
Paprika or cayenne pepper for garnish

1 Wash and wipe the aubergine dry. To roast it, stand it on the burner of a gas stove, stem side up, over a medium-low flame, until the bottom side is thoroughly charred (about 5 minutes). Lay the aubergine on its side and roast, turning it every minute with a pair of tongs until it is fully charred and very soft (about 15 minutes). (Alternately, the aubergine may be roasted in a preheated 500°F/260°C/Gas 9 oven for 20–25 minutes, placed on a baking tray in the middle level of the oven.) When the aubergine is cool enough to handle, peel it and chop the pulp coarsely. Pat dry the pulp with kitchen paper to rid it of the juice and excess moisture, and put it in a bowl. Add the tomatoes and spring onions, and toss to mix well.

2 Blend the yogurt, sour cream, and salt in another bowl until it is thoroughly mixed. Set aside.

3 Heat the oil in a large frying pan over medium-high heat until it is very hot. Add the ginger and cayenne and let sizzle for 10 seconds. Increase the heat to high and add the aubergine mixture. Fry, turning and tossing, until the tomatoes and spring onions look a little fried and the aubergine loses its excess moisture and begins to look drier (about 5 minutes). Turn off the heat. Fold in the coriander and half the cumin. When cool, add it to the yogurt mixture. Stir well to mix. Serve sprinkled with the remaining cumin and paprika or cayenne.

Keeps well in the refrigerator, covered, for two days.

PINEAPPLE AND YOGURT SALAD IN CURRY DRESSING

ANNANAAS RAITA

◆

Combining fruits with yogurt is the speciality of the people of the southwestern region. Pineapple is combined with yogurt and the abundant coconut, then laced with a spicy dressing of mustard seed and curry powder. The combination is surprising, but the taste is uncommonly good. For variety you can use peaches, nectarines, apricots, bananas, mangoes, papayas, or oranges in place of the pineapple.

FOR 6 PERSONS

◆

1 small ripe pineapple
½ pint/300 ml plain yogurt
3 oz/90 g flaked coconut (fresh or tinned, unsweetened)
¼ teaspoon ginger powder

1 tablespoon finely minced fresh coriander
2 tablespoons usli ghee *(p. 57) or light vegetable oil*
1½ teaspoons black mustard seeds
½ teaspoon Curry Powder Master Recipe (p. 73) or sambaar powder (p. 75)
Coarse salt, to taste

1 Peel, core, and dice the pineappel in ¾ in/2 cm pieces. Set aside.

2 Blend the yogurt, coconut, ginger, and coriander in a bowl. Set aside.

3 Heat the *usli ghee* in a small frying pan over medium-high heat. When it is very hot, add the mustard seeds. Keep a lid handy, as the seeds may spatter and fly all over. When the spattering subsides, add the curry powder, stir to blend it in, and immediately pour the entire contents of the pan over the yogurt, scraping it out with a spatula to get all the curry mixture. Stir yogurt well and add salt to taste. Fold in pineapple and let it rest, refrigerated, for at least an hour before serving.

Keeps well in the refrigerator, covered, for a day.

ACCOMPANI-
MENTS

To an Indian a meal without the proper accompaniments is inconceivable. They are virtually as important as the meal itself, served, essentially, to intensify the complex sensations of the meal. The crunch of wafers and crisps against the smoothness of vegetables, the mouth-puckering tingle of fiery pickles and the fresh herbal scents of relishes combined with the soothing blandness of rice and bread – these are all important elements in an Indian meal.

The wafers and crisps recipes are included with snacks on pages 163–170, since they are also important savouries.

SPICY HOT CONDIMENTS

◆

All Indian vegetarian meals include several accompaniments. Most can be mixed and matched and enjoyed. But there are some condiments that, although they may go very well with a variety of meals, are traditionally associated with certain dishes. These condiments provide a certain texture, a tangy flavour, or a peppery bite necessary against the mellowness of the dish and have been handed down from generation to generation. As a result, all Indian cooks are naturally aware of them and automatically know the classic combinations, such as Volcanic Sauce (p. 283) with Rice and Mung Bean Casserole with Cumin and Black Pepper (p. 219); Quick Onion, Tomato, and Cucumber Relish (p. 290) with Punjabi and Uttar Pradesh meals; Fiery Hot Cucumber Spread (p. 284) and Hot and Spicy Tamarind Sauce with Peanuts (p. 286) and plain boiled rice; Tomato-Onion Sauce (p. 287) with Semolina Pilaf with Tomato and Spices (p. 124); and so on. Although these matches are traditional, it by no means suggests that you cannot, for example, serve the Quick Onion, Tomato, and Cucumber Relish with a southern meal. These classic combinations have been proved by time, but do not be afraid to be adventurous.

VOLCANIC SAUCE

MOLAHA KOYAMBOO

◆

Beware of this delicacy, for it can be shockingly hot to the unprepared palate. It is a wonderful accompaniment to Rice and Mung Bean Casserole with Cumin and Black Pepper (p. 219). You can substitute green beans, broad beans, fresh black-eyed beans, green peas, asparagus, carrots, or shallots of equal quantity for the okra.

FOR 8 PERSONS

◆

1½ teaspoons cumin seeds
2 tablespoons coriander seeds
1 tablespoon black peppercorns
4 dry red chili pods
1½ teaspoons yellow split peas
1 tablespoon split white gram beans (urad dal)
1¼ pints/700 ml water
2 teaspoons tamarind paste (p. 86)
⅓ teaspoon ground asafetida
3 tablespoons light sesame or light vegetable oil
1 lb/500 g okra, tops trimmed and left whole, or cut into 1½ in/4 cm pieces
1½ teaspoons cornflour dissolved in 1 tablespoon water
1½ teaspoons coarse salt, or to taste

1 Put the cumin, coriander, peppercorns, chili pods, peas, and beans in a small greased frying pan. Roast the spices over medium-high heat, shaking and tossing, until they turn several shades darker (about 4 minutes). Transfer to a small plate, cool completely, and grind to a fine powder using a spice or coffee mill or blender.
2 Bring 1¼ pints/700 ml water to the boil in a saucepan. Add the tamarind paste, asafetida, and the ground spice mixture, and blend well. Lower heat and cook the sauce, uncovered, for 10 minutes.

3 While the sauce is cooking, heat the oil in a large frying pan. When the oil is hot, add the okra. Fry the okra, turning and tossing, until covered with several brown streaks, regulating heat between medium and high (9–10 minutes). Turn off heat.

4 Add the fried okra to the sauce and continue cooking for an additional 4 minutes. Stir in the cornflour mixture and cook until the sauce thickens. Turn off the heat and stir in salt to taste.

Serve warm, cold, or at room temperature. Keeps well in the refrigerator, covered, for up to two days.

FIERY HOT CUCUMBER SPREAD

TOHAYAL

Reserve this hot and spicy mustard-laced relish for traditional south Indian meals. For an exciting experience, try it by itself mixed with plain cooked rice.

MAKES ½ PINT/300 ML

2 medium cucumbers
3 tablespoons light sesame or light vegetable oil
1 teaspoon black mustard seeds
1 teaspoon split white gram beans
2–4 dry red chili pods, broken into bits
⅛ teaspoon ground asafetida
½ tablespoon tamarind paste (p. 86)
½ teaspoon coarse salt

1 Peel the cucumbers and dice into ¾ in/2 cm pieces. Place a frying pan with 1½ tablespoons of the oil over medium-high heat. When the oil is hot, add the cucumber pieces and cook, stirring and tossing, until the cucumbers are cooked but still firm to the touch (8–10 minutes). If necessary, regulate heat between medium-low and medium-high. Transfer to a bowl and let cool.

2 Wipe the frying pan clean, add the remaining 1½ tablespoons of oil, and place over high heat. When it is hot, add the mustard seeds. Keep a lid handy, as the seeds may spatter and fly all over. When the seeds are spattering, add the beans. When the beans turn light golden (about 10 seconds), add the chili bits and the asafetida and turn off heat. Immediately stir in the tamarind paste. Let cool briefly.

3 With the steel blade in position and the processor running, drop the spice mixture through the feed tube. Let the processor run for 30 seconds or until the spices are crushed coarsely. Add the cucumber pieces and salt to taste. Process, pulsing 8 or 10 times, or until the cucumbers are coarsely puréed and the spices are well blended into the vegetable. Or, alternatively, make a coarse powder out of the spice mixture, using a spice mill or coffee grinder or a mortar and pestle. Chop the cooked cucumber coarsely, using a knife, then mix them together.

Serve at room temperature or cold. *Tohayal* keeps well in the refrigerator, covered, for up to two days.

FIERY HOT SMOKED AUBERGINE CAVIAR

KATRIKAI TOHAYAL

An appropriate and flavourful accompaniment to any southern dish. Follow the instructions for making Fiery Hot Cucumber Spread (p. 284), except substitute one small aubergine grilled over a charcoal or gas flame, peeled, drained of excess juices, and roughly chopped, in place of the cucumbers.

The relish keeps well in the refrigerator, covered, for up to two days.

HOT AND SPICY TAMARIND SAUCE WITH PEANUTS

PULIKACHAL

◆

Tart and spicy, this peanut-studded sauce is good with rice pilafs and rice casseroles such as Coconut Pilaf with Toasted Sesame Seeds (p. 332) and Rice and Mung Bean Casserole with Cumin and Black Pepper (p. 219).

MAKES ¾ PINT/450 ML

◆

4 oz/125 g tamarind pulp (about 1 lemon- or tangerine-size ball)
½ pint/300 ml boiling water
3 tablespoons light sesame or light vegetable oil
¾ teaspoon mustard seeds
½ teaspoon ground asafetida
12–16 dry chili pods
1 tablespoon yellow split peas (channa dal)
1 tablespoon split white gram beans (urad dal)
1 tablespoon sesame seeds
2 oz/60 g raw peanuts
1 tablespoon ground coriander
¼ teaspoon turmeric
1½ tablespoons jaggery or soft brown sugar
12 curry (kari) leaves (fresh or dry)
Coarse salt, to taste

1 Put the tamarind pulp in a nonmetallic bowl. Add ½ pint/300 ml boiling water and let soak for 30 minutes. Strain the liquid into another small bowl, squeezing and mashing the pulp to extract as much pulpy meat as possible. Discard the fibrous residue. Stir in ½ pint/300 ml water and set aside.

2 Heat the oil in a medium-size heavy saucepan over high heat.

When it is hot, add the mustard seeds. Keep a lid handy, as the seeds may spatter and fly all over. Reduce the heat to medium-low while the seeds are spattering and add the asafetida and chili pods. Let sizzle for 15 seconds. Add the peas and beans, and fry, stirring, until they turn light golden (about 3 minutes). Add the sesame seeds and peanuts, and fry for an additional 2 minutes or until the sesame seeds are lightly coloured.

3 Stir in the coriander and turmeric. Gently pour in the tamarind juice and bring to a boil. Add the jaggery, curry leaves, and salt to taste. Lower the heat and let the sauce boil gently, uncovered, until the oil separates and the contents of the pan reduce to thick pulpy sauce (about 50 minutes). Stir 2–3 times during boiling.

Pulikachal keeps well in the refrigerator, covered, for up to a week.

FRAGRANT TOMATO-ONION SAUCE

GOZZOO

A mildly hot and slightly tart sauce that goes well with most meals that are served with rice as a staple, this is also great served with Rice and Mung Bean Casserole with Cumin and Black Pepper (p. 219).

FOR 8 PERSONS

6 tablespoons light sesame or light vegetable oil
1 teaspoon black mustard seeds
½ teaspoon ground asafetida
½–¾ teaspoon cayenne pepper
12 oz/375 g chopped onions
12 oz/375 g chopped red ripe tomatoes
¾ teaspoon coarse salt, or to taste
2–8 hot green chilies, slit

1 Heat the oil in a saucepan over medium-high heat for 3 minutes. When it is hot, add the mustard seeds. Keep a lid handy, as the seeds may spatter and fly all over. When the seeds stop spattering, add the asafetida and cayenne, and immediately add the onions. Cook the onions, stirring constantly, for 2 minutes or until they become a little wilted.

2 Add the tomatoes, salt, and chilies. Mix well and cook, stirring, until the contents of the pan are bubbling hot. Lower the heat and cook, partially covered, for 15–18 minutes or until the tomatoes are cooked and the onions are still holding their shape. Turn off the heat and let the sauce rest, covered, for 30 minutes before serving.

Serve at room temperature.

Gozzoo keeps well for a day, covered, in the refrigerator.

SPICY FENUGREEK-SCENTED SHALLOT SAUCE

MENDIAM KOYAMBOO

◆

A very hot and spicy sauce. The addition of a few fresh fenugreek leaves makes it a superlative accompaniment to Semolina Pilaf with Tomato and Spices (p. 124).

FOR 8 PERSONS

◆

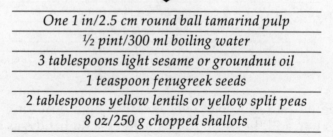

One 1 in/2.5 cm round ball tamarind pulp
½ pint/300 ml boiling water
3 tablespoons light sesame or groundnut oil
1 teaspoon fenugreek seeds
2 tablespoons yellow lentils or yellow split peas
8 oz/250 g chopped shallots

6–8 curry (kari) *leaves (fresh or dry, optional)*
½ pint/300 ml water
2 teaspoons sambaar *powder (p. 75) or* Curry Powder Master Recipe (p. 73)
1½ teaspoons cornflour dissolved in 1 tablespoon water
Coarse salt, to taste
½ teaspoon black mustard seeds
¼ teaspoon ground asafetida

1 Put the tamarind pulp in a nonmetallic bowl and add ½ pint/300 ml boiling water. Let soak for 30 minutes. Strain the liquid into another bowl, squeezing and mashing the pulp to extract as much juice as possible. Discard the fibrous residue and set the tamarind juice aside until needed.

2 Heat 2 tablespoons of the oil in a saucepan over medium heat. When the oil is very hot, add the fenugreek, fry for 30 seconds, and add the lentils. Fry, stirring, until the lentils turn brown (about 3 minutes).

3 Increase the heat to medium-high, add the shallots, and cook, stirring, until they become glazed and begin to fry (about 4 minutes). Add the tamarind juice, curry leaves, and ½ pint/300 ml water, and bring to the boil. Reduce the heat and cook, covered, for 10 minutes or until the shallots are cooked and the tamarind loses its raw smell.

4 Stir in the *sambaar* powder and continue cooking for 5 more minutes. Pour in the cornflour mixture, stirring the sauce constantly, and cook until it comes to the boil and thickens. Stir in salt to taste. Keep the sauce at a gentle simmer while you make the spice-laced oil.

5 Heat the remaining tablespoon of oil in a small frying pan over high heat. When it is hot, add the mustard seeds. Keep a lid handy, as the seeds may spatter and fly all over. When the mustard seeds stop spattering add the asafetida, and turn off the heat. Pour the entire contents of the pan over the sauce and mix well. Let the sauce rest, covered, for a half-hour before serving.

Serve warm, at room temperature, or cold. This sauce keeps well in the refrigerator, covered, for up to three days.

QUICK ONION, TOMATO, AND CUCUMBER RELISH

KACHOOMAR

◆

This fragrant and mildly hot mélange of salad vegetables is good with Punjabi and Moghul dishes. It can be made in a matter of minutes.

FOR 8 PERSONS

◆

8 oz/250 g chopped onion
5 oz/150 g chopped cucumber
5 oz/150 g chopped tomato
3 oz/90 g chopped sweet green pepper
2–3 table spoons chopped fresh coriander
6 hot green chilies, minced
1/3 teaspoon ground cumin
Juice of 1 small lemon
1/2 teaspoon coarse salt, or to taste

Put all the ingredients in a bowl, toss well, and let rest for a half-hour before serving.

Serve at room temperature or cold. This relish is best served as soon as it is made, as the onions begin to wilt and turn limp with keeping.

CHUTNEYS

◆

Chutney, or *chatni* as it is pronounced in India, is a Sanskrit word meaning 'for licking.' Indian chutneys are specifically made for that purpose: to be savoured on the side with a meal, providing many sensations – tart, hot, sweet, savoury, bitter, and mellow-fragrant. Chutneys traditionally consist of highly fragrant herbs, fruits, and aromatic spices, and come in many forms, such as a minced herb sauce or a dip, the classic examples being Coriander Chutney (p. 291) and Sweet and Spicy Tamarind Chutney (p. 293). These are used as dips with fried foods. Chutneys can also be thick and pulpy and used as a spread over bread and crepes. These include Hot Garlic Chutney (p. 292), and Mangalore Coconut Chutney with Green Chilies (p. 294). Finally, chutneys can appear at the table in cooked, preserved form, both sweet as well as peppery hot. These include Anglo-Indian Sweet and Spicy Lime (or Lemon) Chutney (p. 297) and Madras Hot Star Fruit Chutney (p. 299).

CORIANDER CHUTNEY

DHANIA CHATNI

◆

Fragrant and slightly hot, this coriander chutney, very popular in Indian restaurants, generally accompanies Indian appetizers and a traditional north Indian meal.

MAKES ABOUT ½ PINT/300 ML

◆

4 oz/125 g fresh coriander leaves, roughly chopped
¼ pint/150 ml water
2–4 fresh hot green chilies, roughly chopped
1–2 slices fresh ginger
1 teaspoon sugar
1 tablespoon fresh lemon juice, or 2 teaspoons white vinegar

Salt, to taste

4 tablespoons fresh mint leaves (optional)

Put all the ingredients in the container of an electric blender or food processor and blend until finely puréed and reduced to a sauce. Taste the mixture for seasoning and pour into a bowl.

Cover and chill until needed. Keeps well for two to three days, covered, in the refrigerator.

HOT GARLIC CHUTNEY

LASSAN CHI CHATNI

◆

This very hot, garlicky spread is served with Gujarati, Marathi, Coorgi, and Mangalorian food.

MAKES ½ PINT/300 ML

◆

4 oz/125 g flaked coconut (fresh or dry, unsweetened)

4–8 hot green chilies, or ½–1 teaspoon cayenne pepper

4 large cloves garlic, peeled

1 teaspoon coarse salt, or to taste

Light sesame or light vegetable oil

Put all the ingredients except the oil into the bowl of a food processor or blender and process until well ground and blended. If you want a thinner consistency, stir in a few teaspoons oil while puréeing the chutney.

Serve at room temperature.

Keeps well, covered, for a day at room temperature and for a week in the refrigerator.

SWEET AND SPICY TAMARIND CHUTNEY

IMLI CHATNI

◆

This is a very popular north Indian sauce for dipping fried food. For variation add ½ pint/300 ml of peeled chopped unripe mango.

MAKES ABOUT 1¼ PINTS/750 ML

◆

4 oz/125 g tamarind
1 pint/600 ml boiling water
1½ tablespoons paprika
1 tablespoon cayenne pepper
1 teaspoon dry ginger powder
2 teaspoons dry mango powder (or 2 tablespoons lemon juice)
½ teaspoon garam masala (p. 77)
2 teaspoons ground roasted cumin
1 teaspoon coarse salt, or to taste
4 tablespoons sugar

1 Put tamarind in a nonmetallic bowl and add ¾ pint/450 ml boiling water. Let soak for 30 minutes. Strain liquid into another bowl, squeezing and mashing pulp to extract as much juice as possible. Add another ¼ pint/150 ml boiling water to the residue. When cool enough to handle, squeeze pulp again and strain the liquid. Measure the tamarind liquid. There should be 1 pint/600 ml cups; if not, repeat until you have the required amount. Discard the fibrous residue.

2 Add all the other ingredients, mix well to blend, and serve.

Keeps well for three days, covered, in the refrigerator, and for six months in the freezer.

MANGALORE COCONUT CHUTNEY WITH GREEN CHILIES

MANGALORIAN CHATNI

◆

A great-tasting chutney with a fire that lingers within, this is guaranteed to bring tears to your eyes – of joy, of course. It makes a spicy and fragrant accompaniment, wonderful with southern vegetable stews.

MAKES ½ PINT/300 ML

◆

6 oz/175 g packed fresh grated or flaked coconut
4 tablespoons plain yogurt
8–16 hot green chilies
Handful of fresh coriander leaves and stems
4 tablespoons water
½ teaspoon coarse salt, to taste
2 tablespoons usli ghee *(p. 57) or light vegetable oil*
¾ teaspoon black mustard seeds
1 tablespoon sesame seeds
⅓ teaspoon ground asafetida (or 2 tablespoons minced onion)

1 Put the coconut, yogurt, chilies, coriander, and water into the bowl of a food processor or blender and process until finely puréed. Transfer to a serving bowl and stir in salt to taste.
2 Heat the *usli ghee* in a small frying pan over high heat. When it is very hot, add the mustard seeds. Keep a lid handy, as the seeds may spatter and fly all over. While the seeds are spattering, add the sesame seeds. When the sesame seeds are fried and lightly coloured, add the asafetida, and immediately lift the pan off the heat and pour the entire contents of the pan over the coconut mixture. (If, however, you are using minced onion, add it to the pan and continue cooking until it is wilted and begins to turn colour – about 2 minutes. Turn off the heat and pour the spice-onion mixture over the coconut.)

Mix the chutney well and serve at room temperature. Keeps well, covered, for two or three days in the refrigerator.

MUSTARD-FLECKED HOT TOMATO CHUTNEY

TAMATAR KOOT

◆

Fresh red ripe tomatoes are a must in this chutney. Serve it with pilafs and stuffed breads.

MAKES ¾ PINT/450 ML

◆

6 tablespoons vegetable oil
1½ teaspoons black mustard seeds
½ teaspoon cumin seeds
8 hot green chilies, slit
6 large cloves garlic, thinly sliced
1–2 teaspoons Curry Powder Master Recipe (p. 73, or bought)
½ teaspoon cayenne pepper
1–1¼ lb/500–625 g ripe tomatoes, cut into wedges
Coarse salt, to taste

1 Measure out the spices and place them next to the stove in separate piles. Heat the oil in a heavy-bottomed pan over high heat. When the oil is very hot, add the mustard seeds. Keep a lid handy, as the seeds may spatter and fly all over. As the spattering subsides, add the cumin. When the cumin turns dark brown (12 seconds), add the green chilies and garlic, curry powder, and cayenne. Reduce the heat to medium and let sizzle for a minute or two. Add the tomatoes and cook without stirring for 2 minutes. Turn the tomatoes, using a spatula, being careful not to crush them.

2 Lower heat to medium-low and cook the tomatoes, partially covered, for 15 minutes. During the cooking, turn the tomatoes once again to ensure even cooking. At the end of cooking the sauce will have thickened and the tomatoes should look very soft but hold their shape as much as possible. Turn off the heat and sprinkle on salt to taste.

The *koot* is now ready to serve, although for best flavour it should rest for an hour at room temperature. Serve hot, cold, or at room temperature. The *koot* keeps well for a day at room temperature and can be refrigerated, covered, for up to one week.

QUICK RIPE MANGO CHUTNEY
IN SPICY PEPPER SAUCE

MANGA PACHADI

◆

A simple and snappy chutney of medium-ripe mangoes, this can be made in minutes. It goes well with all Indian vegetarian dishes, particularly pilafs, such as Spicy Pea Pilaf (p. 324).

MAKES 1½ PINTS/1 LITRE

◆

1½ lb/750 g unripe raw mangoes
½ pint/300 ml water
⅓ teaspoon turmeric
1 teaspoon coarse salt
2 hot green chilies, shredded
3½ oz/100 g packed jaggery or soft brown sugar
2 teaspoons flour dissolved in 1 tablespoon water
1 tablespoon usli ghee (p. 57) or light vegetable oil
1 teaspoon black mustard seeds
4 dry red pepper pods
¼ teaspoon ground asafetida (optional)

1 Peel and pit the mangoes. Cut the pulp into thin slices.
2 Bring the water, turmeric, and salt to the boil in an enamel pan. Add the mango slices along with the chilies and cook over medium-high heat for 3 minutes or until the mangoes are barely cooked. Add the jaggery, increase the heat to high, and cook the chutney, bubbling, for

5 minutes. Add the cornflour mixture and continue cooking until the sauce thickens. Turn off the heat.

3 Heat the *usli ghee* in a small frying pan over high heat. When it is hot, add the mustard seeds. Keep a lid handy, as the seeds may spatter and fly all over. When the spattering subsides, lift the pan off the heat, add the pepper pods, and let sizzle until they turn several shades darker. Stir in the asafetida if you are using it and pour the entire contents of the pan over the chutney.

Mix well and serve warm, at room temperature, or cold. Keeps well, covered, in the refrigerator, for four to five days.

ANGLO-INDIAN SWEET AND SPICY LIME (OR LEMON) CHUTNEY

NIMBOO CHATNI

Anglo-Indians have their chutneys, too, and here is one. It's easy to make, as are most Anglo-Indian foods.

MAKES 1½ PINTS/800 ML

12 limes or lemons
1 medium-size onion, peeled and quartered
4 hot green chilies
One 1 in/2.5 cm cube fresh ginger
4 oz/125 g dark seedless raisins
5 black (or 7 green) cardomom pods
1 tablespoon black peppercorns
1 tablespoon coriander seeds
1 tablespoon mustard seeds
4 dry red pepper pods
½ pint/300 ml cider vinegar
3 tablespoons coarse salt
1 lb/500 g soft brown sugar

1 Cut the limes in half. Extract the juice, strain, and discard 6 of the lime halves. Put the remaining 18 lime halves along with the onion, chilies, ginger, and raisins into the bowl of a food processor, with the steel blade in position. Process until the contents are finely minced. Transfer the minced mixture to a glass or ceramic bowl.

2 Remove the seeds from the cardamom pods. Put the cardamom seeds along with the peppercorns, coriander, mustard seeds, and pepper pods in a *kadhai* or heavy frying pan. Roast the spices over high heat, shaking and tossing, until they begin to release their aroma (about 3 minutes). Transfer the spices to a dry plate. When completely cool, grind them to a fine powder.

3 Add the ground spices, the juice of the limes, and the vinegar to the minced mixture, and mix well. Cover and let the mixture marinate at room temperature for two days.

4 On the third day transfer the mixture to a nonmetallic pan. Add the salt and sugar, and bring to the boil over low heat. Cook, uncovered, gently bubbling, for a half-hour. Pour into sterilized jars and seal.

Let the chutney settle for at least two weeks before you serve it. For best results, do not open before four weeks. Once opened, store in the refrigerator.

SWEET AND FRAGRANT PINEAPPLE CHUTNEY

CHATNI ANNANAAS

◆

What do you do with a pineapple that is too tart? Turn it into this absolutely ravishing chutney for a Christmas gift.

MAKES 1 PINT/600 ML

◆

1 medium-ripe pineapple
1½ teaspoons ground cumin
1½ teaspoons ground fennel
¼ teaspoon ground cinnamon
½–¾ teaspoon cayenne pepper

| ½–¾ teaspoon black pepper |
| Juice of 1 lemon |
| 1½ teaspoons coarse salt, or to taste |

1 Peel and core the pineapple. Put the pineapple into the bowl of a food processor and process until coarsely puréed (or chop the pulp finely, using a sharp knife).

2 Put the puréed pineapple along with all the other ingredients in a medium-size enamel pan over medium heat. Heat the mixture, stirring often, until the sugar completely dissolves, and bring to the boil. Cook, uncovered, over low heat until the contents of the pan look thick and glazed like jam (about 30 minutes).

Turn off the heat, pour into sterilized jars, and seal. Although it is ready to serve, the flavour improves with two to three days of resting at room temperature. Keeps indefinitely until opened, when it needs to be refrigerated.

MADRAS HOT STAR FRUIT CHUTNEY

TOKKOO

◆

Tokkoo is a very hot and spicy spread made with minced star fruit and the classic southern blend of pickling spices – turmeric, mustard, fenugreek, and cayenne. Although it is traditionally enjoyed with rice and yogurt dishes or noodles, I find that *tokkoo* goes well with many other dishes, including breads and subtle pilafs. It is a perfect accompaniment to Moghul meals that are mild and need an additional punch. For a variation, substitute 1 pint/450 ml unripe tart mango pulp for the star fruit.

MAKES 1 PINT/600 ML

◆

¾ pint/450 ml minced tart unripe star fruit (or tart unripe mango pulp)
1 tablespoon coarse salt
2 tablespoons cayenne pepper
1 teaspoon turmeric
¾ teaspoon ground asafetida
½ teaspoon ground fenugreek seeds
¼ pint/150 ml light sesame or light vegetable oil
1 teaspoon black mustard seeds.

1 Mix the minced star fruit with salt in a nonmetallic bowl and set aside.

2 Blend cayenne, turmeric, asafetida, and fenugreek in a small bowl and set aside next to the burner.

3 Heat the oil in a small enamel pan. When it is hot, add the mustard seeds. Keep a lid handy, as the seeds may spatter and fly all over. When the seeds stop spattering, add the ground spices all at once, give them one quick stir, and immediately add the star fruit pulp. Lower the heat and cook, stirring, until the contents of the pan reduce to a thick pulp and the oil begins to separate (about 10 minutes). If necessary regulate the heat between medium-high and medium. The pickle should be bubbling during the entire cooking time. Also stir constantly to prevent sticking and burning.

Pour into a sterilized jar and seal. It is ready to use immediately.

PICKLES

◆

The difference between chutney and pickle (both of which may contain salt, vinegar, sugar, seasonings, spices, and vegetables or fruits) is the texture. Chutney, as described in the previous section, can be in the form of a sauce, dip, thick pulpy spread, or finely minced preserve, while a pickle contains clearly distinguishable pieces of vegetables or fruit. Pickle can be hot or sweet.

CARROT PICKLE IN MUSTARD OIL

GAJJAR KA ACHAAR

◆

These turmeric-laced crisp carrot sticks in mustard oil are a speciality of Punjab. They go well with north Indian meals. I like them as an appetizer and also served with drinks.

MAKES 1 PINT/600 ML

1 lb/500 g carrots
1½ tablespoons cayenne pepper or red pepper flakes
1 tablespoon crushed black mustard seeds
½ teaspoon turmeric
1 tablespoon coarse salt
¼ pint/150 ml mustard oil
½ teaspoon ground asafetida
5–6 tablespoons lemon juice

1 Peel the carrots and cut into neat sticks.
2 Put the carrots in a bowl, add the cayenne, mustard seeds, turmeric, and salt, and toss well.

3 Heat the oil in a medium-size enamel pan over medium-high heat. When it is hot, add the asafetida, and carrots with the spices. Cook, turning the carrots to coat them with oil, for 1 minute. Add lemon juice, and continue cooking for 2 more minutes or until the carrots just barely lose their raw texture and look blanched. Turn off the heat.

Pack carrots with spices and oil in sterilized jars and seal. The pickle is ready to eat in three days.

INSTANT SHREDDED GINGER AND GREEN CHILI PICKLE

ANDRAK ACHAAR

There are certain Indian pickles that take just a few minutes to put together. They generally contain a large amount of lemon or lime juice, which helps soften the vegetables, thus hastening the pickling process. This ginger and green chili pickle from Gujarat is one such example. The instant pickle is particularly nice with pilafs and rice casseroles, such as Rice and Mung Bean Casserole with Cumin and Black Pepper (p. 219), Indian Cheese and Sweet Pepper Pilaf (p. 222), Jain Coriander-Scented Millet and Mung Bean Pilaf (p. 226), Spicy Pea Pilaf (p. 219), and Coconut Pilaf with Toasted Sesame Seeds (p. 219).

MAKES 1½ PINTS/800 ML

◆

8 oz/250 g fresh tender ginger
8 oz/250 g hot green chilies
8 limes (or small lemons)
3 oz/90 g coarse salt
½ pint/300 ml mustard oil, light sesame oil, or light vegetable oil (or a combination)
2 teaspoons carom seeds, crushed
2 teaspoons black cumin seeds (or white cumin seeds), crushed
2 teaspoons turmeric

1 Peel the ginger and cut into matchsticks. Wash chilies, wipe dry thoroughly, and slit them. Cut limes (or lemons) in half and slice thin.
2 Put ginger, chilies, and lime slices into a bowl. Add salt and toss well.
3 Heat the oil in a large enamel pan until smoking hot. Turn off heat and let oil cool for 2 minutes. Add carom, cumin, and turmeric, stir quickly to blend them in, and immediately add ginger, chili, and lemon mixture.
4 Increase heat to high and cook, turning and tossing the vegetables rapidly for 5–7 minutes or until the lime pieces look a little soft and the chilies are limp. Turn off the heat, pack into a sterilized jar, and seal.

The pickle is ready in one week, although two weeks of resting improves the flavour.

QUICK PICKLED MANGO GINGER IN HOT OIL

INGEE MANGA

◆

This is a very simple and delicious relishlike pickle made with mango-flavoured ginger (p. 66). A speciality of Madras, in the south of India, this pickle frequently accompanies a meal during the months of July and August, when mango ginger is in season. Although it is a classic accompaniment to a southern meal, this pickle goes well with the foods of all the other regions. I particularly like to eat it with stuffed breads.

MAKES 1 PINT/600 ML

1 lb/500 g fresh mango ginger (p. 66, or use 8 oz/250 g fresh tender ginger and 1 medium-size unripe, tart mango)
1 tablespoon coarse salt
4 tablespoons light sesame oil
12 dry red chili pods broken into large bits
1 teaspoon ground asafetida
½ teaspoon turmeric

1 Peel the mango ginger and either dice or cut into thin slices. If you are using a plain ginger and unripe mango combination, prepare the ginger the same way. Peel and stone the mango. Cut the pulp in the same manner as the ginger. Put ginger (and mango) in a non-metallic bowl, sprinkle on the salt, and toss well.

2 Heat the oil in a small frying pan over high heat. When it is hot, add the chili bits, asafetida, and turmeric, and immediately pour the entire contents of the pan over the prepared vegetables.

Mix well and let rest for a half-hour before serving.

THE STAPLES: BREADS AND RICE

BREADS

◆

Second only to curries, the breads of India are what immediately come to a Western mind when the topic of Indian food is raised. Of course without question, the bread that always steals the show is the magnificent *poori* – the paper-thin film of dough puffed to a giant balloon (p. 310). Its dramatic arrival at the table is a surefire conversation stopper.

Indian breads are in fact very simple to make. Most can be prepared in a very short time, since they are usually made with unleavened dough. Also, Indian bread baking requires no special equipment; you can even use a food processor. The breads generally are made of wholemeal flour and are frequently enriched with minced herbs or cheese or stuffed with vegetables. Therefore they are wholesome and nutritious besides being utterly delicious.

It is in north India and the central regions that bread is consumed as the primary staple (see more on the subject of grains on p. 40). The flavouring of Indian breads therefore reflects regional northern spicing. This chapter includes several types of Indian breads, unleavened as well as leavened, from simple, plain, baked to flaky rich and, finally, stuffed with vegetables and spices. The plain ones are generally used as tasty utensils to mop up curries and *dals*, while the stuffed varieties can be served as meals in themselves, accompanied by a simple vegetable or yogurt salad. Serving suggestions for each bread are included after the recipe.

BASIC BAKED WHOLEMEAL BREAD

ROTI YA CHAPATI

◆

This basic wholemeal bread called *roti* (or *chapati*) is popular in the eastern and southwestern parts of India. There they add a little oil and salt to the dough to keep it soft and fresh-smelling. The bread is made with *chapati* flour (finely ground wholemeal grain), which is sifted to remove the excess bran in order to yield a soft, smooth bread. I

don't like to sift and discard all that bran. Instead, I add a little to white flour, which works just as well. *Chapati* flour is available commercially, but you can also make excellent bread using a combination of wholemeal and white flour.

MAKES 16 *ROTI*, FOR 4–6 PERSONS

◆

6 oz/175 g chapati *flour plus 2 oz/60 g strong plain flour, or 4 oz/125 g wholemeal flour plus 4 oz/125 g strong plain flour*
2 teaspoons light vegetable oil
Salt to taste (optional)
¼ pint/150 ml very warm water
Usli ghee *(p. 57) (optional)*

1 Place the flour in a bowl. Add oil (and salt, if you are using it) and rub it into the flour. The oil should be evenly distributed into the flour. Add water, fast at first, to moisten the flour enough so that it adheres into a mass; then slowly, little by little, until the dough is formed and can be kneaded.

2 Place the dough on the work surface and knead for 10–15 minutes. Cover and let the dough rest for 30 minutes.

To make the dough in a food processor, first attach the steel cutting blade. Put both flours, oil, and salt in the container, cover, and process to mix the ingredients. With the machine running, add water through the feed tube in a steady stream, fast at first to moisten the flour enough so that it begins to adhere into a mass. Now add water in dribbles until a ball of dough forms and moves over the blade. Be careful not to run the machine too long at one stretch; turn it off every 15–30 seconds.

To knead the dough, turn on the processor and continue processing for 40–50 seconds. Remove the dough carefully from the container and put it in a bowl.

The dough at the end of kneading should look smooth and shiny and feel soft and pliable.

3 Knead the dough by hand for a few seconds and divide it into two equal portions. Roll each into the cylinder and cut into eight equal parts. Roll each piece into a small ball.

4 Working one at a time, place the ball on the work board, dust it generously with flour, and roll into a 7–8 in/18–20 cm circle. Set aside, covered lightly with kitchen paper. Roll three more breads the same way. While you are rolling the bread, start heating the griddle (about 5 minutes before you finish rolling).

5 Heat a griddle or large frying pan over high heat until very hot (4–5 minutes). Place one rolled bread on the griddle and let cook for 30–45 seconds or until the bottom is cooked and several tiny brown spots appear. Flip the bread with a flat spatula or use a pair of unserrated tongs and bake the other side the same way.

6 Turn on another burner with maximum flame (if you are using an electric stove, then place a fine mesh cake rack over a burner and turn it on high; this must be done in advance of baking the bread in the pan). Place the pan-baked bread directly over the burner and bake until the bread is covered with more brown spots. The bread will also puff during this time. Turn and bake the other side the same way. The entire process will take less than 15 seconds; therefore, be careful not to burn the bread.

Serve immediately in the puffed state or store, deflated, in a napkin-lined dish. The *roti* may also be brushed with *usli ghee* before eating.

Roti or *chapati* goes well with just about all Indian vegetable dishes. It is usually served when a light meal is intended. It is particularly good when the main dish is rich with cream, butter, and nuts. For a light lunch serve a vegetable dish such as Bitter Gourd with Spicy Onion Stuffing (p. 238) and a *dal* such as Banaras Yellow Lentils with Peppered Mango Slices (p. 257).

FENNEL-SCENTED SWEET FLAKY BREAD

MEETHA PARATHA

◆

In addition to being a wonderful adjunct to a north Indian meal, this bread makes a mouth-watering snack served with a cup of coffee.

MAKES 8 BREADS

◆

12 oz/375 g wholemeal flour, plus more flour for dusting
1 teaspoon fennel seeds, coarsely ground
¼ pint/150 ml usli ghee (p. 57) or light vegetable oil
½ pint/300 ml warm water
soft brown or white sugar

1 Blend flour and the fennel in a large bowl. Add 2 tablespoons *usli ghee* and rub the mixture with your fingertips until the *ghee* is thoroughly incorporated. Add half the water all at once; work it into the flour mixture, using your hands. Continuing to mix with your hands, keep adding the water a tablespoonful at a time until the mixture cleans the sides of the bowl and becomes a nonsticky, kneadable dough. Don't add any more water than you have to.

2 Gather the dough into a ball; place it on a clean work surface. Clean your hands thoroughly, then smear your fingers and knuckles with 2 teaspoons of *ghee*. Knead the dough until it is smooth and satiny and springs back when pressed lightly with a finger (about 10 minutes). Place in a clean bowl; let stand, covered with cling film, at room temperature for 30 minutes.

To mix and knead the dough in a food processor, put flour, fennel, and 3 tablespoons *usli ghee* in the processor bowl. With the metal blade in position, process for 10 seconds. With the machine running, gradually add the water through the feed tube just until the dough begins to hold together. Continue to process 40–50 seconds more to knead the dough.

3 Transfer the dough to a clean work surface, shape into an 8 in/20 cm cylinder, and cut into eight equal pieces. Cover them with a tea towel.
4 Shape a piece of dough into a ball, dust with flour, and roll it into a 5 in/13 cm round. Place 2–3 teaspoons sugar in the centre. To enclose the sugar, gather the edge of the circle and pinch it tightly together at the centre to seal. Place the filled, sealed bread, dusted with flour, on the work surface and roll gently with a rolling pin to flatten slightly. Then carefully roll the bread into a 6–7 in/15–18 cm round. Cover with a tea towel. Repeat for the remaining dough. Do not stack the breads.
5 Heat a cast-iron pan or griddle over medium-high heat for 3 minutes. Place on it one bread at a time and cook for 2–3 minutes or until the underside is flecked with brown. With a spatula, flip the bread and cook the second side for 1 minute. Pour about 1 tablespoon of the *ghee* around the edge of the bread and let fry for 1 minute more on each side or until the bread is golden brown. Keep finished breads covered in a warm oven. Wipe the pan with a kitchen paper and repeat for the remaining breads.

SPECIAL BALLOON BREAD

POORI

◆

One of the most popular items on the menu of an Indian restaurant is the balloon-like *poori*. It is made with lightly leavened white flour dough, which lends the *poori* a delicate fermented aroma.

MAKES TWELVE 7 IN/18 CM *POORIS*

12 oz/375 g strong plain flour, plus more for dusting
½ teaspoon bicarbonate of soda
1 teaspoon coarse salt
5 tablespoons groundnut or corn oil
½ pint/300 ml warm water
Groundnut or corn oil to fill a kadhai, a wok, or deep fryer to a depth of 3 in/8 cm

1 Stir flour, bicarbonate of soda, and salt in a large mixing bowl until thoroughly blended. Add 4 tablespoons oil and rub it in with your fingertips until it is thoroughly incorporated. Add ¼ pint/150 ml of the water all at once; work it into the flour mixture, using your hands. Continuing to mix with your hands, keep adding the remaining ¼ pint/150 ml water a tablespoon at a time, until the mixture forms a very soft and sticky dough. Add the remaining 2 tablespoons of water and work it into the dough while punching and kneading it. If the dough sticks to your hands, clean hands thoroughly, then smear fingers and knuckles with the remaining 1 tablespoon oil and knead the dough in the mixing bowl for 10 minutes. Divide the dough into twelve equal portions. Roll each with cling film; let it rest at room temperature for at least 2 hours, or refrigerate until needed (keeps well, covered, for up to 4 days).

NOTE: Do not attempt making this dough in the food processor, as the dough is too soft and sticky and will adhere to the bowl like a paste.

2 Heat the oil slowly in a *kadhai*, wok, or a deep fryer to 375°F/190°C until very hot. While the oil is heating, start rolling the breads, working with one at a time. You will make two batches of six *pooris* each. Reshape one piece of dough into a smooth ball. Dust generously with flour by dipping and pressing the ball in the bowl of flour, then place it on the work board. Roll the dough into a neat 7 in/18 cm round, using a rolling pin and dusting with flour as you go along. Roll out five more balls of dough, placing rounds as they are completed in one layer on baking trays or other clean flat surface; do not allow rounds to touch. Keep covered with cling film.

3 Carefully slip one round of rolled *poori* into the hot oil. When the bread rises to the surface, tap it gently with the back of a perforated spoon; the *poori* will slowly fill with steam and puff up. When lightly browned on the first side (about 20 seconds), turn the *poori* carefully with the perforated spoon and fry on the second side, basting it with oil, for another 20 seconds. Transfer to kitchen paper and drain. Repeat until all six *pooris* have been fried, adjusting heat as necessary to maintain temperature of oil. Serve immediately or keep in a warm oven while you make the remaining six *pooris* the same way and then serve all twelve *pooris* together.

These *pooris* are richer tasting than other *pooris*, as they are made with a white dough that is rich in oil. The plain flour dough also makes the *pooris* slightly crisp and flaky, thus making them hold their characteristic puffed baloon shape better. Therefore, they make ideal breads for entertaining, particularly with all north Indian and Moghul dishes such as Cauliflower, Aubergine, and Potato in Herb Sauce (p. 180) or Courgette Koftas in Creamed Tomato Sauce (p. 188).

SWEET POTATO PUFFED BREAD

ALOO POORI

◆

A variation on the classic *poori*, this bread is made with a golden-orange yam. Mildly sweet and fragrant, *aloo poori* is a great hit with children. The potatoes keep the *pooris* soft and silky for several days. A very nice bread for picnics.

MAKES 16 BREADS

◆

1 medium (8 oz/250 g) dark-skinned yam or sweet potato
½ teaspoon ground cinnamon
3 teaspoons groundnut or corn oil
7 oz/200 g unbleached strong plain flour
Groundnut or corn oil to fill a kadhai, wok, *or deep fryer to a depth of 3 in/8cm.*

1 Boil the sweet potato in water to cover for 20–25 minutes or until it is tender. Drain and set aside until it is cool enough to handle. Peel and chop it coarsely.
2 Put the chopped potato, cinnamon, and 2 teaspoons of the oil in a large bowl; mash and mix until thoroughly blended. Add 6 oz/175 g flour and work it into the potato mixture. Continuing to mix with your hands, keep adding the remaining flour a tablespoon at a time until the mixture cleans the sides of the bowl and becomes a nonsticky, kneadable dough.

3 Gather the dough into a ball; place on a clean work surface and clean your hands thoroughly. Then smear your fingers and knuckles with the remaining teaspoon of oil. Knead the dough until it is smooth and satiny (about 5 minutes). Place in a clean bowl; let stand, covered with cling film, at room temperature for 30 minutes.

To mix and knead the dough in a food processor, first, with the steel blade attached, purée the potato with cinnamon until smooth (about 45 seconds), stopping to scrape the bowl two or three times. With the machine running, add the flour and oil and process until the dough forms a ball (about 35–40 seconds). (If the mixture does not form a ball, with the machine running, add the flour by tablespoons until a ball forms.) Process the ball of dough for 20 seconds more.

4 Transfer the dough to a lightly floured surface and divide it in half. Shape each portion into an 8 in/20 cm cylinder. Cut each cylinder into eight equal pieces and cover them with a tea towel. Shape each piece of dough into a small ball and roll it into a 4 in/10 cm round, dusting often with flour to prevent sticking. Cover the rounds with a tea towel as you roll them. Do not stack them.

5 Heat the oil in a *kadhai*, wok, or deep fryer. When it is hot (375°F/190°C), carefully slip one round into the hot oil. When the bread rises to the surface, tap it gently with the back of a slotted spoon; the *poori* will slowly fill with steam and puff up. When it is lightly browned on the first side (about 20–25 seconds), turn the *poori* carefully with the slotted spoon; fry on its second side, basting it with oil, for 10–15 seconds. Transfer to kitchen paper to drain. Repeat until all the *poori* have been fried, adjusting heat as necessary to maintain temperature of oil. Serve immediately.

YOGURT BREAD

BHATOORA

My brother-in-law Subhash invented this simple and effortless technique for making the famous bread from New Delhi called *bhatoora*. Instead of using white flour and raising the dough with yogurt only (which takes 8 hours), he uses self-raising flour, which needs only 2 hours of resting. Also his addition of onion seeds makes the bread more appealing and aromatic.

MAKES 12 BREADS

◆

8 oz/250 g self-raising flour
1 teaspoon black onion seeds (kalaunji, *optional*)
4 tablespoons plain yogurt
¼ pint/150 ml water
3 tablespoons light vegetable oil
2–3 teaspoons oil for kneading dough
Plain flour for dusting
Groundnut or corn oil to fill a kadhai *or deep fryer to a depth of 2½ in/6 cm*

1 Put the flour and onion seeds in a mixing bowl. Add the yogurt and mix until the flour looks crumbly and lumpy.

2 Blend the water and oil in a small bowl. Add this mixture to the flour little by little, and mix with your hands until the flour adheres into a very soft and somewhat sticky mass. It should not, however, stick to the bowl.

3 Clean your hands thoroughly, then smear your fingers and knuckles with about 2 teaspoons oil; pour the remaining oil over the dough. Knead the dough in the bowl, punching and folding it until it develops elasticity and looks satiny (about 8 minutes). Cover and let rest for at least 2 hours.

4 Divide the dough into twelve equal portions. Keep covered with cling film to prevent drying.

5 Start heating the oil over low heat in a *kadhai* or deep fryer until hot (375° F/190° C.)

6 While the oil is heating, roll the breads. Working with one at a time, shape a piece of dough into a small ball and place on work surface. Dust with flour and roll into a neat 4 in/10 cm round. The bread should be fairly thick (about ⅛ in/3 mm). Roll all the breads the same way. Keep them covered. Be sure not to stack them.

7 When the oil is ready, increase the heat to medium to medium-high and maintain a steady temperature of 375° F/190° C. Drop one rolled bread into the oil. When the bread rises to the surface, tap it gently with the back of the slotted spoon; the *bhatoora* will slowly fill with steam and puff up. It will also swell and become spongy. When lightly coloured on the first side (½–1 minute), turn and cook the other side for about ½ minute. Transfer to kitchen paper and drain. Repeat until all the *bhatoora* have been fried, adjusting the heat throughout the cooking to maintain the temperature of oil.

Bhatoora traditionally accompanies chick-pea-based dishes from Punjab, New Delhi, and the other northern states. Therefore, Manali Unripe Peach and Chick-peas with Fennel (p. 200) would be ideal served with this bread. I also happen to like Courgette Koftas in Creamed Tomato Sauce (p. 188) with *bhatoora*.

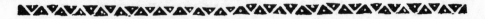

TANDOOR BREAD

NAN

◆

This simple recipe reproduces in your own kitchen the Moghul bread that is traditionally baked in the Indian clay oven *(tandoor)*. The results are as good as they can be without the sweet wood coal and earthy clay aromas.

MAKES 8 BREADS

◆

12 oz/375 g self-raising flour
¼ pint/150 ml milk
3 oz/90 g unsalted butter
1½ teaspoons dry yeast
2 teaspoons sugar

1 Put the flour in a mixing bowl.
2 Heat the milk with the butter in a small saucepan over low heat until the butter melts and the milk is warm. Stir in the yeast and the sugar.
3 Pour the milk mixture over the flour. Mix and knead until you have a soft-satiny dough (about 15 minutes). Cover and let the dough rest in a warm place for 4 hours or until it has risen.
4 Preheat the oven to 500°F/260°C/Gas 9.
5 Punch down the dough first, then knead again for a minute and divide into eight portions.
6 Roll each portion into a neat ball and, using a rolling pin, spread it into a 5 in/13 cm round. Using your hands, stretch the round into an oval-shaped form like a large teardrop. Place the rolled and formed breads on an ungreased baking tray, a few at a time. Bake in the middle of the oven for 3 minutes or until baked. They will look like Middle Eastern *pita* bread.
7 To give the *nan* an attractive appearance, place the cooked breads under the grill for a few seconds until the top develops a few brown spots. Keep them warm, covered, while you bake all the breads. Serve immediately.

NOTE: For a more authentic look and flavour, brush each formed *nan* with water and sprinkle with 1 teaspoon black onion seeds *(kalaunji)* or ¼ teaspoon sesame seeds before baking. *Nan* goes particularly well with all Moghul and north Indian dishes with rich, creamy sauces such as Cauliflower, Aubergine, and Potato in Herb Sauce (p. 180).

CHEESE-AND-HERB-STUFFED TANDOOR BREAD

PANEER KULCHA

This is another version of *nan* with absolutely the most delicious stuffing imaginable: moist cheese *(paneer)*, fresh coriander, and green chilies. For added flavour fold in 3 oz/90 g chopped onion, lightly sautéed in clarified butter.

MAKES 12 BREADS

Indian cheese (paneer) *made with 2½ pints/1.5 litres milk (p. 52), or ½ pint/300 ml mashed potato*
3–6 hot green chilies, minced
4 tablespoons finely chopped fresh coriander
1½ teaspoons lemon juice
Coarse salt, to taste (optional)
All the ingredients for making Tandoor Bread (p. 316)

1 Place the ingredients for the stuffing in a bowl and mix thoroughly. Divide the mixture into twelve equal portions.
2 Make the bread following all the instructions for *nan*, except stuff each portion of dough with a portion of stuffing before rolling and do not stretch the dough into teardrop shapes. Instead, roll it a little longer, into a 6–7 in/15–18 cm round.

3 Bake as Tandoor Bread.

These breads are wonderful cut into small pieces and munched with drinks. Accompanied by a yogurt salad such as Herb-and-Spice-Laced Creamy Yogurt Salad (p. 275), they make a light lunch. For a more substantial meal, add Vegetarian Patties (p. 144) and a *dal* such as Punjab Five-Jewel Creamed Lentils (p. 266).

DILL AND GARLIC BARLEY BREAD WITH SHREDDED GREEN CHILIES

(JUAN ROTI)

Favourite of the Patels (a Hindu sect) in the western state of Gujarat, this barley bread with dill, garlic, and chilies is as exciting as it sounds. Potato is added to the dough to keep the bread moist.

MAKES TWENTY-FOUR 6 IN/15 CM ROUNDS

◆

3 medium potatoes scrubbed
7 oz/200 g barley flour
4 oz/125 g unbleached strong plain flour, plus more flour for dusting
4 tablespoons chopped fresh dill or 1½ teaspoons dried, crumbled
2–4 fresh hot green chili peppers, cored, seeded, slivered
2 medium cloves garlic, slivered
3 tablespoons light vegetable oil
¾ teaspoon coarse salt, or to taste
Unsalted butter (optional)

1 Place the potatoes in a saucepan with water to cover and bring to the boil. Cook the potatoes, covered, until tender (about 30 minutes). Drain, and when cool enough to handle, peel and mash the potatoes.

2 Combine the mashed potatoes with all the other ingredients except the butter in a large bowl. Work with your hands until the mixture cleans the sides of the bowl and becomes a nonsticky, kneadable dough. The dough may be refrigerated, tightly wrapped in cling film, for 5 days, or frozen. Defrost thoroughly before using.

3 Gather the dough into a ball and place on a lightly floured work surface. Clean your hands thoroughly, then knead dough for 2–3 minutes; it should be soft but not sticky.

4 Divide the dough into four equal portions. Roll each portion into a rope 6 in/15 cm long; divide each rope into six equal pieces. Shape each piece into a smooth ball and roll it into a 6 in/15 cm round, dusting often with flour to prevent sticking. Cover the rounds with a tea towel as you roll them. Do not allow the rounds to touch.

5 Heat a cast-iron griddle, or heavy frying pan over high heat for 3 minutes. Reduce the heat to medium-high; place one round of dough on the griddle. Cook until the underside is spotted with brown (about 1 minute). Remove from the griddle and, if desired, brush with butter. Wrap breads in a clean tea towel to keep warm while you cook the remaining rounds, brushing each round as it finishes cooking with the optional butter and then wrapping it in the towel. Serve immediately.

To enhance the flavour further, roast as follows: As you remove each round from the griddle, hold it directly over a high flame, using unserrated tongs; toast, turning frequently, for 8–10 seconds. Do not allow to burn. Brush with optional butter and wrap in a tea towel as directed.

These green-chili-laced breads are delicious by themselves. They make an excellent lunch accompanied by a salad such as Pineapple and Yogurt Salad in Curry Dressing (p. 278) and a spicy cup of tea.

GUJARAT SPICY MILLET BREAD

(DHEBRA)

◆

Millet bread is popular all over north India, particularly in Rajasthan and Gujarat. The most interesting version is made by the Patel farmers of Gujarat, who prepare it with bottle gourd (or courgettes), chilies, ginger, and garlic. The addition of chick-pea and wholemeal

flour lightens the flavour and texture of the bread. This bread is a special treat served with Herb-Laced Yogurt Cheese Spread (p. 107) and Hot Garlic Chutney (p. 292) on cold wintry days.

MAKES 12 BREADS

◆

4 oz/125 g millet flour (bajra atta)
4 oz/125 g chapati flour or wholemeal flour, plus more flour for dusting
2 oz/60 g chick-pea flour
1 tablespoon grated fresh ginger
1 tablespoon thinly sliced garlic
4 hot green chilies, shredded
2 teaspoons sugar (optional)
1 teaspoon coarse salt, or to taste
2 teaspoons Gujarati garam masala (p. 79) or garam masala (p. 77)
¼ teaspoon turmeric
3 tablespoons light sesame or light vegetable oil
2 tablespoons plain yogurt
1 lb/500 g grated bottle gourd (lauki), or courgette or pumpkin
Water as needed
4 oz/125 g usli ghee (p. 57) or unsalted butter

1 Put all the ingredients except the water and the *usli ghee* into a large mixing bowl and mix with your hands, pressing and squeezing until the flour adheres into a mass and can be kneaded. If necessary, add water, a few teaspoons at a time.
2 Pick up the dough and put it on a clean work surface dusted with wholemeal flour. Knead for a few minutes until smooth (3–5 minutes). Because of the grated bottle gourd, the dough will be quite coarse. Cover the dough and let rest for a half-hour.
3 Cut twelve 9 × 9 in/23 × 23 cm pieces of cling film.
4 Divide the dough into twelve equal pieces; roll into smooth balls.

Place one piece of cling film on work surface. Sprinkle on some flour to dust it and place one ball in the centre. Sprinkle the ball with flour and place another piece of cling film on top and roll into a 4–5 in/10–13 cm round, peeling off the cling film and dusting with flour as necessary. Roll five more breads the same way. When six breads are rolled, start heating a cast-iron griddle, or heavy frying pan over medium-high heat.

5 Gently peel the cling film off one rolled bread and set it aside. Put the rolled bread on the hot griddle and cook for 3–4 minutes or until lightly spotted. Turn the bread over and cook the other side the same way (about 3 minutes). Pour about 2 teaspoons of *usli ghee* around the bread and fry for about 1 minute on each side or until it is nicely browned. Remove and keep in a covered dish. Continue with the remaining rolled breads the same way. When all the rolled breads are cooked, roll the remaining six pieces of dough and cook the second batch. Serve warm or at room temperature.

RICE

◆

All meals in India, whether in the north, south, east, or west, include rice and/or bread, as these relatively bland foods provide a canvas upon which the hot, spicy flavours of the other foods can be painted. The hotness of most, if not all, Indian foods makes this counter-point necessary.

Rice, although it is enjoyed throughout the country, is essentially the staple of the southern and eastern regions of India (see more about rice on p. 42). The rice dishes in these and other regions aren't always prepared plain and served as a staple. They are often combined with different vegetables, lentils, fruits, herbs, and spices, and turned into spectacular preparations, often to be served as a dish in itself. Each region in India has a interpretation of these combinations. The addition of protein-rich beans, peas, nuts, and seeds, along with vitamin- and mineral-rich vegetables and fruits, make these rice preparations highly nutritious. The addition of a green salad or a yogurt salad would complete the meal in a most healthful manner.

PLAIN BOILED BASMATI RICE

(OBLA CHAWAL)

FOR 6 PERSONS

12 oz/375 g basmati rice

1 Wash the rice in several changes of water and put it in a bowl. Pour in enough water to cover the rice by at least 1 in/2.5 cm. Let soak for 30 minutes. Drain.

2 While the rice is soaking, bring 6–6½ pints/3.5–4 litres of water to the boil. Add the drained rice. Stir the rice for 30 seconds to make sure the rice does not settle at the bottom of the pan. Bring the rice to the boil. Cook the basmati rice in rapidly boiling water, uncovered, for 5 minutes. Turn off the heat and immediately drain the rice in a large sieve held over the sink. Shake the sieve a few times to rid the rice of water. Transfer the rice to a heated platter and serve immediately.

PLAIN STEAMED BASMATI RICE

(OBLA CHAWAL)

FOR 6 PERSONS

12 oz/375 g basmati rice

1 Wash the rice in several changes of water until the water no longer looks milky. Put the rice in a bowl and pour 1½ pints/800 ml of water on it. Let soak for half an hour. Drain the rice, reserving the water.

2 Put the reserved water into a heavy-bottomed pan with a tight-fitting lid, and bring to the boil. Add the soaked rice and stir carefully with a fork to ensure that the rice does not settle at the

bottom of the pan. Let the water come to a second boil.

3 Reduce heat to low and gently boil the rice, partially covered, until most of the water is absorbed and the surface of the rice is full of steamy holes (10 minutes). There is no need to stir the rice during this period.

4 Cover the pan tightly and steam the rice until fully cooked. This can be done one of two ways: (a) Reduce the heat to the lowest possible level, and raise the pan slightly from the source of heat by placing a pair of tongs or a Chinese wok ring over the burner and resting the pot on it. Let the rice steam for 10 minutes. Or (b) Place the tightly covered pot with the rice in a 300°F/150°C/Gas 2 preheated oven, on the centre shelf, for 25 minutes.

Let the cooked rice rest for 5 minutes, covered and undisturbed. Uncover, fluff the rice with a fork, and serve.

SPICY PEA PILAF

MATAR PULLAO

◆

This spicy Moghul pilaf made without cardamom and with an accent of cinnamon and clove represents the classic Andhra cooking of Hyderabad in the south of India.

FOR 6 PERSONS

◆

12 oz/375 g basmati rice
4 tablespoons light vegetable oil
1½ teaspoons cumin seeds
3 oz/90 g minced onion
1 teaspoon minced garlic
1 teaspoon grated or crushed fresh ginger
2 bay leaves
¼ teaspoon ground cloves
⅓ teaspoon ground cinnamon
¼ teaspoon black pepper
2–4 hot green chilies, minced
12 oz/375 g shelled green peas (or one 10 oz/300 g packet frozen green peas)
1½ teaspoons coarse salt

1 Wash the rice in several changes of water and put it in a bowl. Add enough water to cover the rice at least by 1 in/2.5 cm. Soak for half an hour and drain.

2 While the rice is soaking, bring a large quantity (6–6½ pints/3.5–4 litres) of water to the boil. Keep the water boiling while you prepare the seasonings.

3 Measure out the spices and place them next to the stove in separate piles. Heat the oil in a large pan over medium-high heat. When it is hot, add the cumin. When the cumin turns dark brown (about 12 seconds), add the onion. Fry the onion, stirring constantly, until golden brown (6–8 minutes). Add the garlic, ginger, and bay leaves and continue cooking for an additional 2 minutes.

4 Add the cloves, cinnamon, pepper, and chilies, let sizzle for 15–30 seconds, then immediately add the peas and salt. Stir well to mix. Reduce the heat to very low and let the peas steam in the spiced oil, covered, while you cook the rice.

5 Add the rice to the boiling water. Stir for 30 seconds to make sure the rice does not settle at the bottom of the pan. Bring the rice to the boil. Let it cook in rapidly boiling water, uncovered, for 4 minutes. Turn off the heat and immediately drain the rice in a large sieve, shaking it thoroughly so that all excess moisture clinging to the rice drains away.

6 Immediately add the rice to the steaming pea mixture. Gently mix, turning and folding the rice to blend it. Cover and let the rice steam over low heat for 10 minutes. Turn off heat. Let the rice rest, covered and undisturbed, for 5 minutes. Uncover, fluff the rice with a fork, and serve immediately.

This pilaf, like most Hyderabad food, is on the spicy side. Therefore, serve it with a cool salad, such as Smoked Aubergine and Yogurt Salad (p. 277). For a hotter effect, add Madras Hot Star Fruit Chutney (p. 299). These combinations make perfect light meals accompanied by a tall glass of *lassi*.

TOMATO PILAF

TAMATAR BHAT

◆

An uncommonly good-tasting pilaf made with tomatoes and onions and scented with coriander, this is a speciality of Bangalore, south India.

FOR 6 PERSONS

◆

3 tablespoons light vegetable oil
3 oz/90 g finely chopped onion
2 teaspoons ground coriander
1 lb/500 g fresh ripe or tinned, drained tomatoes puréed with skin
¼ pint/150 ml water
1½ teaspoons coarse salt
1 teaspoon black pepper
10 oz/300 g cooked rice (preferably day-old basmati rice)
½ pint/300 ml water
3 tablespoons unsalted butter
FOR THE FRIED POTATOES:
4 tablespoons light vegetable oil
1 lb/500 g potatoes, diced with skin

1 Heat the oil in a large pan over medium-high heat. Add the onion and cook, stirring until light brown (about 7 minutes). Add the tomatoes and the ¼ pint/150 ml water, mix well, and cook over low heat, covered, for 15 minutes or until reduced to pulpy sauce.

2 Add salt, pepper, rice, and water. Gently mix to fold the rice into the sauce. Add butter and fold to coat the rice evenly. Cover tightly and steam the rice over low heat for 15–20 minutes or until the sauce is absorbed into the rice. If you are garnishing the pilaf with fried potatoes, you can begin making them now while the rice is cooking. Turn off the heat, fluff the rice, and serve surrounded with fried potatoes or daikon radish if desired.

3 To fry the potatoes, heat the oil in a large frying pan over medium heat until it is very hot. Add the potatoes and cook, turning and tossing, until they are browned and cooked (20-25 minutes). Remove with a slotted spoon and drain on kitchen paper.

Alternatively, serve the pilaf with grated or sliced daikon radish (mooli) instead of fried potatoes.

This delicate tomato-flavoured pilaf goes well with coconut and yogurt and dishes such as Tanjore Broccoli and Mung Bean Stew with Coconut (p. 190) or Vegetables Braised in Yogurt and Spices, Patna-Style (p. 205).

FRAGRANT LEMON PILAF WITH CASHEW NUTS

ELUMBUCHUPAYAM SHAADAM

This pilaf provides a lovely way to turn day-old cooked rice into a mouth-watering delicacy. It is traditionally prepared for banquets and during the celebration of the *Kanu* festival.

FOR 6 PERSONS

2 oz/60 g yellow split peas (channa dal)
4 tablespoons light sesame or light vegetable oil
1 tablespoon split white gram beans (urad dal)
8 dry red chili pods
½ teaspoon ground asafetida
1 teaspoon turmeric
½ teaspoon cayenne pepper
2 teaspoons finely chopped fresh ginger
8–10 curry (kari) leaves (fresh or dry)
5–6 tablespoons lemon juice
4 oz/125 g day-old cooked rice
1 teaspoon coarse salt
3 oz/90 g roasted cashew nuts, broken into bits

1 Pick clean and wash peas in several changes of water. Put the peas in a bowl, add enough water to cover by at least 1 in/2.5 cm, and soak for 2 hours. Drain and pat dry on towels.

2 Heat the oil in a large pan over medium heat until hot. Add the peas and fry, stirring constantly, until they begin to brown (about 3 minutes). Stir in the beans and chili pods. Continue frying until the peas and beans turn light brown and the chili pods become several shades darker. Sprinkle on the asafetida, turmeric, cayenne, and ginger, mix well, and let sizzle for 15–20 seconds.

3 Add the curry leaves and lemon juice, increase the heat to medium-high, and as soon as the lemon juice warms up, add the rice. Sprinkle on salt to taste and blend all the ingredients, turning and tossing. Sprinkle on a little water (2–3 tablespoons) if the rice looks very dry. Lower heat and steam rice, covered, for 10 minutes or until thoroughly heated and all the flavours have blended.

Let the rice rest for 5 minutes, covered and undisturbed, before serving. Fluff the rice with a fork. Stir in half the cashew nuts, and serve sprinkled with the remaining nuts.

This spicy lemony pilaf is wonderful served as a luncheon dish accompanied with Bengal Green Beans and Potatoes Smothered in Mustard Oil (p. 232) and a cool vegetable salad.

CUCUMBER, YOGURT, AND RICE PILAF
LACED WITH MUSTARD SEEDS

BAGALA BHAT

The original preparation of this rice pilaf is unusual. The rice was first combined with warm milk (not yogurt) and all the flavouring spices. Then a small amount of yogurt was added to the mixture as a starter. The pan was covered and set aside in a warm place, where the milk turned into yogurt, thus creating this lovely dish. A speciality of Mysore, south India, *bagala bhat* can also be made successfully using yogurt alone, as in this recipe.

FOR 6 PERSONS

12 oz/375 g long-grain rice (preferably basmati)
1–2 medium cucumbers
1 small unripe green mango (optional)
1¼ pints/700 ml plain yogurt
2 teaspoons finely chopped fresh ginger
1½ teaspoons coarse salt
4 tablespoons usli ghee (p. 57) or light sesame or light vegetable oil
1½ teaspoons black mustard seeds
2–4 dry red chili pods, broken into large bits, seeds discarded
2–4 hot green chilies, sliced, seeds discarded
8 curry (kari) leaves (fresh or dry)

1 Wash rice thoroughly in several changes of water and put in a bowl. Add enough water to cover by at least 1 in/2.5 cm. Let soak for half an hour and drain.

2 While the rice is soaking, bring 6½ pints/4 litres of water to boil in a deep pot. Peel cucumbers, cut in half, scrape out the seeds, and discard. Dice cucumbers and put in a large mixing bowl. Peel, stone and dice mango and add to the bowl. Add yogurt, ginger, and salt, and beat until thoroughly blended.

3 Add the rice to the boiling water, stir for half a minute (to make sure it does not settle at the bottom), and bring again to the boil. (Basmati will take 5 minutes; all others, 10 minutes.) Turn off the heat and drain the rice immediately in a large sieve held over the sink. Shake the sieve a few times to make sure the rice is thoroughly drained. Add the rice to the bowl containing the yogurt. Mix well with a folding motion to blend thoroughly.

4 Heat the *usli ghee* in a small frying pan over medium-high heat. When it is hot, add the mustard seeds. Keep a lid handy, as the seeds may spatter and fly all over. As the seeds are spattering, add the red chili bits. When the spattering subsides and the chili bits turn almost black, add the green chilies and curry leaves. Let sizzle for 15 seconds.

Pour the entire contents of the pan over the yogurt-rice mixture. Mix well, cover, and let rest for at least 1 hour. Serve cold or at room temperature.

You can make a meal of this cool pilaf. A hot chutney, such as Madras Hot Star Fruit (or Mango) Chutney (p. 299) makes an excellent accompaniment.

ORANGE-FLAVOURED TURNIP PILAF

SANTRE KA PULLAO

This pilaf flavoured with Moghul sweet spices is popular in Rajasthan. The tang of the citrus fruit complements the sweet turnips and spicy rice.

FOR 4–6 PERSONS

◆

2 seedless oranges
1 lb/500 g turnip
9 oz/275 g basmati or any long-grain rice
4 tablespoons usli ghee (p. 57) or light vegetable oil
5–6 tablespoons minced onion
2 bay leaves
¼ teaspoon ground cinnamon
⅛ teaspoon ground cloves
¼ teaspoon ground mace or grated nutmeg
⅓ teaspoon ginger powder
¼ teaspoon ground fennel
1 tablespoon sugar
4 tablespoons orange juice

1 Grate the peel of 1 orange to make about 1 teaspoon grated zest. Set the zest aside in a bowl. Peel the oranges and separate them into sections. Discard the peel and set aside the orange sections in a bowl until needed.

2 Peel the turnip and cut into uniform ¾ in/2 cm cubes. (If desired, shape each piece of turnip into a round ball, using a potato cutter.)

3 Wash the basmati rice in several changes of water (no need to wash the rice if you are using ordinary long-grain rice). Put the rice in a bowl and add enough water to soak. Soak for half an hour. While the rice is soaking, bring 5 pints/3 litres of water to the boil in a deep pot. Drain the rice, stir it in, and bring the water to the boil again. Cook the rice for exactly 4 minutes, or 10 minutes for regular long-grain rice (the rice will be 90 per cent done). Drain and set aside.

4 Heat 1 tablespoon of *ghee* in a large pan until hot. Add the orange sections and fry over high heat for 2 minutes or until lightly browned and cooked. Transfer to a plate and set aside.

5 Measure out the spices and place them next to the stove in separate piles. Put the remaining 3 tablespoons of *ghee* into the same pan with the onion and bay leaves. Over medium-high heat fry the onion, stirring, for 4 minutes or until cooked but barely coloured. Add the cinnamon, cloves, mace, ginger powder, and fennel; mix and let sizzle for 30 seconds. Add the turnip cubes or balls, sugar and orange zest. Fry, turning and tossing, for 5–7 minutes or until lightly browned. Pour in the orange juice, cover, lower heat, and cook until turnip is cooked but still holding shape (about 10 minutes). Uncover and carefully stir in the rice and orange sections. Cover and continue cooking until the rice absorbs all the liquid and is fully cooked (about 3–5 minutes). Turn off the heat and let the rice rest, covered and undisturbed, for 5 minutes before serving.

A cool yogurt salad is all you need to complete this meal.

COCONUT PILAF WITH TOASTED SESAME SEEDS

TIL-NARIAL BHAT

A delightful, nutritious pilaf filled with the sweetness of coconut and the herbal scent of fresh ginger.

FOR 6 PERSONS

◆

12 oz/375 g long-grain rice (preferably basmati)
1¼ pints/700 ml coconut milk (p. 85, or bought)
1 teaspoon grated or crushed ginger
4 tablespoons light sesame or light vegetable oil
1½ teaspoons black mustard seeds
8 dry red chili pods
5–6 tablespoons sesame seeds
1½ teaspoons coarse salt
4 oz/125 g fresh flaked coconut

1 Wash rice in several changes of water and put in a bowl. Add enough water to cover it by at least 1 in/2.5 cm. Let soak for half an hour and drain.

2 Bring ½ pint/300 ml of water, the coconut milk, and the ginger to the boil in a saucepan. Add the rice and stir until the liquid comes to the boil again (this is to make sure the rice does not settle at the bottom of the pan). Reduce heat and simmer, partially covered, for 10 minutes or until the liquid is almost totally absorbed and the surface of the rice is covered with steamy holes. Cover the pan tightly and continue cooking at the lowest possible heat for 10 more minutes. Turn off the heat and let rice rest, covered and undisturbed, while you prepare the spice mixture.

3 Heat the oil in a *kadhai*, wok, or large frying pan over medium-high heat. When it is hot, add the mustard seeds. Keep a lid handy, as the seeds may spatter and fly all over. When the seeds are spattering, add the chili pods. When the chili pods turn several shades darker (5–8

seconds), add the sesame seeds, and continue frying until they turn golden yellow (about a minute), stirring constantly to ensure even browning.

4 Carefully stir in the cooked rice along with the salt and coconut. Continue frying, turning and tossing, until well blended. Serve warm, at room temperature, or cold.

A very fragrant and mellow pilaf filled with the essence of coconut, this is good with all vegetarian entrées except, of course, those containing coconut. Hearty Blue Mountain Cabbage and Tomato Stew (p. 192) is particularly good.

DESSERTS

Indian desserts, contrary to popular misconceptions (that they are gooey, sticky, and cloyingly sweet), are in fact pudding-like preparations that are often far more subtle and delicate than many European desserts. They are made primarily with milk (either plain or in the form of thickened milk, milk fudge, cheese, or yogurt), the reason being that Indians, believing milk to be the divine Aryan food, prefer to eat it as the last course before they conclude a meal. Another, perhaps more logical reason for including it on the menu is to counteract the many spicy ingredients in the preceding dishes. Milk mellows the strong spices by soothing the digestive system.

Of course, some regions of India are not blessed with an abundance of milk, most notably Madras in the south. Here puddings are made with thinned or diluted milk. To compensate for this decreased flavour, either coconut milk or a distinct flavouring, such as raw camphor, is added. Both are typical regional specialities.

Since most households in India have not even heard of refrigeration, desserts are usually served at room temperature or warm (except, of course, the famous Indian ice cream, *kulfi*). The following desserts can all be served chilled, which mellows their flavourings.

INDIAN RICE PUDDING

KHEERNI

◆

Rice pudding is loved by children and adults alike, and comes in many flavours and textures. In this recipe I flavour the rice pudding in the Bangladeshi style – with coconut and cardamom, garnished with almonds and raisins. The unique flavour of this Indian rice pudding comes from the slow cooking of the milk, which gives it that characteristic *rabadi* flavour (see p. 53) essential in *kheer*.

This soothing pudding is perfect after all spicy-hot dishes.

MAKES 12 SERVINGS

◆

3 pints/2 litres whole milk
3 oz/90 g long-grain rice, preferably basmati
⅛ teaspoon ground cardamom
3 oz/90 g white sugar
2 tablespoons flaked sweetened coconut
2 tablespoons raisins
2 tablespoons sliced almonds

1 Combine half the milk and the rice in a large saucepan and bring to the boil. Lower the heat and cook the milk at a gentle boil for 30 minutes, stirring often to make sure it doesn't stick and burn. At the end of cooking the milk will have the consistency of single cream.

2 Add the remaining milk and the cardamom. Continue cooking at a gentle boil until the milk is reduced and thickened to a pudding consistency (1–1¼ hours). Stir often during this period to prevent it from sticking to the bottom of the pan and burning.

3 Add the sugar and coconut and cook for 10–15 minutes. Pour the pudding into a shallow dish, and sprinkle with raisins and almonds. Let cool and refrigerate thoroughly before serving.

SWEET BUTTERY BEAN AND RICE PUDDING WITH RAISINS AND NUTS

SHAKKARA PONGAL

◆

All Hindu homes in India celebrate the beginning of the harvest season. It is a time during which great rejoicing and feasting takes place. In the south it is called *pongal*, and a special sweet buttery rice dish with beans, nuts, and dried fruits is prepared. This heavenly-tasting pudding is shared with the cattle and the birds to acknowledge and respect their harmonious coexistence with mankind.

This wonderful pudding is also nice served as a tiffin or at breakfast.

FOR 6 PERSONS

◆

9 oz/275 g long-grain rice
5 oz/150 g split yellow mung beans (moong dal)
2 tablespoons yellow split peas
½ pint/300 ml usli ghee (p. 57)
About 1 pint 600 ml boiling water
1¼ pints/700 ml milk
9 oz/275 g jaggery or soft brown sugar
1½ teaspoons ground cardamom
4 tablespoons seedless dark raisins
4–8 tablespoons unsalted roasted cashew nuts, coarsely chopped

1 Rinse and drain the rice. Pick clean the beans and peas. Set aside.
2 Heat 2 tablespoons of the *ghee* in a large saucepan. Add the beans and peas and fry, over medium heat, stirring, for 3 minutes or until very lightly coloured.
3 Add ¾ pint/450 ml of the boiling water, stir, and lower heat and cook at a simmer, partially covered, for 15 minutes. Add the rice and the remaining water, and stir. Cook covered, at a low simmer, until the liquid is absorbed and the rice is almost tender (15–20 minutes).
4 Add the milk, bring the mixture to the boil, and cook, stirring often

to prevent sticking but being careful to keep the rice grains whole,
until it is thickened and the rice is cooked (about 15 minutes).

5 Add the sugar, cardamom, and raisins, and continue cooking for
3 more minutes. Stir in the remaining *ghee* 2 tablespoons at a time,
and most of the cashew nuts (save some for a garnish).

Let the pudding rest, covered, for 15 minutes before you serve it.
Serve warm, at room temperature, or chilled, either as a dessert or as a
snack all by itself.

For a more elaborate presentation pour the freshly made pudding
into a lightly oiled 3 pint/2 litre mould and chill. Turn out on an
attractive plate, slice, and serve with softly whipped unsweetened
double cream.

INDIAN BAKED CHEESE PUDDING

CHENNE KI MITHAI

◆

This Bengali dessert from Calcutta is classically made with Indian
cheese (*chenna*) and flavoured with palm sugar. Using ricotta cheese is
a simple and quick solution that preserves the authentic flavour and
texture of the original version. This recipe, given to me by a dear
friend, Dr Nandini Khosla, produces spectacular results. Adding fresh
coconut and pineapple are my own touches. I feel they lighten the
dessert and give it an exotic tropical appeal.

This is a good dessert to follow spicy hot lentil-based dishes such
as Coorg-Style Hot and Garlicky Black Beans with Lotus Root (p. 198).

MAKES 12–16 SERVINGS

◆

3 lb/1.5 kg ricotta cheese
2 oz/60 g plain flour
6–7 oz/175–200 g sugar
Seeds from 10 cardamom pods, crushed, or ¾ teaspoon ground cardamom
4 oz/125 g grated coconut (fresh or tinned, flaked, unsweetened)
8 oz/250 g crushed pineapple (optional)

1 Preheat the oven to 325°F/165°C/Gas 3.

2 Mix the ricotta, flour, sugar, cardamom, and 3 oz/90 g of the coconut in a bowl until thoroughly blended. Pour the cheese mixture into a 9 in/23 cm square or round greased tin. Shake and tap the pan gently to let the cheese mixture settle evenly. Sprinkle the remaining coconut over it.

3 Bake uncovered in the middle of the oven for 1–1¼ hours or until the cheese is settled and a knife or skewer inserted in the middle of the pudding comes out clean. Turn off the oven and take out the pudding. The pudding will be lightly browned on top. Cool the pudding thoroughly in the tin, then cover it and refrigerate until it is chilled (at least 4 hours, preferably overnight) before you serve it.

4 To serve, cut the pudding into 2 × 2 in/5 × 5 cm squares. If there is any sauce accumulated at the bottom, spoon it evenly over the pudding. Serve topped with crushed pineapple.

NOTE: The pudding has the consistency of a flan immediately after baking, with the water from the cheese separating and collecting in the tin. But as the pudding cools and chills, it reabsorbs the liquid. Thus the texture of the finished pudding is like a very juicy, crumbly cake.

BENGAL CHEESE PUFFS IN FRAGRANT SYRUP

RAS GULLA

◆

Ras Gulla, a very popular Calcutta dessert that is also served as a sweetmeat, is a speciality of the Bengalis, who excel in working with Indian cheese (*chenna*). It is made by steaming balls of freshly made cheese in a heavy syrup until they are puffed, light and spongy. There are essentially two ingredients in this dessert – milk and sugar. Therefore, your success in making airy balls of cheese lies in the freshness of the cheese and the delicate way you handle it. *Ras gulla* is wonderful after any meal, with afternoon tea, or with a cup of coffee.

MAKES 12 SMALL *RAS GULLAS* FOR 4–6 PERSONS

◆

1½ pints/800 ml milk
1½ tablespoons white vinegar mixed with 3 tablespoons water
1½ pints/800 ml cold water
2 teaspoons plain flour mixed with ⅛ teaspoon baking powder or 2 teaspoons semolina
12 oz/375 g sugar
1¼ pints/700 ml water
2 teaspoons cornflour mixed with 2 tablespoons water
1 pint/600 ml water
½ teaspoon screw-pine essence (kewra)

1 Bring the milk to the boil in a large heavy-bottomed pan. Reduce the heat and add the vinegar solution. Stir gently until a white curd forms and separates from the greenish-yellow whey (about 10 seconds). Add 1½ pints/800 ml cold water and turn off heat. Let rest for 1 minute.

2 Drain the curd through two to three layers of muslin placed in a colander or sieve under the tap and let cold water run at medium force through the curd for 10 seconds. Bring the sides of the muslin up and squeeze the cheese in for a few seconds to extract excess water. The cheese should be moist but not wet and weigh about 4 oz/125 g.

3 Put the cheese on a clean block or marble surface. Working with the heel of your hand, break the lumps gently. Knead the cheese for 3 minutes. Sprinkle the flour/baking powder mixture or semolina over it, and knead again until the ingredients are well blended. The kneaded dough should be soft, moist and sticky.

4 Divide the cheese dough into twelve equal portions and roll them into balls that have no cracks. Set aside, covered, until needed.

5 Mix the sugar with 1¼ pints/700 ml water in a shallow pan that is wide enough to accommodate the twelve cheese balls, and bring to the boil. Cook the syrup at a boil for 5 minutes. Stir in the flour mixture and cook for 1½ minutes more.

6 Lower the heat, add the cheese balls, and bring to the boil again. Cover and let the cheese balls boil for 13 minutes as follows: Let them cook undisturbed for the first 5 minutes. Then, during the next 8 minutes, add 2 tablespoons of water every 2 minutes (about ¼ pint/ 150 ml water altogether). This is to keep the syrup from overheating as well as over-thickening. The cheese balls will swell like dumplings. Uncover and, with a ladle, transfer ½ pint/300 ml syrup to a shallow dish large enough to hold the cheese balls, being careful not to break any of them in the process. Thin the ½ pint/300 ml of syrup with 1 pint/600 ml of water and then add the *ras gullas*. Gently stir in the screw-pine essence. Cover and let sit at room temperature or in the refrigerator for at least 8 hours, preferably 24, before serving.

Serve at room temperature or cold. Serve 2–3 *ras gullas* per serving in a small shallow dish. Spoon about 3–4 tablespoons syrup over them.

DARK MILK-FUDGE BALLS IN CARDAMOM-FLAVOURED SYRUP

GULAB JAMUN

Gulab jamun are the all-time favourite dessert as well as sweet of the northern Indians. These sweet-sticky dark fudge balls drenched in a cardamom- or cinnamon-scented syrup are the perfect ending to a spicy meal. Traditionally *gulab jamun* are made with milk that has been cooked and boiled down to *khoya,* but my method of using milk powder and shortening produces just as good a result. Besides, this way you can make *gulab jamun* in just half an hour!

For a variation I use 1 stick of cinnamon in place of the cardamom pods to flavour the syrup.

Gulab jamun is perfect served after a north Indian meal such as Manali Unripe Peach and Chick-Peas with Fennel (p. 200), Spicy Mushrooms with Ginger and Chilies (p. 244), or Bitter Gourd with Spicy Onion Stuffing (p. 238).

MAKES 16 *GULAB JAMUN*

◆

3 oz/90 g non-fat milk powder
2 oz/60 g plain flour
3 tablespoons vegetable shortening
1 teaspoon baking powder
9 tablespoons plain yogurt, or more as needed
FOR THE SYRUP:
1 lb/500 g sugar
3/4 pint/450 ml water
3 green cardamom pods, crushed lightly, or one 3 in/8 cm piece cinnamon
1/2 teaspoon rosewater or more to taste (optional)
Shortening to fill a wide pan to a depth of 2½ in/6.5 cm

1 Mix the milk powder and flour in a bowl. Add the shortening and, with your fingers, rub it in until it is well blended. Add the baking powder and mix well.

2 Add the yogurt a couple of tablespoons at a time, and mix with your fingertips until the mixture looks like a very sticky-pasty dough. Scrape the paste off your fingers, pat the dough into a ball, cover, and let rest for 10 minutes.

3 While the dough is resting, make the syrup. Mix the sugar, water, and cardamom in a shallow pan and bring to the boil. Cook the syrup without stirring, uncovered, for 5 minutes. Turn off the heat, stir in the rosewater, and pour the syrup into a large shallow dish such as a baking tin that can accommodate 16 *gulab jamun* balls in a single layer.

4 Knead the dough very lightly for 1 minute and divide into sixteen equal portions. Roll the pieces into crack-free balls and place them on a plate.

5 Heat the shortening in a large wide pan over medium heat until just hot (325°F/165°C). Slip the balls one at a time into the hot fat. The temperature of the fat will automatically fall to 250–275°F/120–135°C when eight to ten balls are added. Maintain that temperature by regulating the heat between medium and medium-low. The balls may be cooked all at once or in two batches, as long as they have enough room to fry in the fat without touching one another. The balls should be cooking in fat surrounded by tiny bubbles and barely sizzling. Fry the balls, turning them carefully until they are puffed and walnut brown (about 20 minutes). Do not rush or else the dough will not be cooked through. Also the distinct fried flavour will not develop if they are cooked at a higher temperature. Take them out with a slotted spoon and put them in the syrup. Baste the balls, turning often, so they soak up as much syrup as possible.

Let *julab jamun* soak for at least two hours at room temperature before serving; for best results let them soak for eight hours to a day. Serve warm, at room temperature, or cold.

INDIAN ICE CREAM WITH CELLOPHANE THREADS

KULFI AUR PHALOODA

Kulfi, Indian ice cream, is a frozen milk dessert created by the Moghuls of north India. It is made by cooking milk very slowly over a long period of time until it achieves a thick, creamy consistency. This milk is then sweetened, flavoured with cardamom and pistachios, and then poured into special conical *kulfi* moulds (p. 95). Originally, before refrigeration was introduced to India, these moulds were sealed with a little piece of dough and placed in a large terra-cotta water jug (*ghara*). The *ghara* was then filled with ice, salt and water and maintained in this state until the *kulfi* froze and was ready to be served. Today *kulfi* can be made effortlessly by placing the filled moulds in the freezer for 4 hours.

It is the slow cooking of the milk that imparts that distinct characteristic *rabadi* aroma only classic *kulfi* has. Also, because the milk mixture is frozen without being churned, the *kulfi* develops a special grainy texture not unlike that of Middle Eastern *halwa*, something between ice cream and sherbet. In any event, its delicate flavour and cool, soothing sensation are marvellous after a spicy Indian meal.

Kulfi is traditionally accompanied by the delicate cellophane threads called *phalooda* (scented with screw-pine essence) to provide a mellow contrast to the rich sweetness of the ice cream.

FOR 4 PERSONS

◆

1½ pints/800 ml milk
8 teaspoons sugar
8 green cardamom pods, peeled, seeds ground
1 tablespoon thinly sliced unsalted pistachios (optional)
Phalooda *for garnish (home-made, recipe follows, or store-bought, optional)*

1 Bring the milk to the boil over high heat in a medium-size heavy pan, stirring constantly to make sure no skin forms (this should take 10–15 minutes). Lower the heat to medium and cook the milk, gently bubbling and boiling, until it is reduced to ¾ pint/450 ml. This will take about 45 minutes to an hour. Stir often during the entire period so the milk does not stick or burn. Stir in the sugar and the ground cardamom seeds and cool thoroughly.

2 Pour the mixture into *kulfi* moulds, distributing it evenly, or use a bun tin lined with cling film. Cover with foil and freeze until set (about 4 hours).

3 To serve remove *kulfi* one at a time by running a sharp paring knife around the inside surface of the *kulfi* mould. If necessary, dip the moulds in hot water for 15–30 seconds to loosen them. Slip the *kulfi* onto a serving plate and cut into three or four slices width-wise, at an angle. Serve immediately, preferably with cellophane threads.

⊠⊠⊠⊠⊠⊠⊠⊠⊠⊠⊠⊠⊠⊠⊠⊠⊠⊠⊠⊠⊠⊠⊠⊠⊠⊠⊠⊠⊠⊠⊠⊠⊠⊠

CELLOPHANE THREADS IN PINE ESSENCE SYRUP

PHALOODA

◆

Phalooda, a traditional accompaniment to Indian ice cream (*kulfi*), can also be enjoyed by themselves as a separate dessert topped with a thickened milk sauce (*rabadi*), page 53, or with fruits and cream as described later in the recipe.

Phalooda is commonly made with cornflour. The cornflour is combined with water and cooked into a thick paste. Then the warm paste is put through a noodle press directly into a bowl of chilled water. The threads, as they come in contact with the water, cool and form. Before serving they are sweetened and flavoured with essence.

Phalooda threads are extremely fragile, so be very careful while handling them.

MAKES 4 INDIVIDUAL SERVINGS AS DESSERT OR

8 ACCOMPANIMENTS TO *KULFI*

◆

6 oz/175 g sugar
¾ pint/450 ml boiling water
4 oz/125 g cornflour
1 pint/600 ml cold water
1½ pints/800 ml ice-cold water
½ teaspoon screw-pine essence (kewra) *or rose essence* (ruh gulab)

1 Dissolve the sugar in ¾ pint/450 ml boiling water. Refrigerate until needed. This can be done ahead and kept refrigerated, covered, for up to 1 week.

2 Make the two cornflour solutions. For the first, put 2 oz/60 g cornflour in a small bowl and add ¼ pint/150 ml cold water. Mix thoroughly until it is free of lumps and set aside. (This solution will be added later to the cooking sauce.)

3 To make the second cornflour solution, put the remaining cornflour in a medium-size pan along with the remaining ¾ pint/450 ml water. Stir until well blended, then place the pan over low heat. Cook the contents, stirring constantly, until mixture comes to the boil and thickens like a cream sauce (about 4 minutes). Continue cooking the sauce, stirring, for 1 minute more.

4 Keep the cornflour sauce at a gentle bubble and start adding the cornflour solution made in step 2. Add about 1 tablespoon at a time and stir it in. As soon as it is blended and cooked, add another tablespoon. Continue adding and cooking, stirring constantly, until the entire cornflour solution is used up (this will take 7–10 minutes).

5 Increase the heat to medium and cook the mixture for 15 minutes, stirring constantly. The paste will first become very thick then, during the last 5 minutes of cooking, begin to thin. Turn off heat and let paste cool briefly.

6 Place the bowl of chilled water on the work surface. Put some of the warm cornflour paste into the noodle press (or use a pastry bag with a very small hole) and press it directly into the cold water. It will come out like soft noodles, but as soon as it cools in the chilled water, it will get firmer. Continue with all the paste the same way. *Do not try to mix or lift the noodles* at this stage, as they are very, very fragile. Refrigerate and chill thoroughly for at least 1 and preferably 2 hours. Tilt the pan and carefully pour off excess water from the bowl. Add the prepared chilled syrup and essence. *Do not stir*. Refrigerate until needed.

7 When ready to serve, lift the *phalooda*, using two spoons, and serve over *kulfi*. Pour 1–2 tablespoons syrup over it.

8 To serve as a dessert, place *phalooda* on a bed of sliced tropical fruit (such as mangoes, papaya, or pineapple) and top with whipped cream, chopped toasted almonds, or pistachios.

INDIAN SAFFRON ICE CREAM

KESARI KULFI

◆

Saffron *kulfi* is in a class by itself. You don't really taste or smell the saffron in this dessert. Instead, you experience a sensual herbal bouquet. For a more delicate, purer flavour omit the pistachio altogther and reduce the quantity of cardamom to half the original recommended amount. For best results use only the highest quality Spanish saffron threads in this recipe.

Follow all the instructions given for making classic *kulfi* on page 344 and while the milk is cooking, fold in ½ teaspoon crushed saffron threads and ¼ pint/150 ml double cream before pouring the mixture into moulds and freezing.

SWEETMEATS
AND
DRINKS

Indian sweetmeats are candy and fudge-like preparations mainly prepared by professionals in sweet shops called *halwai ki dukan*. These sweets are generally eaten either as a snack with a savoury and a drink in the afternoon or late evening, or at religious functions and feasts at the beginning of the meal as a first course, to bring in good omens.

Although many sweetmeats contain milk, they are primarily made by cooking nuts, vegetables, fruits, or pulses with sugar, in clarified butter, and with various flavourings. Some popular sweetmeats include *jalaibee, gulab jamun, halwa, barfi,* and *laddoo.*

Indian sweet shops have traditionally made sweets using large portions of sugar and fat to prevent them from spoiling in the hot, humid climate. Indian sweet shops here have mindlessly continued the practice, although adequate refrigeration is available.

Since Indians grow up eating such intensely sweet sweets, by the time they become adults, their palates have become accustomed to them. Obviously one can't expect anyone unaccustomed to this level of sweetness to react kindly to it. This is the reason most Europeans dislike or simply stay away from desserts (which are really sweetmeats disguised as desserts) in Indian restaurants.

All the sweetmeat recipes in this book are toned down in sweetness as well as fat content, to my taste. They have, however, all the characteristic flavour, texture and aroma of the classic, authentic Indian versions. I think they taste better, since the subtle sweetness allows one to enjoy the flavours of all the other ingredients. Needless to say, most sweetmeats need refrigeration. They also keep fresh indefinitely in the freezer.

SWEETMEATS

◆

PANCAKES FILLED WITH COCONUT AND JAGGERY

POLI

◆

In the southern and southwestern regions of India, where ancient traditions still prevail, a formal wedding or religious feast always includes a sweet to be served at the end of the festivities. For the Madras Brahmins, the first choice is *poli*, delicate wheat pancakes flavoured with *usli ghee* and cardamom and filled with coconut, split peas, and jaggery.

I call *poli* pancakes not because of the cooking technique, which in fact is totally different from conventional pancake-making, but because of the appearance of the finished product. They are made by wrapping balls of the filling in a very soft dough, then placing them on greased banana leaves (although greased greaseproof paper works just as well) and spreading them into round circles by pressing and stretching them with the fingers. The pancakes are then inverted in a hot frying pan with the banana leaf (or greaseproof paper) still attached, which is then gently peeled off as the pancakes begin to cook.

Poli are neither excessively rich nor very sweet. They keep well in the refrigerator, tightly wrapped in foil, for a week. They can also be frozen successfully for up to three months.

Before serving, bring them to room temperature, then warm them in a hot frying pan and brush with *usli ghee*.

The following recipe developed by my mother is foolproof and produces delicious results.

MAKES 20 *POLI*

◆

FOR THE DOUGH:
12 oz/375 g plain flour
½ teaspoon coarse salt
3 tablespoons oil
½ pint/300 ml or more water
FOR THE FILLING:
6 oz/175 g yellow split peas (channa dal)
¾ pint/450 ml water
8 oz/250 g ground jaggery or soft brown sugar
10 oz/300 g fresh flaked or grated coconut
1½ teaspoons ground cardamom
Oil for brushing
3 fl oz/100 ml usli ghee *(p. 57) for flavouring (optional)*

1 Put the flour, salt, and 1 tablespoon of the oil in a mixing bowl and blend with your fingertips, rubbing the oil into the flour. Add the water and mix to make a very soft, sticky dough. Pour in 1 tablespoon oil a teaspoon at a time, and work it in. Knead the dough by stretching and folding it and giving it a quarter turn for 3–4 minutes. The dough will be very soft and elastic, like a pizza dough. Pat the dough into a neat round, brush with the remaining tablespoon oil, cover, and let rest for 1 hour or until needed.

2 While the dough is resting, prepare the filling. Pick clean the peas and bring them along with the water to the boil in a medium-size pan. Cook the peas, partially covered, over medium heat, gently bubbling, for 40 minutes. Check and stir a few times to make sure the water does not evaporate too quickly. At the end of cooking, the water should be totally absorbed into the peas. If it isn't, uncover and boil until it is. Add the jaggery or the sugar and cook for 5 more minutes or until it is fully dissolved and absorbed into peas. Stir in the coconut, reduce the heat to low, and cook for an additional 5 minutes. Add the cardamom and turn off the heat. The filling will look very moist and crumbly, like cooked rice.

3 Transfer the mixture to the bowl of a food processor with the steel blade attached. Process for 30 seconds or until puréed. (The purée

should be left slightly coarse; it should not be pasty.) Transfer to a bowl.

4 Cut twenty 6 × 6 in/15 × 15 cm pieces of greaseproof paper. Divide the dough into twenty equal portions. Divide the filling into twenty equal portions and roll into smooth balls.

5 Working with one at a time, place on a piece of greaseproof paper on your work surface. Smear oil on your fingers and on the greaseproof paper surface. Place one ball of dough in the centre. Press the dough, stretching it slightly, to make a 2 in/5 cm patty. Place a ball of filling on the top. Pull the sides up and pinch together to enclose the filling completely. Smear more oil on your fingers and press the patty, applying uniform pressure and gently stretching it to form a 5 in/13 cm round. Make four more *polis* the same way. When five *polis* are formed, start heating an ungreased frying pan or griddle over high heat for 3 minutes.

6 To cook the *poli*, reduce the heat to medium-high. Pick up one *poli* with the greaseproof paper and invert it over the pan with the paper still attached. Quickly but carefully peel the paper off. (If the dough sticks and begins to stretch, use a spatula to release it from the paper.) Cook the *poli* for 1½ minutes or until the underside is cooked and flecked with brown. Turn with a wide spatula and cook for 1 more minute. Transfer to a dish lined with a towel, cover, and make the remaining four *polis* the same way. When all five *polis* are cooked, make the next batch of five *polis*. In all, there will be four batches of *polis* to form and cook.

Serve warm or at room temperature. For a truly delicious taste, brush generously with melted *usli ghee*.

PANCAKES FILLED WITH WALNUTS AND JAGGERY

POORAN POLI

◆

The Maharashtrian Brahmins of Poona have their own version of *poli* called *pooran poli*. Their technique for making them is the same as the Madras version, except they use no coconut in the filling. A friend of mine, Asha Joshi of Bombay, adds ground nuts to the filling, which I find exciting and very tasty.

Make *pooran poli* using all the ingredients and following all the instructions given for making *poli* on page 351 but substitute 8 oz/ 250 g ground walnuts for coconut in the filling.

COCONUT DUMPLINGS

KOYAKATTAI

◆

Koyakattai, also known as *modakam*, are traditionally made during the religious festival of *Vinayaka Chachurthi*, the celebration of the elephant-headed god Ganesha – powerful and wise and possessing the power to remove all obstacles in any undertaking. Ganesha is also known as a compulsive eater, and it is believed he had a weakness for these dumplings. They are marvellous served as a dessert, as a snack, or as a tiffin with a cup of coffee. Since these dumplings travel well, they are an ideal picnic food.

MAKES 12 *KOYAKATTAI*

◆

FOR THE DOUGH:
¼ pint/150 ml water
Pinch coarse salt
4 oz/125 g rice flour
1 tablespoon light sesame or light vegetable oil
FOR THE FILLING:
3–4 oz/90–125 g powdered jaggery or soft brown sugar
4 tablespoons water
4 oz/125 g fresh flaked coconut
1 teaspoon ground cardamom
5–6 tablespoons finely chopped toasted cashew nuts or walnuts (optional)
Oil for brushing
Usli ghee (p. 57) or unsalted butter for brushing (optional)

1 Bring the water and salt to the boil in a small pan. Drop the rice flour in all at once and mix vigorously to prevent lumping. As soon as flour and water are combined and thickened, like a thick custard, turn off the heat. Mix for 1 additional minute. Transfer the paste to a small bowl and add oil and knead for 3 minutes; let cool completely.

2 Rinse the pan thoroughly and add the jagggery or sugar and water, and bring to the boil, stirring constantly. Add the coconut and cook over low heat until the coconut absorbs the syrup and looks thick and pulpy (about 5 minutes). Turn off the heat and stir in the cardamom and nuts, if you are using them. Let the mixture cool completely, then divide the filling into twelve equal portions.

3 Roll the dough into twelve crack-free balls, using a little oil. Working with one at a time, brush the ball with oil and roll into small rounds 3½–4 in/9–10 cm in diameter (these are best rolled between two sheets of cling film). Place a portion of filling in the centre. Pull sides up and pinch together to enclose the filling completely. Fill all the dumplings the same way.

4 Arrange the dumplings in a single layer on a steaming rack. Steam the dumplings for 20 minutes or until a toothpick inserted into the dough part comes out clean.

NOTE: Freshly steamed dumplings are usually soft, moist, and slightly sticky. They become firm and non-sticky as they cool. Serve the dumplings while still warm, with a little sweetened whipped cream or brushed with *usli ghee* or melted butter, if desired.

QUICK GLAZED CARROT HALWA

GAJAR HALWA

◆

The art of making *halwa* with nuts was introduced in India during the Moghul period by the traders from the Middle East and Asia Minor. It is the Indian cooks, however, who are credited with making *halwa* by using vegetables such as carrots, pumpkin, courgettes, gourds, potatoes, and yams.

This glazed carrot *halwa*, a speciality of the Sikhs of Punjab, is the most popular *halwa* in India and is enjoyed as a dessert as well as a sweet.

Traditionally it is made with milk fudge (*khoya*, p. 53), but I substitute ricotta cheese combined with powdered milk and butter, which is quicker and produces just as good a result.

FOR 12–16 PERSONS

◆

12 oz/375 g unsalted butter
6 oz/175 g ricotta cheese
1½ oz/45 g non-fat dry milk powder
1½ oz/45 g blanched slivered almonds
2 tablespoons chopped unsalted pistachios
2½–3 lb/1.25–1.5 kg shredded or grated carrots
9 tablespoons sugar
1½ teaspoons ground cardamom

1 Melt 4 oz/125 g of the butter in a frying pan. Add the ricotta and milk powder, mix it in, and cook over medium-high heat to a thick paste (about 15 minutes), stirring constantly. Transfer the mixture to a small plate and set aside.

2 Wipe the pan clean and add 1 oz/30 g of the butter along with the almonds. Cook over medium-high heat until the almonds turn light golden (about 2 minutes), turning and tossing constantly. Drain the almonds on kitchen paper and set aside for garnish. Add the pistachios to the same pan and cook until they become crisp (about 1 minute). Drain the pistacios on kitchen paper and set aside separately.

3 Wipe the pan clean and add 4 oz/125 g butter and place over medium-high heat. When the butter melts, add carrots and stir-fry until they are well coated with butter. Reduce heat to medium or medium-low, cover, and cook for 8 minutes or until the carrots are cooked but not mushy. Add sugar and cardamom and cook until the carrots are glazed (about 5 minutes), stirring constantly.

4 Blend in the milk-cheese paste and continue cooking and adding the remaining butter in small portions, until the *halwa* looks thick and glazed (12–15 minutes). Turn off the heat and stir in the pistachios.

The *halwa* can be made ahead and refrigerated for up to 1 week. To serve: Heat the *halwa* and put on an attractive serving dish and pat it down with a metal spatula. Garnish the *halwa* with almonds. The *halwa* has the consistency of a thick, moist pudding. Serve scooped into individual dessert plates with a spoon.

CRISP JALAIBEES IN SWEET SYRUP

JALAIBEE

◆

These crisp orange spiral rings filled with fragrant sweet syrup can be addictive, particularly when served with tea and a spicy hot savoury such as Hot Tapioca and Peanut Croquettes, Maharashtra-Style (p. 148).

In north India *jalaibees* are a favourite breakfast treat accompanied with scalded milk.

MAKES ABOUT 4 DOZEN *JALAIBEES*

◆

9 oz/275 g plain flour
1 oz/30 g chick-pea flour
¼ teaspoon baking powder
2 tablespoons plain yogurt
½ pint/300 ml hot water
1 oz/30 g rice flour
12 oz/375 g sugar
½ teaspoon tandoori *colouring, or* *½ teaspoon powdered saffron threads*
Groundnut or corn oil to fill a kadhai, *wok,* *or deep frying pan to a depth of 2 in/5 cm*

1 Mix 8 oz/250 g of the plain flour with the chick-pea flour, baking powder, yogurt, and hot water in a bowl. Cover and leave the mixture to ferment in a warm place for 24 hours.
2 When ready to make the *jalaibees*, stir in the remaining 1 oz/30 g flour and the rice flour.

3 Heat the sugar with ¾ pint/450 ml water in a large shallow pan and bring to the boil. Cook the syrup, boiling, uncovered, for 5 minutes. Turn off the heat and stir in the *tandoori* colouring or saffron. Keep the syrup next to the burner where the *jalaibees* will be cooked.

4 Heat the oil in the *kadhai*, wok, or deep frying pan over medium heat. Fill a pastry bag fitted with a 1 in/2.5 cm pastry tube with some of the fermented batter (¼ pint/150 ml). When the oil is hot (350°F/ 180°C), squirt the batter into the hot oil in a swift spiral motion (about three rounds of 4 in/10 cm diameter). Make three to four such circles. Let them fry for 2 minutes or until very lightly coloured. They should not become dark brown. If, however, they become a little dark all over or develop a few dark spots, that's acceptable. Turn and fry for another half-minute.

5 Remove the *jalaibees* with tongs and place them flat in the syrup. Gently press to push them into the syrup. Be careful not to crack the fragile pastries. Let soak, immersed in syrup, for 15–30 seconds. Remove and set aside to drain on a wire rack for 1 minute. Repeat with the remaining batter the same way. Serve warm or at room temperature.

Jalaibees are best eaten as soon as they are made, while the syrup is still warm and the pastry is flaky-crisp. They may, however, be kept in a very good state tightly covered in foil for five days.

SUNFLOWER SEED FUDGE

BHANG BARFI

◆

In India during certain religious festivals such as the Festival of Lights (*Diwali*) and the Festival of Water (*Holi*), a special sweet fudge made with melon seeds and laced with various intoxicants is prepared. It is joyfully consumed mostly by farmers living in the countryside. The intoxicants primarily consist of *bhang* or *hashish*, *ganja* and *charas* from the hemp or marijuana plant, *Cannabis sativa*, and *affeem* from the opium plant, *Papaver somniferum*. Eating *barfi* and drinking the locally brewed liquor such as *tharra* ensures absolute bliss!

This *barfi*, even without the intoxicants, is delicious.

MAKES 5–6 DOZEN *BARFIS*

◆

9 oz/275 g melon seeds (p. 46) or sunflower seeds
6 oz/175 g unsalted butter
8 oz/250 g ricotta cheese
2 oz/60 g milk powder
6 oz/175 g soft brown sugar
½ teaspoon ground cinnamon
½ teaspoon ground cardamom
¼ teaspoon ground cloves
4 oz/125 g fresh hot green chili pepper leaves (optional)

1 Put the seeds in a large ungreased frying pan and toast them, shaking and tossing, over medium-high heat, until lightly browned (about 6 minutes). Turn off heat and transfer the seeds to a plate and cool thoroughly. Add the seeds to the container of a food processor or a blender and grind them to a fine powder. Set aside.

2 Wipe the frying pan clean and melt 4 oz/125 g butter. Add ricotta and milk powder and mix into the butter. Cook the mixture over medium-high heat until it turns into a thick paste (about 4 minutes). Add sugar, cinnamon, cardamom, and cloves, and continue cooking until the sugar is fully melted and incorporated into the cheese mixture. When the mixture begins to bubble vigorously, add the remaining butter.

3 When the butter has melted, start adding the leaves (if you are using them) about 1 oz/30 g at a time and fold into the cheese mixture. If the *barfi* mixture begins to fry and brown too fast, reduce heat to medium or medium-low. After the pepper leaves have been added, continue cooking the *barfi*, stirring, until it looks thick and pulpy.

4 Turn off the heat and stir in the ground sunflower seeds.

While it is still warm, pour the mixture into a 9 × 9 in/23 × 23 cm cake tin and, using a flat spatula, pat it down into an even thickness. When cool, cut the *barfi* into small squares and wrap the individual pieces in attractive silver paper. Store *barfi* in the refrigerator for up to three months.

DRINKS

THANDA-GARAM

When one thinks of Indian drinks, *lassi*, the popular yogurt drink, and tea are all that usually come to mind. But did you know Indians have innumerable beverages, from the simple freshly squeezed juice of sugarcane to the complicated lightly fermented and treated palm sap?

Indian drinks are made with any ingredient that has a wonderful fragrance. This includes flowers, wood chips, leaves, fruits, beans, nuts, seeds, and vegetables.

There are specific drinks served as appetizers at religious functions and wedding ceremonies to invoke the right spirit. In my mother's house herb teas are regularly brewed as remedies for colds, stomach disorders, and body heat. Then there are drinks – mostly fermented – that are prepared on important holidays. But most commonly, drinks in India are enjoyed with snacks at teatime, tiffin, brunch, or any time one decides to have a bite. For this reason, the most common beverages in India are tea and coffee, which Indians prepare in distinctly different ways.

LEMONADE WITH GINGER

SHIKANJEE

◆

This Indian version of lemonade is traditionally made with *kagzee nimboo*, meaning lemons with paper-thin skins. The addition of ginger, a typical Indian touch, gives the lemonade a cooling sensation.

MAKES EIGHT ½ PINT/300 ML SERVINGS

◆

4 fl oz/125 ml freshly squeezed lemon and/or lime juice
1 tablespoon juice extracted from fresh ginger
6 oz/175 g sugar
¾ pint/450 ml water

1 Combine lime juice and ginger juice in a glass or ceramic dish and set aside.

2 Put sugar and water in a small saucepan and bring to the boil over low heat, stirring constantly. Let syrup boil for 30 seconds. Turn off heat.

3 When syrup is cool, stir in lime-ginger juice mixture. Transfer the lemonade to a jar or bottle, cover, and chill thoroughly.

4 To serve, distribute evenly in eight tumblers filled halfway (about ¼ pint/150 ml) with ice-cold water. Add enough ice cubes to fill to the top. Stir carefully and serve.

This ginger-scented lemonade is the all-time favourite of many Indians. Great to cool off with after exercise or jogging, it is a good drink to accompany Punjabi and Gujarati meals.

CHILLED CARROT TEA WITH HOT PEPPERS

KAANJI

This is the most popular non-alcoholic beverage served in Punjabi homes and in New Delhi. It is made by pickling special red carrots that 'bleed' in mustard water. The water absorbs the flavour of the carrots and ferments with the help of mustard. *Kaanji*, with a delicate spicy-sour taste and aroma, is generally served chilled, with a stick of carrot to be used as a stirrer and also to be munched on at the end.

Red carrots are not available in Britain. However, carrots combined with a few slices of beetroot work well.

This classic recipe from the farms of Punjab calls for a sprig of the local herb *marwa* (marjoram) to be added.

MAKES 3 PINTS/2 LITRES

◆

2 tablespoons black mustard seeds
1 lb/500 g carrots
1 very small red beetroot
1 tablespoon coarse salt
3 pints/2 litres water
4 dry red chili pods, broken into bits
Fresh sprig marjoram or oregano

1 Crush the mustard seeds coarsely, using a mortar and pestle, a food processor, or a rolling pin on a work surface. Set aside.

2 Peel the carrots, wash them thoroughly, and cut them into 2½ in/ 6 cm long pieces. Cut each piece into ¼ in/5 mm slices. Stack several slices together and cut them into ¼ in/5 mm sticks to resemble julienned potatoes.

3 Scrub the beetroot clean under cold running water. Peel and cut into ¼ in/5 mm slices.

4 Put the carrots and salt along with 3 pints/2 litres water in a deep pot and bring to the boil. Turn off the heat and add the beetroot slices, crushed mustard seeds, chili pieces, and marjoram. Stir well. Transfer the mixture to a ceramic or glass jar. Cover the jar with a piece of muslin to keep dust away but allow air to circulate through. Set aside in a cool place to allow the carrots to marinate in the mustard water for one to three days.

For best results the carrots must marinate for three days to perfume and mellow the water and transform it into a delicate pink.

Chill the *kaanji* thoroughly in the refrigerator before serving. Strain the liquid through a fine mesh sieve or muslin and serve it in tall glasses with carrot sticks.

CHILLED CUMIN TEA WITH MINT

JAL JEERA

◆

I love this drink from the Northern Province, called *jal jeera* (meaning 'cumin infusion'), which tastes like a bouquet of delicate flowers. The combination of tamarind, mango powder, and brown sugar imparts a lovely sweetish-sour taste. *Chat masala*, or black salt, is an important ingredient in this drink both for flavour and because of its ability to stimulate one's appetite. When I was growing up in New Delhi, I often sipped this before dinner, especially during hot, sultry summer evenings.

MAKES 3 PINTS/2 LITRES

◆

1 lime-size ball of tamarind (about 1½ oz/45 g)
½ pint/300 ml boiling water
¾ pint/450 ml water
2 tablespoons soft brown sugar
1 tablespoon mango powder
1 tablespoon ground roasted cumin seeds
2 teaspoons red pepper
1½ oz/45 g mint leaves
½ in/1 cm cube fresh ginger
½ teaspoon chat masala *(p. 82) or black salt (p. 19–20)*
2 teaspoons coarse salt, or to taste
8 mint sprigs for garnish

1 Put the tamarind in a non metallic bowl, add ½ pint/300 ml boiling water, and let soak for 1½ hours or overnight. Mash the pulp with a spoon or your fingers. Strain the liquid, squeezing the pulp as much as possible into another deep dish. Return the residue to the bowl and add ¾ pint/450 ml more water. Squeeze the pulp again and strain the liquid into the deep dish. Discard the stringy fibre. Add enough water to the tamarind liquid to make generous 2½ pints/1.5 litres.
2 Stir in sugar, mango powder, cumin, and pepper, and mix well.

Purée the mint leaves and ginger in ¼ pint/150 ml water, using a food processor or blender, and add to the tamarind water. Stir in the *chat masala* and coarse salt to taste. Let the liquid sit for an hour before serving.

3 Strain the liquid through a fine mesh sieve or a piece of muslin. Serve in cocktail glasses with ice cubes, garnished with mint.

COLD JAGGERY-LACED TAMARIND DRINK

PANAKAM

◆

An agreeable combination of tamarind, jaggery, ground ginger, and lime, this is a standard classic at all religious and social festivals in southern India.

MAKES 2½ PINTS/1.5 LITRES

◆

1 lime-size ball of tamarind (about 2 oz/60 g)
½ pint/300 ml boiling water
¾ pint/450 ml water, room temperature
Juice of 3 limes (5–6 tablespoons)
1½ teaspoons ground ginger
½ teaspoon ground cardamom
¼ teaspoon ground fennel
1½ teaspoons black pepper
5–8 tablespoons jaggery or soft brown sugar

1 Put the tamarind in a non metallic bowl, add ½ pint/300 ml boiling water, and let soak for a half hour or overnight. Mash the pulp with a spoon or your fingers. Strain the liquid, squeezing the pulp as much as possible, into a deep pan. Return the residue to the bowl and add ¾ pint/450 ml more water. Squeeze the pulp again and strain it into the same deep pan. Discard the fibrous residue. Add enough water to the tamarind liquid to make 2½ pints/1.5 litres.

2 Place the pan with the tamarind water over medium-high heat and bring to the boil. Lower the heat and boil gently for 2 minutes. Turn off the heat. Stir in all the other ingredients.

Chill thoroughly. Serve in cocktail glasses.

A very tasty beverage to serve with all south Indian meals, it is also good served at tiffin or at tea in place of brewed tea.

ICED YOGURT DRINK WITH MINT

CHAACH

Yogurt drink is the most popular beverage in India. It is made either sweet or savoury or sometimes a combination of the two, as in this recipe, and flavoured in any of several different ways. Each region in India has a special formula of its own. The following slightly sweet yogurt drink flavoured with fresh ginger and mint is the speciality of Moslems in Gujarat, in western Indian.

FOR 6 PERSONS

1¼ pints/700 ml buttermilk
¾ pint/450 ml plain yogurt
⅓ teaspoon salt
5 tablespoons sugar
1 teaspoon juice squeezed from fresh ginger
1½ teaspoons lemon juice
Handful of mint leaves, slightly crushed

1 Put all the ingredients except the mint in the container of a food processor or a blender and process until thoroughly blended and the sugar is fully dissolved.

2 Pour the drink into a large attractive pitcher. Stir in the mint leaves and chill thoroughly.

To serve, strain the yogurt drink into tall glasses over ice cubes.

This low-calorie minty yogurt drink goes well with all Indian vegetarian meals, particularly hot chili-laced southern stews. It is also good at Sunday brunch and on picnics.

SAFFRON-LACED ALMOND MILK PUNCH

KESARI DOODH

◆

A very refreshing drink made with sweetened milk, ground almonds, and saffron, *kesari doodh* is popular throughout India. It is served as a non-alcoholic beverage at cocktails, as soup in a cup, or as a drink at religious festivals.

FOR 2 PERSONS

◆

2 tablespoons slivered almonds
¼ teaspoon saffron threads
¾ pint/450 ml milk
1 tablespoon sugar, or to taste

1 Put almonds and saffron in a small bowl. Bring ¼ pint/150 ml milk to the boil in a pan and add it to the almonds and saffron. Let soak, covered, for half an hour.
2 Put the milk along with almonds and saffron into a blender. Add sugar and process until finely puréed. Add the remaining milk and continue blending for ½ minute more.
3 Serve chilled, at room temperature, or, if desired, put it in a pan and heat, stirring constantly, until warmed through. Pour the milk back and forth from the pan to another container to froth it as much as possible. Pour into tall glasses and serve.

MANGO-LACED YOGURT DRINK

AAM LASSI

◆

This is the famous nutritious yogurt drink *lassi* that is frequently seen on Indian restaurant menus. *Lassi* is in fact very quick and simple to make. Fruit pulp is combined with yogurt, sugar, and the desired flavouring and churned with ice to create the frothy drink. This particular *lassi* is made with sweet ripe mango fruit.

For best results the fresh mango should be very ripe and flavourful (see p. 00). Use tinned Indian (*alfanzo*) mango purée if you cannot get a fresh ripe mango.

MAKES THREE ¼ PINT/150 ML SERVINGS

◆

½ pint/300 ml plain yogurt
½ teaspoon lemon juice
4 oz/125 g mango pulp (fresh or tinned)
5–6 tablespoons cold water
4 tablespoons honey or sugar
9-10 ice cubes

Put yogurt, lemon juice, mango pulp, water, and honey or sugar in the bowl of a processor or an electric blender and blend for 1½ minutes or until the sugar is fully dissolved. Add ice cubes and continue blending until yogurt drink is frothy (the ice cubes will not disintegrate fully). Pour into tall glasses with ice cubes and serve.

A very tasty and somewhat filling drink, mango *lassi* is great with lunch, a Sunday brunch, and on hot summer afternoons.

INDIAN CINNAMON TEA

MASALA CHAH

◆

After a spicy meal, what better drink than a tea from Darjeeling with a gentle bouquet that is aromatic with cinnamon and a suggestion of citrus. To truly enjoy this wonderful tea, omit milk or sugar, which I think masks the flavour.

MAKES FOUR ¼ PINT/150 ML SERVINGS

◆

1½ pints/800 ml water
3 in/8 cm piece cinnamon stick, broken into small bits
3 in/8 cm piece fresh lemon peel
4 heaped teaspoons leaf tea, or 4 teabags (orange pekoe)
Milk and sugar, if desired

1 Bring the water to the boil in a pan. Add cinnamon bits, stir, and turn off heat. Let cinnamon soak in the water for 2 minutes.
2 Bring water with cinnamon to boil again. Add lemon peel and tea, and turn off heat. Let tea brew, covered, for 3 minutes. Strain the tea into a pot and serve. If desired, pass milk and sugar on the side.

BASIL TEA

TULSI KI CHAH

◆

For centuries in India, herbal teas have been brewed as remedies for minor ailments. This basil tea, made with ginger shreds and honey, is a standard remedy in my mother's house for common colds. For rich basil flavour use only holy basil leaves, although the common sweet basil makes an acceptable pot of tea.

FOR 2 PERSONS

◆

Handful of holy basil leaves (Olimum sanctum) or common sweet basil leaves
1 pint/600 ml water
2 teaspoons leaf tea or 2 teabags (orange pekoe)
1 thin slice fresh ginger
1 tablespoon honey, or to taste
Milk, as needed

Bring basil leaves and water to the boil in a small pan. Lower the heat and brew the leaves, covered, for 5 minutes. Add tea leaves (or bags), ginger, and honey. Stir well and bring to the boil. Turn off the heat, let the tea brew for 3 minutes before serving. Strain the tea into cups. Pass milk on the side.

A very refreshing tea in summer, when fresh basil covers the herb gardens. I like it in late afternoons with Savoury Cumin Country Biscuits (p. 166).

SOUTH INDIAN COFFEE

MADRAS KAPEE

◆

This is the Indian – more specifically south Indian – technique of making coffee. The process is somewhat similar to making French café au lait, except here the coffee is juggled or churned after being combined with milk and sugar to produce a frothy mixture. The special flavour of the coffee comes from the south Indian coffee beans, grown in Mysore or in the Nilgiri Hills along the Blue Mountains.

There is no better way to enjoy a south Indian vegetarian meal than to follow it with a hot cup of southern coffee. This coffee is also served at tiffin, breakfast, and with southern savouries.

FOR 2 PERSONS

◆

1 oz/30 g Mysore coffee, percolator ground
¼ pint/150 ml boiling water
¼ pint/150 ml milk
3 teaspoons sugar, or to taste

1 Put ground coffee in the south Indian coffee percolator or a coffee filter. Gently press down to compact it lightly. Pour the boiling water on it and let it filter down into the lower receptacle (if using a coffee filter, follow the manufacturer's instructions).
2 While the coffee is percolating, boil the milk with the sugar in a small saucepan, stirring constantly. Add the percolated coffee and stir to mix. Pour the coffee back and forth from the pan to another container to froth it as much as possible. Pour into glasses or cups and serve immediately.

ACKNOWLEDGEMENTS

◆

When I was writing my first cookbook, *Classic Indian Cooking*, I was surprised and touched by the generosity of so many people – family and friends – who came forward to help and advise me. Today I am overwhelmed with emotion to say that they have remained by my side, helping through this second book with the same vigour and warmth. My gratitude to them will be forever.

My parents I thank for teaching me the meaning of courage, dignity, and the joy of sharing. For years they spent hours collecting and researching material for the book and testing recipes before recommending them to me. The family cook, Maharajin, for flavouring all the food with love and for teaching me the fundamentals of making Indian snacks and baking bread. I am indebted to my sisters, Reena, Roopa, and Chitra, particularly Chitra, who spent hours discussing cooking techniques and nutritionally balanced menus and shared her treasured recipes. I would also like to mention my brothers-in-law, Subhash for his delicious recipes for bread, relish, and *dals*, Kumar for lively discussions on cultural heritage, and Ramu on ingredients, and my grandmothers and aunts for their advice.

I am grateful to Asha Abhal, Rita Agnihotri, Myrtle and Moses Ashknasi, Mrs Bakshi, Steve Gomes, Dr Nandini Khosla, Dr T. N. Murthy, Rajalakshmi Raja, Arvind Shah, and Asha Vyas for sharing their recipes and thoughts. To Vinod Shah of Patel Discount Centre for enlightening me on Gujarati culture and the richness of the farmer's life, to Arun Sinha of Foods of India, an importer and owner of one of the best-stocked grocery and utensil stores in New York, for generously taking time to discuss various ingredients and cooking equipment, and to Jaramaya of Madras Woodlands for giving me insights into Malabar cooking.

I am also grateful to Pat Baird of Manning, Selvage and Lee, Inc., and Don Braddock of Texas Rice Production Co. for discussions on rice, to Fredrick Scheer and William Paterson of the U.S. Department of Agriculture, the New York Botanical Gardens, Cornell University Cooperative Extension, and Pusa Institute in New Delhi, India, for information on tropical produce and grains. To the staff at the Indian Consulate in New York for their advice on Indian festivals and practices.

I extend my gratitude to friends in the food world and to business associates for their encouragement and support. Particular thanks to Bev Bennet, Rosemary Black, Anthony Dias Blue, Pat Brown, Marian Burros, Craig Claiborne, Barbara Costikyan, Florence Fabricant, Pierre Franey, Jan Freiman, Gael Green, Suzanne Hamlin, Zack Hanle, Barbara Hansen, Debby Hartz, Judith Huxley, Jay Jacobs, George Lang, Bob Lowe, Bryan Miller, Phyllis Richman, Mimi Sheraton, Margaret Sheridan, Carl Sontheimer, Bill Stendhal, and Paula Wolfert. I thank Betty Franey and John Guarnaschelli for their warmth and encouragement.

I would like to make special mention of Rodney M. Madden for reading the manuscript, making constructive suggestions, and providing moral support among other things, and Margaret Morrello and Mary Towner for helping test the recipes. Barney Karpfinger, my agent, for believing in me, Tim Gray for tireless typing, Rina Cascone for meticulous copy editing, and Molly Finn and Anne DeRavel for their expert testing and comments. Brad Conard for his advice and assistance, Lela Rolontz and John Ekizian for their generous help and support, and Harvey Hoffman whose prodigious care has kept this book on schedule.

In America, I would like to thank my editor mentor, Maria Guarnaschelli for her editing, and for giving the manuscript form and shape. There is nothing she hasn't done for this book. She is special and will always hold that place in my heart.

I wish to thank in England the staff at Dorling Kindersley for their warm support and efforts, in particular Joanna Lorenz for splendid copy editing, Peter Luff for design and Norah Carey for converting the recipes. Finally, I wish to thank my English editor Jill Norman for her consistently sound advice and superb editorial comments in shaping this book.

INDEX